Robert Beck, who used the moniker **Iceberg Slim**, was a major-league pimp during the '40s and '50s. He decided to leave the pimping game having served his third and final stretch in jail. He moved to Los Angeles where he straightened out and began a career as a writer. *Pimp* was originally published in 1967.

Also by Iceberg Slim

Fiction
Trick Baby
Mama Black Widow
Death Wish
Long White Con
Airtight Willie & Me
Shetani's Sister

Non-fiction
The Naked Soul of Iceberg Slim

pimp

THE STORY OF MY LIFE

Introduced by Irvine Welsh

ICEBERG SLIM

CANONGATE

This Canons edition published in Great Britain in 2019 by Canongate Books

First published in Great Britain in 1996 by Payback Press, an imprint of
Canongate Books Ltd, 14 High Street, Edinburgh EH1 1TE

First published in the United States in 1967 by Holloway House Publishing Co.

canongate.co.uk

1

British Library Cataloguing-in-Publication Data
A catalogue record for this book is available on request from the British
Library

ISBN 978 1 78689 612 4

Typeset in Mir   ion   Serif Modular by Palimpsest Book   Production Ltd,
                          Fa   lk, Stirlingshire

Printed a   p.A.

Introduction

I was driving through some black neighbourhoods on Chicago's South Side this spring with American writer Don De Grazia, en route to a White Sox game. Our destination was Bridgeport, an old Irish-Italian enclave in the city's ethnically divided zones, where we planned to stop off for some food prior to taking in the baseball at US Cellular Fields. Chicago has changed a great deal since Don wrote *American Skin*, his acclaimed novel about the city's white working-class skinheads. The youths that hung around the Bridgeport corners were now dressed indistinguishably from the black kids we'd passed on the other side of the overhead bridge.

This phenomenon is ubiquitous. From inner London housing estates to mainstream Hollywood, the influence of black American 'street' culture is – perversely – almost hegemonic. Don, our friend Marty and myself were musing at the irony that the global culture wars have been won by the most dispossessed and maligned section of western society: black youth in America's ghettos.

My interest in African-American culture began after reading *Soul on Ice*, the biography of Black Panther Eldridge Cleaver. There was something about the writing, its irreverence, anger and downright sass (despite how close Cleaver flirted with sexual violence as a supposed complement to black liberation), that instantly chimed with me. At the time, being a white, working-class youth from one of the most monoethnic places in Europe, I didn't recognise his style as something that I grew up around. But it slowly dawned on me that I had heard versions of the same thing in the school playground, the street corner and the local boozer.

Despite being angry, restless and politically conscious in my youth, I was always ambivalent with regard to revolutionary politics. To me this seemed to be about middle-class people using whatever fringe party as a personal forum for the same kind of hysteria and self-righteous moralising prevalent in the pages of their parents' *Daily Mail*. Eldridge Cleaver was certainly no middle-class kid playing out some psychodrama; he and his ilk came from places where people were directly hurt and disadvantaged by the politics of the system. Through him I got into Huey Newton, Angela Davis, Bobby Seale and, eventually, Malcolm X.

But on my personal journey, far more significant than any of them would be the autobiography of a Chicagoan I picked up in a used bookshop in Soho. The author's name, Iceberg Slim, was arresting enough, and the book bore a stark but evocative title: *Pimp*. How could you not pick up a book called *Pimp* written by a guy named Iceberg Slim? As the subtitle indicated, it was the story of the author's life. The inside pages backed up the cover's promise: this tale was recounted without compromise but with the wit, verve, rage and humour that characterised the black revolutionary writing that had capitvated and enthralled me.

Later I learned that Slim had produced *bona fide* novels too. I obtained a tatty old copy of *Trick Baby* from another second-hand bookshop; it had long been out of print in the UK. I'd formed a belief that one of the ambitions of any real writer should be to speak the truth to power and orthodoxy, but do it in the most entertaining way the imagination can devise. After reading *Trick Baby*, I was convinced that Iceberg Slim was a writer with a mission, rather than just an entertaining street raconteur. I relentessly hunted down the rest of his fiction.

Prior to being known as Iceberg Slim, or Robert Beck (which he would subsequently become), he was Robert Lee Maupin, born in Chicago on the 4th of August, 1918. Much of his childhood was spent in Milwaukee's poor North Side and the industrial town of Rockford, Illinois – consistently ranked as one of America's most blighted and depressed cities – before he returned to Chicago as a teenager. Abandoned by his father, Robert's mother supported the family through working as a domestic and operating a beauty shop. He would later – somewhat uncharitably – credit her in having prepared him for the pimp lifestyle by pampering him during his childhood.

As a teenager, Robert briefly attended the Tuskegee Institute in the mid-1930s, his spell coterminous with that of Ralph Ellison, the author of *The Invisible Man*, although the two moved in different circles, each oblivious to the presence of the other.

Robert was a tall, lithe youth (his looks would be retained into his late middle age, despite a fondness for cocaine, heroin and whisky), and with his gift of the gab, women were drawn to him, and a certain type of woman in particular. He commenced pimping at eighteen, and plied his trade until he was forty-two, adopting the moniker 'Iceberg Slim' along the way. It was said that he obtained the nickname through standing at a bar unflappably drinking whisky as a shoot-out raged around him. This Wild-West saloon-bar cliché perhaps represents a somewhat mythologised account of events, but the very fact that it has been attached to him is instructive in itself. The greater likelihood is of a more mundane reference to his pimp's cold ruthlessness and his slender physical build.

Slim was, and has probably shaped, the archetype of every blaxploitation movie pimp and/or street hustler from the violent and edgy to the benign form of Antonio Fargas's Huggy Bear in the original *Starsky and Hutch*, updated with added 'ice' by Snoop Dogg in the remake. He operated on Chicago's unforgiving streets, and in conjunction with his activities, several periods of incarceration followed. He did a stretch in Leavenworth and then spent the best part of 1960 languishing in solitary confinement at Cook County House of Corrections. For such a naturally exuberant and garrulous man, this proved to be an onerous burden and it was this last stretch that finally motivated Slim to reject earning a living through crime and to attempt to write about his experiences.

He moved to California in the 1960s to pursue a writer's life, changing his name to Robert Beck, the adopted surname belonging to his mother's then husband. It was a strange tribute, reflecting the ambivalence in what was probably the most significant of all his relationships.

Pimp: The Story of My Life, described as an 'autobiographical novel', was published in 1969 by Holloway House and marked his most significant transition: from pimp to artist. The *New York Times* decided the subject matter was too rich for their blood, and refused to print an advert for the book. Nonetheless, Iceberg Slim found *Pimp* being shelved next to work by other black authors of the turbulent '60s, like Cleaver's *Soul On Ice*, Bobby Seale's *Seize The Time* and Malcolm X's *Autobiography*. As the more militant black political movements in the 1970s began to gain ascendancy in African-American communities, Slim met Huey P Newton and other members of the Black Panther Party, whom he admired greatly and regarded as kindred spirits. He had initially, either through political naivety or perhaps hustler's self-justification, considered his success as a pimp as striking a blow against white oppression. The Black Panthers, however, had little mutual regard for him, considering his former profession as little more than the exploitation of his own people for personal gain.

Yet Slim's books were successful, immediately garnering widespread attention amongst black youth. Even Hollywood got interested; following the success of *The Godfather*, gangster chic was in vogue. Universal Pictures snapped up the film rights to *Pimp*, only for the project to be considered too contentious and put on indefinite hold. For many years persistent rumours have abounded that a film is about to be produced, with the rival Slim-inspired 'Ices', T and Cube, vying for the lead role. However the blaxploitation era cinematically spawned *Trick Baby*, which made it onto the screen in 1973, directed by Larry Yust.

For a man who made his money as a ruthless, brash smooth-talker, and despite his justified but often boastful regard for his own intellect, Iceberg Slim possessed a paradoxical honesty and a genuine humility as writer. He always saw himself as a work-in-progress, a man who was learning, hoping eventually to become a positive force in the black community, like the Panthers. It is regrettable that the warm approval he accorded them was seldom reciprocated, because Slim was worthy of respect, due mainly to the fact that he was more concerned with understanding his life rather than allowing himself to be pulled into the manipulation game of either self-flagellating or trying to exonerate himself from his past deeds.

His writer's candour is as boundless as his sharp mind, and his insights help us to understand pimping (and therefore prostitution and the darker side of male sexuality) as a phenomenon. For example, his theory that the power of the pimp archetype in ghetto culture is a direct by-product of slavery, of the white man being able to gain forcible access to the 'stable' of black women, while enslaved black males were treated basically like stud animals, now has universally recognised validity.

Lest we forget (and too often we do), slaves did not have a choice in whom they married or had long monogamous relationships with. They were essentially like livestock, the purpose of their sexual activity being to breed strong slaves. This was exacerbated by vast quantities of religious and 'scientific' discourse that constantly reiterated the animal status of Africans, the 'naturalness' of their slavery, and the necessity of severe torture and punishment for blacks (it was claimed that their skins were thicker and less sensitive so more violence was needed to draw blood). Even Immanuel Kant, from a village in Germany, felt moved to pontificate on the most effective way to beat slaves. The psychic effects for the African-American community on sexuality and racialised gendered experiences cannot be overestimated (and possibly never totally comprehended by white people), nor the fraught relationship between men and women when black masculinities had historically been physically or even literally castrated by white patriarchy. Michael Eric Dyson, the African-American theorist and activist in *Know What I Mean?: Reflections On Hip Hop*, explains the impact of this legacy in terms of the pimp.

> The symbolism of the pimp in black American culture is tied up with notions of upward mobility, especially when the pimp is viewed as an escape hatch for the economically degraded working-class man . . . in brutally direct fashion, the pimp seizes control of the female's

reproductive organs to make money and generate status for himself. Pimping, in certain ways, both simulates and replicates chattel slavery, or the owning of bodies for generating wealth. Pimping is the plantation in motion.

Rehabilitation from a gangster's life, particularly one mired in the foulest of gender politics, takes a great deal of moral courage and soul-searching. In his post-pimp life in LA, Slim had to psychologically reconfigure himself, in order to sustain a satisfactory relationship with his wife and become a proper father to his daughters. The honesty about his failings in his relationships with the women in his life is compelling. Despite an avowed love of his mother, he posits, in an *LA Free Press* interview, the proposition that pimps must, on a subconscious level, hate their mothers and women in general:

> The best pimps that I have known, that is the career pimps, the ones who could do twenty, maybe thirty years as a pimp, were utterly ruthless and brutal, without compassion. They certainly had a basic hatred for women. My theory is, and I can't prove it, if we are to use the criteria of utter ruthlessness as a guide, that all of them hated their mothers. Perhaps more accurately, I would say that they've never known love and affection, maternal love and affection. I've known several dozen in fact that were dumped into the trash bins when they were what? . . . only four or five days old.

In response to this, the interviewer, Helen Koblin, alleges that Slim claims to have loved his mother in the book.
Slim replies:

> Of course, but underneath the threshold of consciousness, I know that I must have hated her, as demonstrated by my neglect of her through the years.

Iceberg Slim would go on to revise his weak view of pimping as a revolutionary act. He came to concur with the perspective that it was the responsibility of the black artist to destroy the glamorous image of the pimp, and his victims.

> It is counterrevolutionary for black people to prey on other black people, or upon poor white people. I recognize the necessity for crime in black America. I understand why, for survival, black people must steal. But I don't condone crime. I feel that what it takes to be a successful criminal could be used in a more constructive way. Like if the pimp has enough circuitry going in his brain to control nine women, surely, he's got no business being a pimp. So if you're black, and you must be a criminal, don't steal my stuff. Go over there. Steal from affluent white people.

In the same *LA Free Press* interview Slim candidly responded to the claim that as former pimp, he had made his fortune through the total degradation of the black woman in this society:

> That's true. And the tragedy there is, that the black woman is the bedrock of the black family unit. This is what is under direct assault. It occurred under the structured racism of America. When a black man turns out a black woman, he is denigrating the bedrock of family life in his community. Again, this is counterrevolutionary.

But I feel that Helen Koblin missed the mark when she pressed the point that Slim had conceded, namely, that he had therefore assisted in the degradation of his own race. Assisted whom, was surely the bigger question being skirted. As a writer Slim has encouraged more people to pick up the pen and microphone than the gun or the bag of powder. It will always be social conditions that generally inspire the latter, not some artist's observations of them.

But why are pimps invariably black? The answer is that they aren't, it's simply because black street culture has embraced that particular term into its lexicon. In Slim's words:

The pernicious white man, instead of pimping, shoots for one mark, one victim, and he takes that broad and spends it on flashy young broads and makes the Vegas scene. If he's really a top-notcher, he makes the French Riviera. They are called 'players'. Most white guys became players because they've got the prey. They don't really have to come down to street level to get their bread. White widows with $80,000 or $90,000 are not uncommon. They don't even cause a social ripple. You know – some white woman with $90,000 – she ain't got no money according to this country's standards. If a black widow or a black woman has $90,000, man, my God – she's rich. You know these food places that are really busy like barbecue joints where they give you a ticket? Well, that's what she'd have to do. She'd have to interview niggers because they'd be playing for that ninety grand. Here again the same old opportunity and plethora of opportunity. Who wants to pimp? Why would a personable, attractive, young white guy have to get down on the street level? It ain't worth it if you're white. All right, so you're getting a grand a week from all three girls – that's $3000 a week. Then you got your nut – the police. All of the convoluted thinking that it takes just to keep a stable together and move from one posh watering and feeding spot to another and rip 'em off.

This debate is shrouded in hypocrisy. Al Capone, who ruled Slim's home city, and particularly its South Side, has been given the Hollywood and heritage treatments, and his Chicago is now something of a sanitised tourist attraction. But with his control of prostitution as well as racketeering, he too was a pimp, and a bigger, more brutal and successful one than Slim could ever have been.

In contrast to Capone's blood-soaked demise, the latter years of the California-based Iceberg's life seem to have been bookish and contented. As well as writing, he was a popular figure on the American lecture circuit. When times were lean (as they usually are for writers, at least at some point), Slim took work as a janitor, his ability and willingness to do a 'proper job' another indication that the life of crime had grown to hold scant appeal. Outside of this, he lived a family life, before passing away on April 28th, 1992, at age seventy-three.

But now it's time to crave the reader's indulgence, as I strive to put into context how important Iceberg Slim was to me. Like many people from a 'non-bookish culture' I was probably always a writer, but I didn't know how to become one. In the housing scheme where I grew up, books were passed around. Often not brilliant books (occasionally yes), but nonetheless they circulated. In small systems-built flats, there was scant room for bookcases. So books were never artifacts, they always had a utility, even if that was sheer pleasure, and they were generally passed on rather than being hoarded or displayed.

My own writer's journey probably started with Evelyn Waugh via my Uncle Jack, a fireman, who was taking an Open University degree course. Waugh's Guy Crouchback trilogy ended up in my hands, through him and via my father. This was to be a life-changing experience for me. Waugh, so different from my background, became, and remains, one of my favourite writers. These were the books that took me into literary fiction. I recall, at the Sydney Writers' Festival, telling a somewhat surprised, and perhaps not entirely delighted, Auberon Waugh about his father's influence on my writing.

So I wrote, or rather doodled, in small spidery script that nobody would be able to decipher, as writing was a guilty pleasure for me. I was insecure about it and hated to tell many friends that I read, let alone wrote. Basically, from my social milieu, it seemed quite an indulgent pastime, for effete, rich ponces only. The Ernest Hemingway and Jack London cult of the macho writer pretty much passed me by. That was all very well for the wild frontierslands of America, but writers in Britain were people like Evelyn Waugh, not Irvine Welsh. So Waugh was inspirational in his own way, but he was also prohibitive – he confirmed to me that you had to be posh and wealthy to be a writer. This, of course, was nonsense, and I can see now that I was relentlessly looking for reasons to fail, as one does when failure becomes the norm and the overwhelming cultural expectation. To get past this means that significant invisible barriers have to be broken down. I found the inspiration to do that under my nose, where I came from, in Scotland.

William McIlvanney was a revelation. He was writing about a place and people I could identify with and they were the central characters, the stars of the show, not wheeled on as villains or comedians. James Kelman and Alasdair Gray, in their different ways, would come along and take this to new levels. Kelman's insistence on the importance of voice in the narrative was particularly liberating. Then I moved backwards, through Hogg, Stevenson, Scott, Grassic Gibbon and Burns. But wherever I travelled in literature, through Beckett and Joyce in Ireland to Dostoyevsky and Tolstoy in Russia, Iceberg Slim remained one of my biggest influences.

Why should this be?

One way I can describe it was when my American wife, white and from Chicago's suburbs, on meeting my friends at a party in Edinburgh for the first time, informed me, 'You don't really get white people like you and your friends in America. Culturally and socially, you are a lot closer to working-class black Americans in the projects.' And by this, she didn't mean that we greeted each other with a cringeworthy 'yo'. (Yet it should be emphasised that one would obviously wince even further if this analogy were taken too far. Many Europeans, particularly those from Celtic nations, have often been guilty of overplaying this 'brothers in misery and oppression' conceit. No white European tribe, whether Irish peasants after the famine, or Scottish Highlanders following the clearances, have had to face the recent horror and continuing cultural and psychological legacy of kidnap, transportation and slavery.)

As liberating as the likes of McIlvanney and Kelman were (and still are), back then they were writing about my place but not my time. In '70s Britain there was still a welfare state and a strong trade union movement, a Labour Party who at least espoused (if never delivered) some form of wealth redistribution. This was laid to waste in the '80s, when Thatcher's policies ripped up the postwar consensus, destroyed the welfare state and the notion that the wealthy in society had any responsibility for its poorer members. There was, in her own words, no such thing as society.

So by the end of the miners' strike, I took it as given that the class war was more or less over. It had been won – by the other side. The schemes I grew up in had, through sale of higher-amenity council housing, mass unemployment and the introduction of drugs as the key element of the developing underground economy, been reduced to the ghetto level of the black American projects. I took this social landscape as given: we were not, under New Labour, going back; there would be no attempt to rebuild the social fabric, and even the moderate social democratic policies of Europe would be rejected in favour of a basic neoconservative 'enterprise economy' model of development. There would be resistance, of course, but it would not prevail. But I was less interested in the politics and more intrigued, in a novelistic sense, by the type of society we had created. To me Iceberg Slim's view of the relationships of the black American ghetto, the hustling, scamming, pimping, drug-dealing, stealing and rampant aspiration towards wealth, suddenly seemed more relevant than ever.

Basically, Slim and writers like him gave me the confidence to write in my own voice. If I hadn't picked up *Pimp*, I doubt I could have gone on to write *Trainspotting* or *Glue*.

In his transition from pimp to writer, Slim became some exotic hybrid between the flash, stylish, politically conscious Muhammad Ali and a recidivist money machine/Michael Jordanesque breadhead. In that way he lived the dilemma faced by almost any aspirant who hails from a dispossessed culture: personal social mobility or radical/revolutionary political change?

One of his most endearing features was that Iceberg Slim never sought any insincere exoneration for the life he led. His writing is characterised by a scrupulous honesty to both the social reality and the hyperreal theatricality of street life, which has been the template for the hip-hoppers and rappers that followed him. Slim candidly admitted that one of reasons he became a writer and stopped pimping was due to a fear of being exploited by younger prostitutes, as would inevitably have happened. In Slim's works, the hookers are seldom simply victims of the pimps, just fellow ghetto strugglers with the same grifter sensibility.

Iceberg Slim did for the pimp what Jean Genet did for the homosexual and thief and William Burroughs for the junky: articulate the thoughts and feelings of someone who had been there. The big difference is that they were white.

Unlike them, and despite one Harvard study of *Pimp* as a 'transgressive novel', Slim was, and still is, marginalised as a writer. It's ironic and indicative of the institutionalised racism of English-speaking society that someone whose influence on Western culture is now probably greater than any touted (white) writer of all postwar generations finds himself in this peculiar position. Literature, always the most culturally hegemonic art form, has basically shut Slim out, in a way the music industry tried (unsuccessfully) to do with black artists for years.

This begs the question: just how good a writer was he?

Stylistically, his novels are a treat, his eye for the psychology of a character sharper than just about anyone you'll ever read. His prose style is that adjective-rich mix, with the constant lookout for the telling phrase that is often favoured by many self-taught writers. By the time his last novel *Doom Fox* was published, he had honed and developed his craft, still using his own street experiences as the foundation for his novelistic imagination, but moving outside the ghetto box into the realm of conspicuous LA wealth. Thus he also foreshadowed the rapper's cribs featured on MTV, where the fast-money music millionaires from poor homes drown in the luxury of the most gaudy American consumerism, often for a short while, before the unheralded repossessions take place.

Back in 1973, Hollie West wrote in the *Washington Post*:

The Iceberg Slim of yesteryear is considered an anachronism to the young dudes now out there on the block trying to hustle. They say he is crude and violent, overlooking his staggering gift of gab. Iceberg acknowledges that pimping has changed because 'women have changed'. The advent of women's lib, changing sexual mores, general affluence in this society and widespread use of drugs by pimps to control prostitutes have made an impact.

Even at the time, this may have been wishful thinking on his part, but it certainly no longer holds true. In the age of Jordan before Ali, the 'Get Rich Or Die Trying' philosophy of the projects, the growth of an African-American middle class and an often regressive post-feminism, all occurring within a globalised entertainment market that devours everything, Slim's continued resonance and resurgence with the poorest youths in black ghettos may often seem to be a reactionary force – especially when they identify with the pimp, rather than the artist.

Slim was aware of this. When asked about the success of his avowed aim of saving youngsters from the same kind of life he lived (as stated in the preface to *Pimp*), he was characteristically transparent and forthright:

No. They rationalize. They think they'd be slicker than I. It's almost impossible to dissuade young dudes who're already street-poisoned because almost without exception they have no recourse but to think they're slicker than Iceberg.

Much of the sensibility of modern rap and hip-hop makes Slim's words seem sadly prophetic. Many of the young rappers (often ludicrously) see their (commercially and socially driven) mission being about trying to project cooler, harder and more ruthless personas than Slim. But there are exceptions to this: the brilliant rapper Nas, who, following on from the success of his *Untitled* album and backed by over half a million petition signatures, launched an attack on the Fox Network's racist and sexist smears of Michelle Obama, the wife of the US

Presidential candidate. Fox broadcasters referred to her as the Illinois senator's 'baby mama' and deployed terms like 'lynching parties' when discussing her. Nas would perhaps be an example of the persona Slim the writer strived towards – the 'positive force' who admired the radicalism of the Panthers and rejected the hustler route. Another might be Jay-Z, who marries 'gangsta' rhetoric and posturing with consequential warnings of what this behaviour actually does to black people and the African-American community.

So this intoduction ends with a plea to not just check out *Pimp*, but also the backlist of Iceberg Slim's fiction. The hip-hop street code of 'keepin' it real' was practically invented by him. Robert Beck, aka Iceberg Slim, in terms of his impact on shaping our global cultural landscape, is probably now as essential reading as William Shakespeare. Black and white alike, we have to get beyond his life as a pimp, and accept him as one of the most influential writers of our age.

Irvine Welsh, 2008

Foreword

Dawn was breaking as the big Hog scooted through the streets. My five whores were chattering like drunk magpies. I smelled the stink that only a street whore has after a long, busy night. The inside of my nose was raw. It happens when you're a pig for snorting cocaine.

My nose was on fire and the stink of those whores and the gangster they were smoking seemed like invisible knives scraping to the root of my brain. I was in an evil, dangerous mood despite that pile of scratch crammed into the glove compartment.

'Goddamnit, has one of you bitches shit on herself or something?' I bellowed as I flipped the long window toward me. For a long moment there was silence.

Then Rachel, my bottom whore, cracked in a pleasing ass-kissing voice. 'Daddy Baby, that ain't no shit you smell. We been turning all night and ain't no bathrooms in those tricks' cars we been flipping out of. Daddy, we sure been humping for you, and what you smell is our nasty whore asses.'

I grinned widely, inside of course. The best pimps keep a steel lid on their emotions and I was one of the iciest. The whores went into fits of giggles at Rachel's shaky witticism. A pimp is happy when his whores giggle. He knows they are still asleep.

I coasted the Hog into the curb outside the hotel where Kim, my newest, prettiest girl, was cribbing. Jesus! I would be glad to drop the last whore off so I could get to my own hotel to nurse my nose with cocaine and be alone. Any good pimp is his own best company. His inner life is so rich with cunning and scheming to out-think his whores.

As Kim got out I said, 'Goodnight Baby, today is Saturday so I want everybody in the street at noon instead of seven tonight. I said noon, not five minutes after or two minutes after, but at twelve noon sharp I want you down, got it, Baby?'

She didn't answer, but she did a strange thing. She walked into the street around the Hog to the window on my side. She stood looking at me for a long moment her beautiful face tense in the dim dawn.

Then in her crisp New England accent she said, 'Are you coming back to my pad this morning? You haven't spent a night with me in a month. So come back, Okay?'

A good pimp doesn't get paid for screwing, he gets his pay off for always having the right thing to say to a whore right on lightning tap. I knew my four whores were flapping their ears to get my reaction to this beautiful bitch. A pimp with an overly fine bitch in his stable has to keep his game tight. Whores constantly probe for weakness in a pimp.

I fitted a scary mask on my face and said, in a low deadly voice, 'Bitch, are you insane? No bitch in this family calls any shots or muscles me to do anything. Now take your stinking yellow ass upstairs to a bath and some shut eye, and get in the street at noon like I told you.'

The bitch just stood there, her eyes slitted in anger. I could sense she was game to play the string out right there in the street before my whores. If I had been ten years dumber I would have leaned out of that Hog and broken her jaw, and put my foot in her ass, but the joint was too fresh in my mind.

I knew the bitch was trying to booby trap me when she spat out her invitation. 'Come on kick my ass. What the hell do I need with a man I only see when he comes to get his money? I am sick of it all. I don't dig stables and never will. I know I'm the new bitch who has to prove herself. Well Goddamnit, I am sick of this shit. I'm cutting out.'

She stopped for air and lit a cigarette. I was going to blast her ass off when she finished. So, I just sat there staring at her.

Then she went on, 'I have turned more tricks in the three months I have been with you than in the whole two years with Paul. My pussy stays sore and swollen. Do I get my ass kicked before I split? If so, kick it now because I am going back to Providence on the next thing smoking.'

She was young, fast with trick appeal galore. She was a pimp's dream and she knew it. She had tested me with her beef and now she was lying back for a sucker response.

I disappointed her with my cold overlay. I could see her wilt as I said in an icy voice. 'Listen square-ass Bitch, I have never had a whore I couldn't do without. I celebrate, Bitch, when a whore leaves me. It gives some worthy bitch a chance to take her place and be a star. You scurvy Bitch, if I shit in your face, you gotta love it and open your mouth wide.'

The rollers cruised by in a squad car so I flashed a sucker smile on my face and cooled it until they passed. Kim was rooted there wincing under the blizzard.

I went on ruthlessly, 'Bitch, you are nothing but a funky zero. Before me you had one chili chump with no rep. Nobody except his mother ever heard of the bastard. Yes Bitch, I'll be back this morning to put your phony ass on the train.'

I rocketed away from the curb. In the rear-view mirror I saw Kim walk slowly into the hotel, her shoulders slumped. In the Hog, until I dropped the last whore off you could have heard a mosquito crapping on the moon. I had tested out for them, solid ice.

I went back for Kim. She was packed and silent. On the way to the station, I rifled the pages in that pimp's book in my head for an angle to hold her without kissing her ass.

I couldn't find a line in it for an out like that. As it turned out the bitch was testing and bluffing right down the line.

We had pulled into the station parking lot when the bitch fell to pieces. Her eyes were misty when she yelped, 'Daddy, are you really going to let me split? Daddy, I love you!'

I started the prat action to cinch her when I said, 'Bitch, I don't want a whore with rabbit in her. I want a bitch who wants me for life. You have got to go after that bullshit earlier this morning, you are not that bitch.'

That prat butchered her and she collapsed into my lap crying and begging to stay. I had a theory about splitting whores. I think they seldom split without a bankroll.

So, I cracked on her, 'Give me that scratch you held out and maybe I will give you another chance.'

Sure enough she reached into her bosom and drew out close to five bills and handed it to me. No pimp with a brain in his head cuts loose a young beautiful whore with lots of mileage left in her. I let her come back.

When at long last I was driving toward my hotel I remembered what Baby Jones, the master pimp who turned me out, had said about whores like Kim.

'Slim,' he had said, 'A pretty Nigger bitch and a white whore are just alike. They both will get in a stable to wreck it and leave the pimp on his ass with no whore. You gotta make 'em hump hard and fast to stick 'em for long scratch quick. Slim, pimping ain't no game of love, so prat 'em and keep your swipe outta 'em. Any sucker who believe a whore loves him shouldn't a fell outta his mammy's ass.'

My mind went back to Pepper. Then back even further and I remembered what he had said about The Georgia.

'Slim, a pimp is really a whore who has reversed the game on whores. So Slim, be as sweet as the scratch, no sweeter, and always stick a whore for a bundle before you sex her. A whore ain't nothing but a trick to a pimp. Don't let 'em Georgia you. Always get your money in front just like a whore.'

On the elevator riding to my pad I thought about the first bitch who had Georgied me and how she had flim-flammed me out of my head. She would be old and gray now, but if I could find her I would sure get the bitch's unpaid account off my conscience.

Preface

In this book I will take you the reader with me into the secret inner world of the pimp. I will lay bare my life and thoughts as a pimp. The account of my brutality and cunning as a pimp will fill many of you with revulsion, however if one intelligent valuable young man or woman can be saved from the destructive slime then the displeasure I have given will have been outweighed by that individual's use of his potential in a socially constructive manner.

I regret that it is impossible to recount to you all of my experiences as a pimp. Unfortunately it would require the combined pages of a half-dozen books. Perhaps my remorse for my ghastly life will diminish to the degree that within this one book I have been allowed to purge myself. Perhaps one day I can win respect as a constructive human being. Most of all I wish to become a decent example for my children and for that wonderful woman in the grave, my mother.

1

Torn from the Nest

Her name was Maude and she Georgied me around 1921. I was only three years old. Mama told me about it, and always when she did her rage and indignation would be as strong and as emotional perhaps as at the time when she had surprised her panting and moaning at the point of orgasm with my tiny head wedged between her ebony thighs, her massive hands viselike around my head.

Mama worked long hours in a hand laundry and Maude had been hired as a babysitter at fifty cents a day. Maude was a young widow. Strangely, she had a reputation in Indianapolis, Indiana as a devout Holy Roller.

I have tried through the years to remember her face, but all I can remember is the funky ritual. I vaguely remember not her words, but her excitement when we were alone.

I remember more vividly the moist, odorous darkness and the bristle-like hairs tickling my face and most vividly I can remember my panic, when in the wild moment of her climax, she would savagely jerk my head even tighter into the hairy maw.

I couldn't get a breath of air until like a huge black balloon she would exhale with a whistling whoosh and relax limply freeing my head.

I remember the ache of the strain on my fragile neck muscles, and especially at the root of my tongue.

Mama and I had come to Indianapolis from Chicago, where since the time when she was six months pregnant, my father had begun to show his true colors as an irresponsible, white-spats-wearing bum.

Back in that small town in Tennessee, their home town, he had stalked the beautiful virgin and conned her into marriage. Her parents, with vast relief, gave their blessing and wished them the best in the promised land up North in Chicago.

Mama had ten brothers and sisters. Her marriage meant one less mouth to feed.

My father's father was a skilled cook and he passed his know-how to my father, who shortly after getting to Chicago scored for a chef's job at a huge middle-class hotel. Mama was put on as a waitress.

Mama told me that even with both of them working twelve hours a day, six days a week they couldn't save a nickel or buy furniture or anything.

My idiot father had come to the big city and gone sucker wild. He couldn't stay away from the high-yellow whores with their big asses and bitch-dog sexual antics. What they didn't con him out of he lost in the cheat crap joints.

At the hotel one night he vanished from the kitchen. Mama finally found him thrusting mightily into a half-white waitress lying on a sack of potatoes in a storage room, with her legs locked around his back.

Mama said she threw everything she could lift at them. They were unemployed when they walked away from the shambles.

My father tearfully vowed to straighten himself out and be a man, but he didn't have the will, the strength to resist the cheap thrills of the city.

After my birth he got worse, and had the stupid gall to suggest to Mama that I be put on a Catholic Church doorstep. Mama naturally refused so he hurled me against the wall in disgust.

I survived it and he left us, his white spats flashing and his derby hat at a rakish angle.

It was the beginning of a bitter winter. Mama packed pressing irons and waving combs into a small bag and wrapped me warmly in blankets and set out into the bleak, friendless city to ring door bells, the bag in one arm and I in the other.

Her pitch was something like this, 'Madam, I can make your hair curly and beautiful. Please give me a chance. For fifty cents, that's all, I will make your hair shine like new money.'

At this point in the pitch Mama told me she would slip the blanket aside to bare my wee big-eyed face. The sight of me in her arm on a sub-zero day was like a charm. She managed to make a living for us.

That spring with new friends of Mama's we left Chicago for Indianapolis. We stayed there until 1924, when a fire gutted the hand laundry where Mama worked.

There were no jobs in Indianapolis for Mama and for six months we barely made it on the meager savings. We were penniless and with hardly any food when a tall black angel visiting relatives in Indianapolis came into our lives.

He fell instantly in love with my lissome beautiful mother. His name was Henry Upshaw, and I guess I fell as hard for him as he fell for Mama.

He took us back to Rockford, Illinois with him where he owned a cleaning and pressing shop, the only Negro business in downtown Rockford.

In those tough depression times a Negro in his position was the envy of most Negro men.

Henry was religious, ambitious, good and kind. I often wonder what would have happened to my life if I had not been torn from him.

He treated Mama like she was a princess, anything she wanted he got for her. She was a fashion plate all right.

Every Sunday when we all three went to church in the gleaming black Dodge we were an outstanding sight as we walked down the aisle in our fresh neat clothing.

Only the few Negro lawyers and physicians lived as well, looked as well. Mama was president of several civic clubs. For the first time we were living the good life.

Mama had a dream. She told it to Henry. Like the genie of the lamp he made it a reality.

It was a four stall, opulent beauty shop. Its chrome gleamed in the black-and-gold motif. It was located in the heart of the Negro business section and it flourished from the moment its doors opened.

Her clientele was for the most part whores, pimps, and hustlers from the sprawling red-light district in Rockford.

They were the only ones who always had the money to spend on their appearance.

The first time I saw Steve he was sitting getting his nails manicured in the shop. Mama was smiling into his handsome olive-tinted face as she buffed his nails.

I didn't know when I first saw him that he was the pin-striped snake who would poison the core of our lives.

I certainly had no inkling that last day at the shop as live billows of steam hissed from the old pressing machine each time Henry slammed its lid down on a garment.

Jesus! It was hot in that little shop, but I loved every minute of it. It was school-vacation time for me and every summer I worked in the shop all day, every day helping my stepfather.

That day as I saw my reflection on the banker's expensive black shoes I was perhaps the happiest black boy in Rockford. As I applied the sole dressing I hummed my favorite tune 'Spring Time in the Rockies.'

The banker stepped down from the shine stand, stood for a moment as I flicked lint from his soft rich suit, then with a warm smile he pressed an extravagant fifty-cent piece into my hand and stepped out into the broiling street.

Now I whistled my favorite tune, shines were only a dime, what a tip.

I didn't know at the time that the banker would never press another coin into my hand, that for the next thirty-five years this last day would be remembered vividly as the final day of real happiness for me.

I would press five-dollar bills into the palms of shine boys. My shoes would be hand made, would cost three times as much as the banker's shoes, but my shoes though perfectly fitted would be worn in tension and fear.

There was really nothing out of the ordinary that day. Nothing during that day that I heard or saw that prepared me for the swift, confusing events that over the weekend would slam my life away from all that was good to all that was bad.

Now looking back remembering that last day in the shop as clearly as if it were yesterday my stepfather, Henry, was unusually quiet. My young mind couldn't grasp his worry, his heart break.

Even I, a ten-year-old, however, knew that this huge, ugly black man who had rescued Mama and me from actual starvation back in Indianapolis loved us with all of his great, sensitive heart.

I loved Henry with all my heart. He was the only father I had ever really known.

He could have saved himself an early death from a broken heart if instead of falling so madly in love with Mama he had run as fast as he could away from her. For him she was brown-skin murder in a size-twelve dress.

That last night at eight o'clock Dad and I flicked the shop's lights out as always at closing.

In an emotion muffled voice he spoke my name, 'Bobby.'

I turned toward him and looked up into his face tense and strained in the pale light from the street lamp. I was confused and shaken when he put his massive hands on my shoulders and drew me to him very tightly just holding me in this strange desperate way.

My head was pressed against his belt buckle. I could barely hear his low, rapid flow of pitiful words.

He said, 'Bobby, you know I love you and Mama, don't you?'

His stomach muscles were cording, jerking against my cheek. I knew he was going to burst into tears.

I said as I squeezed my arms around his waist, 'Yes, Daddy, yes, Daddy. We love you too, Daddy. We always will, Daddy.'

He was trembling as he said, 'You and Mama wouldn't ever leave me? You know Bobby, I ain't got nobody in the world but you two. I just couldn't go on if you left me alone.'

I clung tightly to him and said, 'Don't worry Daddy, we'll never leave you, I promise, honest, Daddy.'

What a sight we must have been, the six-foot-six black giant and the frail little boy holding on to each other for dear life, crying there in the darkness.

I tell you when we finally made it to the big black

Dodge and were riding home my thoughts were turning madly.

Yes, poor Henry's fears had foundation. Mama had never loved my stepfather. This kind wonderful man had only been a tool of convenience. She had fallen in love with the snake all right.

His plan was to cop Mama and make it to the Windy. The dirty bastard knew I would be excess baggage, but the way Mama was gulping his con, he figured he could get rid of me later.

Only after I had become a pimp years later would I know Steve's complete plot, and how stupid he really was.

Here this fool had a smart square broad with a progressive square-john husband, infatuated with him. Her business was getting better all the time.

Her sucker husband was blindly in love, and the money from his business was wide open to her. If Steve had been clever he could have stayed right there on top of things and bled a big bankroll from the businesses in a couple of years.

Then he could have pulled Mama out of there and with a big bankroll he could have done anything with her, even turned her out.

I tell you she was that hot for him. She had to be insane over the asshole to walk away from all that potential with only twenty-five hundred in cash.

Steve blew it in a Georgia-skin game within a week after we got to Chicago.

I have wished to Christ, in four penitentiaries, that the lunatic lovers had left me in Rockford with Henry when they split.

One scene in my life I can never forget and that was that morning when Mama had finished packing our clothes and Henry lost his inner fight for his pride and dignity.

He fell down on his knees and bawled like a scalded child pleading with Mama not to leave him, begging her to stay. He had welded his arms around her legs, his voice hoarse in anguish as he whimpered his love for us.

His agonized eyes walled up at her as he wailed, 'Please don't leave me. You are sure to kill me if you do. I ain't done nothing. If I have, forgive me.'

I will never forget her face as cold as an executioner's, which she was, as she kicked and struggled loose from him.

Then with an awful grin on her face she lied and said, 'Henry, Honey, I just want to get away for a while. Darling, we'll be back.'

In his state she was lucky he hadn't killed her and me, and buried us in the back yard.

As the cab drove us away to the secret rendezvous with Steve sitting in his old Model T, I looked back at Henry on the porch, his chest heaving as tears rolled down his tortured face.

There were too many wheels within wheels, too much hurt for me to cry. After a blank time and distance we got to Chicago. Steve had vanished and Mama was telling me in a drab hotel room that my real father was coming over to see us, and to remember that Steve was her cousin.

Steve was stupid all right, but cunning, if you get what I mean.

Mama, at Steve's instruction, weeks before, had gotten in contact with my father through a hustler brother of Mama's in Chicago.

When my father came through the hotel room door reeking of cologne and dressed to kill, all I could think was what Mama had told me about that morning when this tall brown-skin joker had tossed me against the wall.

He took a long look at me. It was like looking in a mirror. His deep down guilt cream puffed him and he grabbed me and squeezed me to him. I was stiff and tense in the stranger's arms, but I had looked in the mirror too when he came in, so I strung my arms limply about his neck.

When he hugged Mama, her face was toward me, and stony like back there with Henry. My father strutted about that hotel room boasting of his personal chef's job for Big Bill Thompson, the mayor of Chicago.

He told Mama and me, 'I am a changed man now. I have saved my money and now I really have something to offer my wife and son. Won't you come back to me and try again? I am older now, and I bitterly regret my mistakes of the past.'

Like a black-widow spider spinning a web around her prey, Mama put up enough resistance to make him pitch himself into a sweat then agreed to go back to him.

My father's house was crammed with expensive furniture and art pieces. He had thousands of dollars invested in rich clothing and linens.

After a week my hustler uncle brought Steve to visit us, and to case the lay-out. My father bought the cousin angle and broke out his best cigars and cognac for the thieves. It was another week before they took him off.

Remember, at the time I had no idea as to what really was going to happen. I would learn the shocking truth only after we got to Milwaukee.

On that early evening when it happened Mama was jittery as we prepared to visit some close white friends of my father. I had a wonderful time getting acquainted with the host's children who were around my age. Too soon it was time to go home.

In my lifetime I have seen many degrees of shock and surprise on the human face. I have never seen on any face the traumatic disbelief and shock on my father's face when he unlocked the door and stepped into his completely empty house. His lips flapped mutely. He couldn't speak. Everything was gone, all the furniture and drapery, everything from the percolator to the pictures on the wall, even my Mama's belongings.

Mama stood there in the empty house clinging to him, comforting him, sobbing with real tears flowing down her cheeks. I guess she was crying in joy because the cross had come off so beautifully.

Mama missed her calling. She should have been a film actress. With only a bit part, an Oscar a season would have been a lead-pipe cinch for her.

Mama told my father we would go to Indianapolis to friends until he could put another nest together.

When we got to Milwaukee by train, ninety miles away, Steve had rented a house. Every square inch of that house was filled with my father's things.

Those lovely things did us little good and brought no happiness. Steve, with his mania for craps, within weeks had sold everything, piece by piece, and lost it across the craps table.

Mama worked long hours as a cook, and Steve and I were alone quite often.

At these times he would say, 'You little mother-fucker, you. I'm going to beat your mother-fucking ass. I am telling you, if you don't run away, I'm going to kill you.'

He was just so cruel to me. My mother had bought me a little baby cat. I loved that kitten, and this man hated animals. One day the cat, being a baby cat, did his business on the kitchen floor.

Steve said, 'Where is that little mother-fucker?'

The little kitten had hidden under the sofa. He grabbed that kitten and took it downstairs where there was a concrete wall. He grabbed it by the heels. I was standing (we lived on the second floor) looking down at him; he took the kitten and beat its brains out against that wall.

I remember, there was a park behind our house, concrete covered. There were some concrete steps. I sat there and I cried until I puked.

All the while I kept saying like a litany, 'I hate Mama! I hate Mama! I hate Mama!' And, 'I hate Steve! I hate Steve! I hate him! I hate him!'

For many tortured years she would suffer her guilt. She had made that terrible decision on that long ago weekend.

I know my lousy old man deserved what happened to his goods. I know Mama got her revenge and it was sweet I am sure, but it was bitter for a kid like me to know that Mama was part of it.

Perhaps if Mama had kept that burglary cross a secret from me, in some tiny way I might have been stronger to fight off that pimping disease. I don't know, but somehow after that cross Mama just didn't seem like the same honest sweet Mama that I had prayed in church with back in Rockford.

I went to her grave the other day and told her for the hundredth time since her death, 'Mama, it wasn't really your fault. You were a dumb country girl, you didn't understand. I was your first and only child. You couldn't have known how important Henry was to me.'

I choked up, stopped talking to her beneath the silent sod, and thought about Henry lying rotten, forgotten in his grave.

Then through my tight throat I said to Mama, 'To you he was ugly, but Mama I swear to heaven he was so beautiful to me. I loved him Mama, I needed him. I wish you could have seen beyond his ugly black face and loved him a little and stayed with him. Mama, we could have been happy, our lives would have been different, but I don't blame you. Mama, I love you.'

I paused looking up at the sky, hoped she was up there and could hear me, then I went on, 'I just wish you were alive now, you would be so proud of me. I am not a lawyer as you always wanted me to be, but Mama, you have two beautiful grandchildren and another on the way, and a fine daughter-in-law who looks a lot like you when you were young.'

The grave next to hers had visitors, an old man and a bright eyed girl about ten.

I stopped my bragging until the pair walked away, then I said, 'Mama, I haven't shot any H in ten years. I haven't had a whore in five years. I have squared up, I work every day. How about it Mama, Iceberg Slim a square? You wouldn't believe it Mama, I wear fifty-dollar suits right off the rack, and my car is ten years old, you gotta believe it now Mama. Goodbye Mama, see you Christmas, and remember, I'll always love you.'

When I walked away from her grave I thought, 'I don't know, maybe that prison head-shrinker was right when he told me I had become a pimp because of my unconscious hatred for my mother.'

I know one damn thing, I can't help crying at her grave almost as if I was crying because I did so much to put her there. Maybe the hidden hate that I can't feel wants me to laugh that she's down there in the earth. Maybe my crying is really laughing.

About ninety days after Steve smashed my kitten Mama cast

off her spell, and one gray April dawn while Steve lay in a drunken, open-mouthed stupor, Mama and I packed what we could carry and moved into a hotel room. It was complete with hot plate and down-the-hall toilet.

Steve had stomped on three and a half years of our lives. I would soon be fourteen.

On the fourth of August, my birthday, our old friend Steve, with diabolical timing, made that event unforgettable. Since that chilly dawn in April he had searched the slum streets for his escaped dupes, thirsty for revenge.

I waited eagerly in the hotel room for Mama who had promised to bake a cake in her white woman's kitchen. She said she would be home early at six o'clock to celebrate my birthday.

Well, she came home all right on the seventh of August, from a hospital, with her broken jaw wired, and her body covered with bruises.

Steve had stalked her and attacked her with his fists and feet and then escaped through the grimy catacombs of the Ghetto.

All that night and all the next day I crouched in the dark shadows beneath his stairwell gripping a gleaming ice pick. He never came back. He had moved.

Twenty years later, while idly looking from the window of a plush hotel suite I would see something familiar in the white-haired stooped figure of a garbage collector on the street three stories down.

I blacked out, when reason returned I was down there on the street in the bright morning sunlight, clutching a pistol, wearing only a pair of red silk pajamas.

As the garbage truck turned the corner a block away out of range, a small crowd of passers-by stood bug-eyed watching the strange scene as Rachel, my main whore, tugged at my arm, pleaded with me to get off the street.

That was the last time I saw Steve, but I just don't know, even now, what I would do if our paths crossed.

Perhaps that beating Mama took was good, as painful as it was. I remember how it worried me in that cruddy hotel room when the hotel's neon sign outside our window would flash on her face. Her eyes would be bright, riveted on the ceiling, she would be in a trance, remembering, still hot for him.

As worthless as that bastard was otherwise, he sure must have been a son-of-a-bitch in the bed.

After all he had done to us, she still had a terrible itch for the bastard. That beating was good for her, it cured the itch.

Mama had learned a bitter lesson the hard way. The country girl had rolled in the hay with the city slicker and now I saw all of her sorrow and guilt in her eyes.

We couldn't go back to the peaceful, green hills of Rockford. She had destroyed a good man back there, a native son. Henry died a year after we left him. Until the grave claimed her, Henry would rise from his own to haunt her in the lonely gloom.

Mama was desperate to save at least fragments of her image, to hold fast the love and respect I had for her in Rockford. I had seen too much, had suffered too much. The jungle had started to embalm me with bitterness and hardness.

I was losing page by page the fine rules of thought and deed that I had learned in church, from Henry, from the Boy Scout Troop in Rockford. I was sopping up the poison of the street like a sponge.

I had begun to play Steve's favorite game, craps, in the alleys after school.

Dangerously I was frantic to sock it into every young girl weak enough to go for it. I had to run for my life one evening when an enraged father caught me on his back porch punching animal-like astraddle his daughter's head. I had become impatient with the unusual thickness of her maidenhead.

2

First Steps into the Jungle

The slide was greased. I was starting my long plunge to the very bottom of the grim pit. I guess my trip downward really was cinched when I met a petty hustler who was very likeable and we became pals.

My hustler pal was called Party Time. By the time he was twenty-three he had done four bits in the joint. On each fall he had been jacked up for either strong-arm robbery or till tapping.

He got his monicker hung on him because as soon as he scored for scratch he would make fast tracks to the nearest underworld bar.

When he got inside the door he would shout, 'All right you poor ass bastards, it's party time and Joe Evans is in port with enough scratch to burn up a wet elephant. All you studs stop playing stink finger with these long-cock whores and everybody belly up to the log and get twisted on me.'

His flat African features were pasted to a skull that could have belonged to a cave man. He was short, powerful, and shiny black.

He was ugly enough to break daylight with his fist, but for some curious reason he was irresistible to many of the thrill-seeking white women who sneaked into the black side of town panting as they chased after that hoary myth: Nigger men do it so good it thrills you to your toe nails.

There was a Fast sheet joint with the trick rooms in the rear, right on the alley. I was peeping one night into one through a frayed shade when I saw Party Time for the first time.

My eyes were bugging when I saw the tall viking type white man, his tiny, but voluptuous female white companion and Party Time taking their clothes off. Finally they stood there naked. I could see their lips moving so I pressed my ear and eye sideways against the window that was open a couple of inches at the top to get the sound.

The white joker was tenderly hefting Party Time's weapon in his hand like maybe it was Ming Dynasty Pottery. He said excitedly to the broad, 'Oh! Honey, can you believe the size, the beauty of it.'

In the glow of the room's red light, that broad looked like an animated portrait by Da Vinci. Her eyes were blue fire in her passion. She purred like a Persian kitten and pounced onto the bed.

Party Time stood at the side of the bed looking down at her. He was an ebony executioner. His horizontal axe cast a cruel shadow across the snowy peaks, rose tipped.

My trouser front was tented as I pressed even tighter against the window. I had never seen anything like this back in Rockford. Then to my amazed ears, the white man said a strange thing as he pulled a chair to the end of the bed and sat on the very edge of it.

He was breathing hard when he said, 'All right now Boy, stab it into her, hurt her, punish her, crucify her, good Boy!, good Boy!'

The broad looked so fragile and helpless to my naive eyes that I felt a pang of pity pulse inside me as she moaned and whimpered in painful pleasure beneath the black demon savagely pile driving between the jerking white legs jack-knifed, imprisoned behind the sweating, hunching black shoulders.

Like he was trying to make a home Party Time was asking in a hoarse voice over and over, 'Beautiful Bitch, is it good? Beautiful Bitch, is it good?'

The white man was an odd, funny sight as he raced around the arena like a demented Caesar, cheering on his merciless black gladiator.

Finally when the show was over and they started to dress, I went to the front and sat on a stoop next door to the joint. I wanted to get a close up of the freaks.

When they got to the sidewalk, in their street clothes, they were disappointingly normal. Just a clean-cut white couple having a parting chat with a grinning, black Negro.

The mixed-up couple went down the sidewalk away from me. Party Time came toward me. He didn't notice me sitting on the stoop. I was itching with curiosity, so I hit on him when he came abreast. It startled him. His face got stiff.

I said, 'Hey Jack, how you doing? That sure is a fine silk girl, huh? You got a square to spare?'

He fished a cigarette from his red shirt pocket, handed it to me and said, 'Yeh Kid, she's fine as a Valentine. Two sights I ain't never seen and that is a pretty bulldog, and an ugly white woman.'

He was spouting cliches, but to a small town boy he came off witty as Hell. I was in that brain-picking mood so I put the snow machine into high gear to hold him. My eyes bucked in mock awe as I lit the square.

I said, 'Thanks Man, for the square. Christ! that's a sporty vine you got on. I wish I could dress like you. You sure are clean aplenty.'

He took the bait like a rapist in a nudist colony for the blind. He flopped down on the stoop beside me. He poked his chest out, his eyes flashing like a pin-ball machine gone haywire, as he got ready to open up. He hiked the pants legs of his green checked suit to his calves to show his blood red socks.

The huge zircon on his right pinky glittered under the street lamp as he cracked his knuckles and said, 'Kid, my name is Party Time. I am the best flat-footed hustler in town. Money loves me and can't stay away from me. You see that fine silk broad, I got a double saw to lay her. Course that ain't nothing, it happens all the time. I could be one of the greatest pimps in the country if I was lazy, and didn't have so much good hustler in me.'

I sat there listening to his bullshit until two A.M. He was likable and I was hungry for a pal. He was an orphan and he had just done a two-year bit straight up, his fourth, two months before. He had a head full of wild risky hustles he wanted to try. He needed a partner. He tried all of them on me for size.

I got home at two-twenty. About one minute later I heard Mama's key in the door. She had served a banquet for her white folks. I just made it into bed with all my clothes on, when she came to look in on me. I was snoring like a drunk with a sick sinus when she kissed me goodnight.

I lay thinking in the darkness until daybreak, putting myself into, and trying to size myself into one of those quick buck schemes that Party had plotted. When the sun came up fat and bright I knew I would give the Party's version of the Murphy a whirl. I didn't know his version was crude and dangerous, and only a weak imitation of the real Murphy.

Years later I discovered that the Murphy when played by experts was a smooth short con game with a slight risk. In any section where Negro whores operate white men will flock to trick with them.

I met Party several times after school at a pool room. He ran my role down to me and the next Friday night we got down with our hustle. Mama was serving a party so I could stay in the streets until at least one A.M.

Around ten that night in an alley in the heart of the vice section, Seventh and Vliet Sts., we unwrapped the package that Party had brought. I rolled up my pants legs beyond my bony knees. I slipped into the twenty-five cent red-cotton dress from the Salvation Army.

I put on the frayed red satin high-heel shoes. I pinned a scraggly piece of hair just inside the front inner band of the faded blue straw bonnet. When I tilted it on my head at a sexy angle, the ringlets of uneven hair hung down over my eyes like bangs.

I stood wide-legged, flexed my thigh and hip muscles against the tight red dress aping the whores stance.

Party looked me over head to toe. I was wondering how I came off as a broad. He shook his head, hunched his shoulders and walked toward the mouth of the alley to catch a sucker.

I got the answer when he reached the sidewalk. He twisted his head toward me and said, 'Listen Man, stay outta the light, okay?'

Within five minutes he gave me the office that some action was coming down the street. I watched Party giving the pitch to a short elderly white man. I wondered if I had enough voltage as a broad to come through with my end of the deal.

He officed my flash cue an instant before the white man peeked up the alley at me. I jerked my skinny ass in a series of bumps and grinds and hopefully waved him toward me.

That skinny black bitch he saw must have lit a fire in him all right. He fumbled his hide from his hip pocket and handed a bill to Party.

The chump started up the alley at a helluva pace for an old bastard. He had paid his money and he was red hot to take his chance to stick that hot Nigger bitch waiting for him in the shadows.

He had no chance, but in a way he was lucky. Lucky that his hide had not been fat with greenbacks. If he had been loaded, when I evaporated through that gang way, Party instead of fading away would have come into the dark alley behind the sucker and robbed him with brute force.

My heart was pounding in excitement as I galloped through the alleys toward our next prearranged duck blind. I took a new station several blocks away. Party Time came moments later, looked up the alley and hooked the tips of his thumb and index fingers into an 'all is well' O.

We beat several other suckers. None had the fare for the strong arm. We worked until twelve-thirty, then unlike Cinderella, I stashed my mildewed costume, got my half of the seventy-dollar take and raced home. Mama came in a half hour after I did.

As in all other things there are many Murphys. Real Murphy players use great finesse to separate a mark from his scratch. The most adept of them prefer that a trick hit on them. It puts the Murphy player in a position to force the sucker to qualify himself and to trim the mark not only for all of his scratch, but his jewelry as well.

When approached and quizzed by a mark as to, where a girl can be found, the Murphy Man will say, 'Look Buddy, I know a fabulous house not more than two blocks away. Brother, you ain't never seen more beautiful, freakier broads than are in that house. One of them, the prettiest one can do more with a swipe than a monkey can with a banana. She's like a rubber doll, she can take a hundred positions.'

At this point the sucker is wild to get to this house of pure joy. He entreats the con player to take him there, not just direct him to it.

The Murphy player will prat him to enhance his desire. He will say, 'Man, don't be offended, but Aunt Kate, that runs the house don't have nothing but high-class white men coming to her place. No Niggers or poor white trash. You know, doctors, lawyers, big-shot politicians. You look like a clean-cut white man, but you ain't in that league are you?'

At this pricking of his ego the mark is ready for the hook. He will protest his worth as a person and his right to go where any other son-of-a-bitch can go. Hell for a high class lay a double saw wouldn't faze him. Few can resist the charm of exclusivity in its myriad forms.

The con player still hedging, shoring up firmly the convincer will then say, 'Man, I believe you and everything you say is true as gospel. In fact, I like you Pal, but try to see my side of it. First to show you I trust you, I'll tell you a secret. I been working for Aunt Kate's house for many years now as her outside man, you know, making sure only nice dates went up there. Aunt Kate and I got an airtight system. Friend, I know you will help me keep Aunt Kate's rules, so let's go. I am taking you to the thrill of your life.'

While keeping up an inflaming description of the whores and sexual delights to be found only at Aunt Kate's, the Murphy player had steered the sucker to a pre-chosen neat attractive apartment building. In the foyer in a subtle but compelling manner the con player nudged the mark into a fast meeting of minds, the question agreed on. As hot as he was, he couldn't go up before he checked in all valuables. It was Aunt Kate's unshakeable rule.

Aunt Kate was rock right never to tempt or trust a whore. Only fools trusted whores, right? The mark wasn't a fool, right? Right!

The con player produced a sturdy brown envelope. The sucker counted all the scratch in his pocket into the hand of Aunt Kate's outside business manager. The efficient affable manager shoved it into the envelope, licked it, sealed it, and stuck it in his pocket for safe keeping from the possible larceny in the hearts of the gorgeous dolls upstairs, third floor, first apartment to the left, number nine to be specific.

The sucker was in a bubbly mood as he took the stairs three at a time. He liked that Nigger down there who was protecting his money. What had he told him, when he gave him the shiny gold-colored metal check? 'Harry, Pal, this one is on me, just go up and hand it to Aunt Kate. Everything is going to be all right. If you want, you can buy me a drink when you come down.'

The two strikes that had whiffed across the white man's mental plate and had set him up for the Kill, the third strike was first his desperate need to relieve himself into a black body, the second was his complete inability to conceive that the black boy before him was intelligent enough to fool him, to fashion the Murphy dialogue.

Party and his rawboned lure after three weekends of fair success with the Murphy ran head on into a round brick balloon. It was only five feet tall, but it weighed close to three-hundred pounds.

It was a Saturday night around ten. The vice section was overrun with Johns. It seemed that every white man in town was out there, scratch in one hand and rod in the other, ripping and running after the black whores with the widest, blackest asses.

Party and I set up a blind on the fringe of the section, because with all that mad action in the center it would be a hectic cat-and-mouse game with the cruising, rousting vice squad. I would have gotten something less than pure kicks to get busted making like a broad.

Party hadn't strong-armed since his last bit. The only reason he hadn't was simply that none of the Johns we had fleeced was carrying a wad.

We were fishing in a sand pile. All the hungry suckers were swimming in center stream.

From my Murphy station in the alley, I watched Party eagerly for the office for action. Around eleven-thirty, I was standing on one leg and then the other like a bored crane with a twenty-five cent dress on.

About five minutes later the office came through. Was it a man? A machine? No, it was a walking, living, round balloon with a fat poke and a flaming itch for black Cush. It stood there fascinated by my furious bumps and grinds.

I felt prickly feet of excitement stomping along my spine when the balloon took his hide out. Party jerked rigid at the sight of its contents. Even as the balloon bounced toward me, I inched toward my point of evaporation. I knew the strong-arm lust had exploded inside Party and sure as Hell he was going to come up that alley and smash the air out of the balloon.

I quit the scene and poked my head into the alley farther up. I could hear guttural grunting. The kind of sound a heart case makes when he's riding hard to convince a nympho that he's a raging tiger. It was the balloon that was grunting as he held Party in a crushing strangle hold. My heart-beat back-fired and melted the starch in my props. I collapsed onto a garbage can. The balloon was also a weight lifter. Poor Party was hanging high over the head of the monster and then flung to the alley floor with a shattering whoomp where he lay like a rag doll. The balloon hollered as he leaped into the air and then fell like a ton of concrete on moaning Party. I was almost puking in pity for Party. But I just couldn't find the strength to get off that garbage can and join the fray. Anyway it wouldn't have been ladylike.

The derrick scooped Party from the alley and flung him across his back. I watched Party's rubber neck bumping against the balloon's rear end as he was carried to the sidewalk.

I jetted out of there and went to the roof of my building. I watched for the rollers I was sure were coming to bust me, but they never came. Old Party had had the funky luck to try the strong-arm on a professional wrestler called the Blimp.

Party went back to the joint for a yard after he got out of City Hospital. One thing about Party he wasn't copper-hearted. He never tipped my name to the heat.

When he got older, and lost his nerve to hustle, he got a crazy desire to pimp. He wasn't the type, but he kept trying until he ran the Gorilla game on a dope dealer's broad and was set up for a hot shot. Party tried his fists and muscle until the pimp game croaked him. The pimp game is like the watchmaker's art, it's tough. Party went through his life struggling to make a watch while wearing boxing gloves. Party's bad break sobered me, and I started hearing what was going on in day classes at school.

At fifteen, amazingly, I graduated from high school with a 98.4 average. There was a sizeable alumni of Tuskegee, a Southern Negro college, who insisted upon Mama letting them underwrite all expenses for my education at their Alma Mater. Mama leaped at the chance.

The alumni went into debt and sent me down to their hallowed school with a sparkling wardrobe. They didn't know I had started to rot inside from street poisoning.

It was like the poor chumps had entered a poisoned horse in the Kentucky Derby and were certain they had a cinch winner. They couldn't know they had bet their hearts and blood money on a born loser.

A rich bonanza was at stake. The success of my very life itself. The rescue of Mama from her awesome guilt. The trust and confidence of that big-hearted alumni.

My mental eyes had been stabbed blind by the street. I was like a freakish joker who had gotten clap in his eyes from a mangy street whore.

On campus, I was like a fox in a chicken coop. Within ninety days after I got down there I had slit the maidenhead on a half-dozen curvy co-eds.

Somehow I managed to get through the Freshman year, but my notoriety was getting awful. The campus finks were envious, and it was too dangerous to continue to impale co-eds on my stake.

In my Sophomore year, I started going into the hills near the campus to juke joints. With my slick Northern dress and manner I was prince charming in spades to the pungent, hot-ass maidens in the hills.

A round butt, bare foot, beauty – fifteen years old – fell hard for me. One night I failed to meet her in our favorite clump of bushes. I had stuck her up to keep a date in another clump of bushes with a bigger, hotter, rounder ass than hers.

Through the hill grape vine she got the wire of my double cross. It was high noon on campus the next day when I saw her. I had just walked out of the cafeteria onto the main drag. The street was lousy with students and teachers.

She stood out like a Pope in a cat house. Her potato-sack dress was grimy and dirty as Hell from the long trip from the hills. Her bare feet and legs were rusty and dusty. She saw me a wild heart-beat after I saw her.

She battle-cried like an Apache Warrior, and before I could get the wax out of my props, she had raced close enough toward me so that I could see the insane fury in her eyes.

Beads of sweat clung to the kinky hair in the pit of her arm that was upraised, gripping like a dagger a broken Coca Cola bottle, the jagged edges were glinting in the sun.

The screaming teachers and students fled like terrified sheep in the wake of a panther. I don't remember what athlete was reputed to be the fastest human in the world that year, but for those few seconds after I got the wax out of my legs, I was.

When I finally looked back through the cloud of dust, I saw the crazy broad as a speck in the distance behind me.

Mine had been a carpet offense and I was on it in the office of the school President.

I stood before him seated behind his gleaming mahogany desk. He cleared his pipes and gave me a look like I had jacked off before the student body. He held his head high. His nose reaching for the ceiling like I was crap on his top lip.

In a sneaky Southern drawl he said, 'Boy, yu ah a disgrace to oauh fine institushun. Ah'm shocked thet sech has occurred. Yo mothah has bin infaumed of yo bad conduck. Oauh bord is considurin yo dismissul. En thu meantime, keep yo nos clean, Boy. Yo ah not to leave campus for eny resun.'

I could have saved my worry over dismissal. That alumni had powerful pull all right. I got a break and got the chance to stay until mid-term of the Sophomore year when I went for the okey doke. I took a bootlegging rap for a pal. 'What goes around comes around' old hustlers had said. Party had taken our beef without spilling.

Anything with a buzz in it was in great demand on campus. A pint of rot gut whiskey brought from seven and a half to ten dollars depending on supply. My roommate had scratch and a Fagin disposition. He was a sharpy from a number-racket family in New York.

We made a deal. He would bank roll our venture if I copped the merchandise and sold it. He got my promise that I would keep his part in it a secret. He was a fox for sure.

He gave me the scratch and I slipped up into the hills to contact a moonshiner who would supply me. Perhaps I don't have to say that I carefully avoided any contact with that broad who pushed me to that track record.

I scored for a connection and the markup on campus was four-hundred percent.

Everything was beautiful. The merchandise was moving like crazy. I was sure that when I got back home for the summer I would have enough scratch to turn everybody green with envy.

I recruited a co-ed I had layed to distribute for me in her dorm. It was the beginning of the end.

There were two jasper co-eds in her dorm who were fierce rivals for the love of a coffee-colored, curvaceous doll from a country town in Oklahoma. The doll was really dumb. She had no idea of the lesbian kick, so naturally she couldn't know she was a target.

Eventually, the craftier of the two jaspers wore the doll down and turned her out. They had to keep the secret of their romance from the other jasper because she was tough and built like a football player. She was doing money favours for the doll hoping to get into her pants. The doll and her jockey were in cahoots playing the sucker jasper hard for the scratch.

One night the doll and her jockey were tied into a pretzel doing the sixty-nine and drunk as Hell on my merchandise, when their passionate outcries reached the ears of the muscular jasper.

The bloody fight and spicy details were topics for state-wide gossip.

In the heat of the investigation my agent fell apart. She put the finger on me and within a week I was on the train going back to the streets for good. I didn't turn over on my roommate. I obeyed the code.

Mama changed jobs a week after I got back, to nurse and cook for a wealthy, white recluse. Now I really stuck my nose in the devil's ass.

Mama had to stay on the place. I saw her once a week, on Sunday, when she would come in for a day. That was the only time I stayed at the hotel.

I had found a fascinating second home, a gambling joint run by a broken-down ex-pimp and murderer called Diamond Tooth Jimmy. The two-carat stone wedged between the upper front rotting teeth was the last vulgar memento of his infamy as the top ass-kicker of the nineteen-twenties.

He boasted endlessly that he was the only Nigger pimp on Earth who had ever pimped in Paris on French girls. I was to discover later, when I would meet and be trained by the Master, that Jimmy was a mere buffoon, an amateur not fit to hold the Master's coat.

After the suckers were trimmed and all the shills had been paid, Jimmy would lock the door and then like a ritual light up a thin brown reefer. As he talked, he would pass it to me, cursing me affably for not inhaling deeply and holding the smoke, as he put it, deep in my belly.

I would go to bed in the tiny cubicle in the rear of his glorious days as a pimp. When dawn broke he would go out through the joint door home to the nineteen-year-old jasper on whom he lavished furs and jewels. He was a real sucker.

I would go to bed in the tiny cubicle in the rear of the joint and dream fantastic dreams. Always beautiful whores would get down on their knees and tearfully beg me to take their money.

For several months I had been screwing the luscious daughter of a popular band leader. She was fifteen. Her name was June and she had a wild yen for me. She had a habit of waiting down the street from the gambling joint until Jimmy left, then she would come up and get on the army cot with me. She would stay until seven o'clock at night. She knew I had to clean the joint for action around nine.

One day, around noon, I asked her, 'Do you love me enough to do anything for me?'

She said, 'Yes.'

So, I said, 'Even turn a trick?'

She said, 'Anything.'

I put my clothes on and went to the street and saw an old gambler whom I knew was a trick and told him what was upstairs. Sure enough he gave me a five-dollar bill, the asking price, and I took him upstairs and let him in on her. She turned him in less than five minutes.

My seventeen-year-old brain reeled. This was still the Depression. I could get rich with this girl and drive a big white Packard.

My next prospect was all wrong. He was an acquaintance of the band leader, June's father. He went up the stairs, saw her and called the father in Pittsburgh.

The father called the local police department and my pimping career died aborning. When the detective came, I was still out there looking for tricks for the down payment on that big white Packard.

Diamond Tooth's bullshit had screwed me for certain. My mother, of course, was shocked. She was sure it was a frame up. That June, that evil girl, had led her sweet little Bobby astray.

At the County Jail two days before my trial, I left my cell on an Attorney Consultation pass. A short, gopher-faced Negro sat in the cage at an old oak desk grinning at me.

My blood ran cold, my palms got slippery wet as I took a seat across from him. The gleaming yellow gold teeth filling his mouth had been a flash of doom. Christ! I thought, a Deep South Nigger lip. Didn't Mama know that most of them turned to jelly when defending a criminal case?

The rodent wiped his blue-black brow with a soggy handker-chief and said, 'Well Bobby, it seems that you are in a little trouble, huh? I am attorney Williams, an old friend of your family. I knew your mother as a girl.'

My eyes sent special delivery murder across the table to that ugly bastard.

I said, 'It isn't a little trouble. Under the Max I could get a fin.'

He fingered his dollar necktie and hoisted his starved shoulders inside the jacket of his cheap vine and said, 'Oh! Now let's not be fatalistic. You are a first offender and I am positive it will mitigate the charge. Rest assured I will press the court for leniency. Now tell me the whole truth about your trouble.'

Anger, everything drained out of me. I was lost, stricken. The phony would lead me to the slaughter. I knew I was already tried and convicted and sentenced to the joint. The only loose end was for how long? Without hearing it myself, I ran down the details to him and stumbled blindly back to my cell.

On my trial day in the courtroom, the shaky bastard was so nervous before the bench when he pleaded me guilty that the same cheap vine that he had worn at our first meeting was soaked by his sweat.

He was so shook up by the stern face and voice of the white hawk-faced judge that he forgot to ask for leniency. That awful fear the white folks had put into him down South was still painfully alive in him. He just stood there paralyzed, waiting for the judge to sentence me.

So, I looked up into the frosty blue eyes and said, 'Your Honor, I am sorry for what I did. I have never been in trouble before. If Your Honor will just give me a break this time, I swear before the Lord I won't ever come back down here. Please, Your Honor, don't send me to the pen.'

The frost deepened in his eyes as he looked down at me and intoned, 'You are a vicious young man. Your crime against that innocent young girl, against the laws of this state are inexcusable. The very nature of your crime precludes the possibility of probation. For your own good and for that of society's I sentence you to the State Reformatory to a term for not less than one year, and for not more than eighteen months. I hope it teaches you a lesson.'

I shrugged off the wet hand of the lip from my shoulder, avoided the tear-reddened eyes of Mama sobbing quietly in the rear of the courtroom, and stuck my hands out to the bailiff for the icy-cold handcuffs.

June's old man was a big wheel with lots of muscle in the courts. He had gone behind the scenes and pulled strings, and put the cinch on the joint for me. My sentence was for carnal knowledge and abuse, reduced from pandering, because you can't pander from anything except a whore, and June's old man wasn't about to go for that.

Yes, I was sure working at that first patch of gray in my mother's hair. Steve would have been proud of me, don't you think?

My sentence to the Wisconsin Green Bay reformatory almost cracked Mama up.

There were several repeaters from the reformatory on my tier at County Jail, who tried to bug the first offenders with terrible stories about the hard time up at the reformatory, while we were waiting for the van to take upstate to the reformatory. I was too dumb to feel anything. A fool I was to think the dummy was a fairy tale!

In the two weeks that I waited, Mama wrote me a letter every day and visited twice. Mama's guilt and heartbreak were weighing heavily on her.

Back in Rockford she had been a dutiful church goer, leading a christian life until Steve came on the scene. But now when I read her long rambling letters crammed with threats of fire and brimstone for me if I didn't get Jesus in my heart and respect the Holy Ghost and the fire, I realized that poor Mama was becoming a religious fanatic to save her sanity. The pressures of Henry's death and now my plight must have been awful.

The van came to get us on a stormy, thunderous morning. As we stepped into the van handcuffed together I saw Mama standing in the icy, driving rain waving good-bye. I could feel a hot throbbing lump at the base of my throat to see her standing there looking so sad and lonesome, cowering beneath the battering rain. I could feel the tears aching to flow, but I couldn't cry.

Mama never told me how she found out the time the van would come. I still wonder how she found out and what her thoughts were out there in the storm as she watched me start my journey.

The state called it a reformatory, but believe me it was a prison for real.

My belly fluttered when the van pulled into the prison road leading to the joint. The van had been vibrating with horse play and profane ribbing among the twenty-odd prisoners. Only one of them had sat tensely and silently during the entire trip. The fat fellow next to me.

But when those high slate gray walls loomed grimly before us it was as if a giant fist had slugged the breath from us all. Even the repeaters who had served time behind those walls were silent, tight faced. I started to believe those stories they had told back in County Jail.

The van went through three gates manned by rock-faced hacks carrying scoped, high-powered rifles. Three casket-gray cell houses stood like mute mourners beneath the bleak sunless sky. For the first time in my life I felt raw, grinding fear.

The fat Negro sitting next to me was a former school mate of mine in high school. He had been a dedicated member of the Holiness Church then.

I had never gotten friendly with him because his only interest at that time seemed to be his church and Bible. He didn't smoke, swear, chase broads or gamble. He had been a rock-ribbed square.

His name was Oscar. Apparently he was still square because now his eyes were closed and I could hear bits of prayer as he whispered softly.

Oscar's prayer was abruptly cut off by the screech of the van's brakes as it stopped in front of the prison check-in station and bath house. We clambered out and stood in line to have our handcuffs removed. Two screws started at each end of the line unlocking the cuffs.

As they moved toward the middle of the line they stifled

the thin whispers of the men. They said to each man, 'Button it up! Silence! No talking!'

Oscar was shaking and trembling in front of me as we filed into a brightly-lit high-ceilinged room. A rough pine counter stretched for twenty yards down a green-and-gray flagstone floor that looked clean enough to eat from. This was part of the shiny, clean skin of the apple. The inside was rotting and foul.

Cons with starch-white faces stood behind the long counter guessing our sizes as we passed them and passing out faded pieces of our uniform from caps to brogans.

We passed with our bundles into a large room. A tall silent screw, dazzling with brass buttons and gold braid on his navy-blue uniform, slashed his lead-loaded cane through the air like a vocal sword directing us to put our bundles on a long bench and to undress for short arm inspection, and a brief exam by the prison croaker seated at a battered steel desk in the back of the room.

Finally we all had been checked by the croaker and showered. The gold-spangled screw raised his talkative cane. It told us to go out the door and turn left, then straight ahead. Two screws marched alongside as we made it toward a squat sandstone building two-hundred yards away. Was that talking cane the dummy's?

I heard it before I saw it. A loud scraping, thunder laced with a hollow roar. Never before had I heard anything like it. Then mysteriously, in the dimness, countless young grim faces seemed to be bobbing in a sea of gray. A hundred feet ahead I saw the mystery. Hundreds of gray-clad cons were lock stepping from the mess halls into the three cell houses. They were an eerie sight in the twilight marching mutely in cadence like tragic robot soldiers. The roaring thunder was the scrape and thump of their heavy prison brogans.

We reached the squat building. We were to stay in its quarantine cells for the next ten days. All fish new cons were housed here to be given a thorough medical check-out and classification before being assigned to work details out in population.

I got a putrid taste of the inside of that apple when cons in white uniforms and peaked caps gave us our supper through a slot in our cell doors. It was barley soup with a hunk of brown bread. It would have made great shrapnel in a grenade.

I was new and learning, so instead of just gulping it down, I took a long close look at the odd little things black-dotted at one end. I puked until my belly cramped. The barley in the soup was lousy with worms.

The lights went out at nine. Every hour or so a screw came by the roll of cells. He would poke the bright eye of his flashlight into a cell and then squint his eyes as he looked into each cell. I wondered if it were a capital crime in this joint to get caught having an affair with lady five fingers.

I flapped my ears when I heard one of the white repeaters running down the joint in a whisper to a fish. Oscar was listening too because he had stopped praying in his cell next to mine.

The white fish was saying, 'Look Rocky, what the Hell gives with that hack in the bath house? Why don't the jack-off never rap? What's with that cane bit?'

The repeater said, 'The son-of-a-bitch is stir crazy. His voice-box screwed up on him a dime ago. He's been the brass nuts here for a double dime, and guess how the bastard lost his rapper?'

That screw and his light was making the rounds again, so the repeater got on the dummy.

When the screw had passed he continued, 'The creep was called Fog Horn by the cons before his trouble made him a dummy. They say the bastard's bellows could be heard from one side of the joint to the other. He's the meanest captain of screws this joint ever had. In the last double dime he has croaked two white cons and four spades with his cane. He hates Niggers.'

Oscar was praying like mad now. He had heard what the repeater said about those four Negroes. The fish wanted a loose end tied for him.

He said, 'Yeh Rocky, just to glim him and you know he's rough, but what in the Hell cut his box off?'

The repeater said, 'Oh! The vine has it he treated his wife and Crumb crusher worse than he did the cons. She got her fill of his screwing and drilled herself and the kid through the head. The little broad was only two years old. The note his broad left said, I can't stand your hollering any longer. Good-bye. A head-shrinker here at the time said when the broad croaked herself it shut off Brass Nuts box.'

I lay there thinking about what the con had said. I thought about Oscar and wondered if he could pull his bit or if he would go back to his parents in a pine box, or worse to the crazy farm.

Oscar had been sentenced to a year by the same judge that had socked it into me. Oscar, poor chump had started going with a crippled Irish girl of seventeen.

In the dark balcony of a downtown theatre they were seen smooching by the son of a close friend of the girl's family. He reported post haste to his parents who wired up the girl's parents. They were Irish, with temper and prejudice.

They third-degreed the girl and she confessed that old black Oscar had indeed trespassed the forbidden valley. The charge of statuatory rape naturally stood up and here was old Oscar next door to me.

I slapped the itching sting on my thigh. I pulled the sheet back. Lord, have mercy! How I hated them. It was a bed bug I had smashed, but he was only a scout. When that flashlight jarred me awake an hour later, a division of them was parading the walls.

I lay wide eyed until morning. The inside of that shiny apple was really something else.

After all our tests we fish were taken out of the quarantine tank on the tenth day to the Warden's office. My turn came to go in. I got up from the long bench in the hall outside his office and walked in. My knees were having a boxing match as I stood before him.

He was a silver-maned, profane, huge, white bull with two tiny chunks of black fire rammed deep into his eye sockets.

He said, 'Well Sambo, you sure got your black-Nigger ass in a sling, didn't you? Well understand me, we didn't send for you, but you came. We are here to punish you smart-aleck bastards, so if you fuck around, two things can happen to you, both of them horrible. We got a hole here that we bury tough punks in, it's a stripped cell without light, twenty feet below ground. Down there, two slices of bread and a pint of water twice a day. You can go out that North gate in a box for your second choice. So take this rule book and study it. Now get your rusty black ass out of my face.'

The only thing I said before I eased out of there was, 'Yes Sir, Boss Man,' and I was grinning like a Mississippi rape suspect turned loose by the mob.

It was a wise thing I had uncled on him. One of those arrogant repeaters went to the hole for having a sassy look in his eyes. The charge was 'visual insubordination.'

Oscar and I were assigned to work and live in cell block B. It was all black. Of the three, it was the only one without toilets. We had buckets in cells that we took out each morning and dumped into running water in a trough behind the cell block.

The only stench in my life I have ever smelled that was worse than that cell block on a warm night was a sick hype.

It was rough all right and a terrible battle of wits. The battle mainly centered around staying out of sight and trouble with the dummy. He walked on the balls of his feet and he could read a con's mind. It was terrifying to have maybe a slice of contraband bread in your bosom, and then from nowhere have the dummy pop up.

He didn't pass out an instruction leaflet running down the lingo of that cane. If you misunderstood what it said, the dummy would crack the leaded shaft of it against your skull.

After I had put in six months on my bit, a young Negro con came in on transfer from the big joint and brought me a wire from Party.

He sent word that we were still tight and I was his horse if I never won a race.

It felt good to know he had forgiven me for turning chicken back there in the alley with the balloon.

The dummy hated everybody. He felt something much more frightful for Oscar.

I don't know whether it was that the dummy had a hate for God too, and he knew how religious Oscar was, and had focused all his hate on a living target.

Oscar and I shared a double bunk cell. I had the bottom bunk. It was a chilling sight at night when the dummy should have been at home to look up from a book and see him out there on the tier motionless, staring up at Oscar in his bunk reading the Bible.

When I was sure that the cold, luminous, green eyes had slipped away for the night, I would crack, 'Oscar, my man, I like you. Will you take some good advice from a friend? I am telling you Pal, it's driving the dummy off his rocker to see you reading that Bible. Pal, why in the Hell don't you stop reading it for your own good?'

That square jerk would go on reading, he hadn't even noticed the dummy's visit.

He would say, 'I know you are my friend and I appreciate your advice, but I can't take it. Don't worry about me. Jesus will protect me.'

Mama was writing at least once a week. Every month she visited me. On her last visit, without worrying her too much, I suggested it would be a good idea to put in a long-distance call to the Warden once a week just so he would know somebody out there loved me and wanted me to stay healthy.

She was looking fine and had saved her money. She had opened a beauty shop. She told me when I came up for parole she was sure a friend of hers would give me a job. At night after her visits I would lie sleepless all night mentally recapping our sad lives. I could still remember too, every mole and crease in Henry's face.

One night after one of her visits, the radio loud speaker on the cell house wall blared out 'Spring Time in the Rockies.' I tried to keep my crying a secret from Oscar, but he heard me. He marked off a chapter in the Bible for me to read, but with the dummy around, I wasn't about to do something stupid like that.

The dummy put one over on Jesus and busted Oscar. We had almost finished mopping the flag when the cell-house runner brought me two wieners from the kitchen. A pal had sent them.

I gave Oscar one. He stuck it inside his shirt. I stood my mop against the wall and ducked into an empty cell and wolfed mine down.

We had finished mopping and were at the supply closet putting our mops and buckets away. Oscar was nibbling slowly on his wiener like he was safe and sound at the Last Supper.

I saw the giant shadow glue itself against the wall next to the closet door. I looked through the trap door in the corner of my eye. The universe reeled.

It was the dummy. He saw the piece of wiener in Oscar's hand. The dummy's green eyes were oscillating.

That deadly cane razored through the air and cut a slice of hair and bloody flesh from the side of Oscar's head.

The scarlet glob was hanging by a slimy thread of flesh dangling like an awful earring near the tip of his ear lobe. Oscar's eyes walled toward the back of his head as he moaned and slipped to the flag. From the grey whitish core of the wound spouts of blood pulsed out.

The dummy just stood there looking down at the carnage. His green eyes were twinkling in excitement. I had seen him every day for eight months. I had never seen him smile. He was smiling now like he was watching two cute kittens frolicking. I stooped to help Oscar. I felt feathery puffs of air against my cheek. The cane was screaming. The dummy was furiously waggling it beside my head.

It was screaming, 'Get out!'

I got. I lay in my cell wondering if the dummy had second thoughts and would try for two. I heard the voices of the hospital orderlies on the flag taking Oscar away.

I remembered the murderous force of the blow the dummy had struck. I remembered that pleased look on his face. I knew from con grape-vine that he was from Alabama. I knew now it hadn't been Oscar's Bible that had put the dummy's balls in the fire. The dummy knew about that crippled Irish girl.

Oscar went from the hospital into the hole for fifteen days. The charges 'possession of contraband food' and 'physical aggression against an officer.' I was there and the only aggression on Oscar's part was the natural resistance of his flesh and bone to that steel cane.

The parole board met in the joint every month to consider applications. Every con, when he had served to within several months of his minimum, started dreaming of the street and that upcoming parole consideration.

Oscar was in the hole and I missed his company. He was a square, but a nice one with lots of wry wit. Several cons slightly older than I came in on transfer from the big joint. They claimed to be mack men.

In bad weather when there was no yard recreation I would join them at a table on the flag. I didn't talk much. I usually listened. I was fascinated by the yarns they spun about their pimping ability. They had a lot of bullshit, and I was stealing as much as I could from them to use when I got out.

I would go back to my cell excited. I would pretend I had a whore before me. I would stand there in the cell and pimp up a storm. I didn't know that the crap I was rehearsing wouldn't get a quarter in the street.

Oscar came out of the hole and was put into an isolation cell on the top tier of the cell house. I didn't see him come in so I wasn't prepared when I got a chance to go up there.

When I got to the cell with his number in the slot, a skinny joker was peeing in his bucket with his back to me. He was in a laughing fit. I checked the number in the slot again. It was Oscar's number all right.

I pulled the key to the supply closet across the bars of the cell door. The skeleton jumped and spun around facing me. His eyes were wild and vacant. It was Oscar. Only that livid bald scar on the side of his head made me sure.

He didn't seem to remember me so I said, 'How are you, Pal? I knew they couldn't stop a stepper.'

He just stood there, his dingus flopping from his open fly.

I said, 'Jack, you are going to give your bright future the flu if you don't get it out of the draft.'

He ignored my words, and then from the very bottom of his throat I could hear a kind of eerie high pitched humming or keening, like maybe the mating call of a werewolf. I was beginning to worry about him.

I was standing there trying to figure something to say to get through to him. He hadn't been out of the hole for more than two hours. Maybe some loose circuit would jar back to contact.

I knew he had been destroyed when he gave me a sly look and went to the back of his cell. He picked up his bucket and thrust his hand into it.

He brought out a fist full of crap. He scraped the crap from his right palm into the rigid upturned left palm.

Using his left palm as a kind of palette, he dipped into the crap with his right index finger and started to finger paint on the cell wall.

I just stood there in shock. Finally, he stopped, snapped to attention, saluted me and stuck his chest out proudly and pointed a crappy finger at his art on the wall.

There was an idiot's look of triumph on his face like he had finished the Sistine Chapel Ceiling.

I gave up on him. I went downstairs and told the cell house screw.

The next day they shipped Oscar to the funny farm where perhaps he is today, thirty years later.

My time went fast after the eighth month. I had gone before the parole board and I was waiting for my pink slip. A white one meant denial and a new date for consideration.

I saw the mail clerk when he shoved it through the bars of my cell. I leaped up and grabbed the small brown envelope. My hands shook so badly, it took seconds to rip it open. It was pink! I banged my fists against the steel wall of my cell. I was so happy I couldn't feel pain.

They dressed me out in a cheap glen-plaid suit. I would have been thrilled to have left that den of pressure in tar and feathers. On the way out I had to face the bull.

When I walked into his office he said, 'Well Snow-ball, you

must have had your rabbit's foot. So long, see you in a couple of weeks.'

I wasn't out yet, so I gave him the same uncle smile going out that I gave him coming in.

When I walked out of the joint the fresh air was like a blast of oxygen. It made me woozy. I turned and looked back at the joint. The dummy was standing at the chapel window staring at me, but for once that steel cane wasn't talking to me.

3

Salty Trip with Pepper

First thing back in Milwaukee, I reported to my parole officer, a Mr Rand, I think. After asking a thousand questions and filling out a mountain of papers he gave me an I.Q. Test. When he computed my score his sea-blue eyes saucered in surprise.

He couldn't understand how a boy with a score of one hundred and seventy-five could do a stupid thing like peddling a girl's ass on the sidewalk.

If that I.Q. Test had been on the basis of the half-baked criminal, pimping theories that I had picked up in the joint at that table from those Chili pimps that were churning in my mind, and that I was so eager to try, my score would have been zero.

I was eighteen now, six feet two inches tall, slender, sweet, and stupid. My maroon eyes were deeply set, dreamy. My shoulders were broad and my waist as narrow as a girl's.

I was going to be a heart breaker all right. All I needed was the threads and a whore.

Mama's small, lucrative beauty shop was on the main drag. Poor Mama, she was doomed I guess to inadvertently set up my disasters.

I had started on my job delivering for the drugstore owned by the friend of my Mama's who had hired me to satisfy the parole condition of a job upon release.

As fate would have it, Mama's shop and the drugstore were in the same building. Mama and I lived in an apartment over the store fronts.

Mama called me in from the sidewalk one day about three months after I had gotten parole. She wanted me to meet one of her customers who was getting her eyebrows arched. I walked through the pungent odors rising from the hot pressing combs pulling through the kinky hair of several customers, to the rear of the shop.

There she was, flashy as a Christmas Tree, sitting before a mirror at a dressing table with her back to me. Mama stopped plucking at her brows as she introduced us, 'Mrs Ibbetts, this is my son Bobby.'

Like a yellow cat hypnotizing a bird, she sat there motionless, her green eyes smoky, as she stared at me through the mirror.

Then the velvet purring voice undulated toward me, she said, 'Oh Bobby, I have heard so much about you. It's so exciting to meet you, but please call me Pepper, everyone does.'

I don't know what excited me more as I stood there, her raw sensuality or the blazing rocks on her tapered fingers that I was sure hadn't come from Kresges. I mumbled something like I had to go back to the drugstore to work, and I would see her around.

Later I saw her slide into her sleek Caddie convertible, her white silk dress riding up exposing the satin sheen of her banana yellow thighs. As she gunned away from the curb, she turned deliberately and gave me a full dose of those hot green eyes. She was signing our deal.

I quizzed around and got the background on her. She was twenty-five, an ex-whore who had worked the jazziest houses on the Eastern Seaboard. A wealthy white fence and gambler had tricked with her out there, and it had gotten so good to him that he crossed her pimp into a five-year bit and squared her up.

Three days later, a half hour before closing, an order came in for a case of Mums. The address was in the plush Heights, miles from the store.

I made the trip on a bicycle. She answered the door wearing only a pair of white lace step-ins. My erection was hard and instant.

It was a fabulous pad, and the lights were soft and blue. The old man wouldn't be back for a week.

I was just a hep punk, I wasn't in her league, but one of my greatest assets has always been my open mind. That freak bitch cajoled and persuaded me to do everything in the sexual book, and a number of things not even listed.

What a thrill for a dog like her to turn out a tender fool like me. She was a hell of a teacher all right, and what a performer. If Pepper had lived in the old Biblical city of Sodom the citizens would have stoned her to death.

She nibbled and sucked hundreds of tingling bruises on every square inch of my body. Fair exchange, as the old saw goes, is never robbery.

It took me a week to get the stench of her piss out of my hair. She sure had been pimped on hard back East. She hated men, and she was taking her revenge on me.

She had taught me to snort girl, and almost always when I came to her pad, there would be thin sparkling rows of crystal cocaine on the glass top of the cocktail table.

We would snort it through alabaster horns and then in the mirrored bedroom we made circus love until our nerve ends shrieked.

Pepper and that pure cocaine would have made a freak out of a Priest. She had sure put me on a fast track.

I couldn't know at the time that at the end of the line stood the grim State Penitentiary.

I was green all right and twice as soft, and Pepper knew it. Here was a hardened ex-whore who knew all the crosses, all the answers, who handled lots of scratch and wasn't laying a red penny on me.

The dazzling edge on our orgies was dulling for me, but I was flipping Pepper with the techniques she had taught me. I knew all the buttons to push for her, and she burned hotter than ever for her little puppy.

No wonder, I was freaking for free, those Eastern pimps had charged her a fortune.

I tried one night to get a C note from her for a suit. I knew I had really come on fine in the bed. She had almost climbed the walls in her passion.

'Sugar,' I said, 'I saw a wild vine for a bill downtown. If you laid the scratch on me, I could cop tomorrow.'

She slitted her green eyes and laughed in my face, and said, 'Now listen Lil' Puppy, I don't give men money. I take it from them, and besides as sweet as you are to this pussy, you don't need a suit. I like you as you are, with no clothes on at all.'

I was a rank greenhorn, sure, but her cold turn down of my plea for the C note was bitchy cute, and I was a salty sucker, so I reacted like any stupid would-be pimp who had been Georgied.

I had fouled up basic business. I had led with my dick instead of my mitt.

I reached down and slapped her hard against the side of her face. It sounded like a pistol shot. On impact a thrill shot through me. I should have slugged her with a baseball bat.

The bitch uncoiled from that bed like a striking yellow cobra, hooked her arms around my waist, and sank her razor sharp teeth into my navel.

The shock paralyzed me. I fell on my back across the bed moaning in pain. I could feel blood rolling from the wound down toward my crotch, but I couldn't speak. I couldn't move.

Pepper was sure a strange twisted broad. She was breathing hard now, but not in rage. The violence, the blood, had turned her on.

She was gently caressing me as she licked, with a feathery tongue, the oozing wound on my belly. She had never been so tenderly efficient as she took me on a beautiful trip around the Universe.

The funny thing was, that throbbing awful pain some how became a part of, melted into the joy of the feathery tongue, the thrill of the thing that Pepper was doing to me.

I guess Freud was right. If it thrills you to give pain, you can get your jollies taking it.

When I left Pepper, I was sapped. I felt like an old man. My mood was as bleak and cheerless as the gray dawn I cycled through.

When I got home and looked into the mirror, a death's head stared back at me. That vampire bitch was sucking my life's blood all right. I also knew that crystal cocaine wasn't exactly a health tonic.

Pepper was too fast, too slick for me. I had to make her shit or get off the pot.

I made the skeleton in the mirror a solemn vow that before the week was out I would in some way get Weeping Shorty, a pimp about fifty-five who, while a gorilla pimp, was the best pimp in town to pull my coat, to give me a plan for putting a ring in Pepper's nose.

Before I got busted, I had seen him at Jimmy's joint. He had looked horrible then, and now less than a year and a half later he looked like a breathing corpse.

Hoss was his Boss. He had chippied around and gotten hooked. It was Friday, almost midnight, when I found him.

He looked at me and made that clacking sound against the roof of his mouth with his tongue. You know, that mischievous, weirdly joyful sound that a young kid makes the instant before he rams a hat pin into your ear drum.

Then he said, 'Well kiss my dead mammy's ass, if it ain't Macking Youngblood. The whore's pet and the pimp's fret.'

The junkie bastard was jeffing on me, lashing me with contempt and scorn. Old pimps always know when a youngster with a yen for the pimp game is desperate for advice.

After all, they remember when they started and what a bitch it was just to learn the million questions. The answers would come slowly, from heartbreaking trial and error, from the ass kissing of the few who had solved the riddle, who pimped by the book.

The cleverest pimp could give a thousand years and never come close to all the answers.

Weeping Shorty was an old man, and he had gotten past the questions and had worked out a few answers, but even so he knew a thousand times more than I did. So I fought for control, I couldn't show anger. If I did he would cut me loose.

We had been standing under the awning of a vacant store front. He pulled me with a jerk of his head, I followed him to a big shabby Buick.

It was parked at an intersection in a cheap-trick district.

When we got inside the Buick I understood why he had parked it there. He could watch and keep tabs on his stable of scrawny, junkie whores working the four corners of the intersection.

He sat under the wheel not saying anything. His eyes straight ahead. I had kissed his ass for a half hour, and now he was freezing up. I thought of the tiny pile of cocaine wrapped in tinfoil under my instep that I had filched from Pepper. I fished it out and held it in my hand. Perhaps the cocaine would open him up.

I turned to him and said, 'Weeping, do you want a light snort of girl?'

He stiffened like a butcher knife had been run into his back. He looked at the wad of tinfoil in my palm and snatched it and in the same motion hurled it through the window on his side.

His top was blown, he shouted, 'Nigger, ain't you got no sense? You trying to go back to the joint and blow my wheels?'

I said, 'What did I do wrong? All I did was to offer the C just to be sociable. What's wrong with that?'

He said, 'Sucker, first booty butt you don't transport no hard in your stomp, keep it in your mitt so you can down it fast to the turf. Second, you're on parole. You're hot! You ain't got no business sitting dirty in my short. There's a law, Sucker, that can confiscate a short with stuff in it. You know if the heat had hit on you you'd unload in my short. Keep stuff off you. When you stop somewhere down it in the street until you ready to split. It's better to get beat for the stash than beat by the heat. Now what took your head outta Pepper's ass long enough for you to look me up?'

Oh! how this junkie creep bugged me. I sat there beside him trying to think of questions that would bleed him so I could get out of his face fast. He looked exactly like a withered baboon. His breath stunk like he had just eaten a bowl of maggots.

I said, 'Weeping, Pepper hasn't got my nose open for her. She's too jazzy and slick for me. I came to you because everybody knows that your game is mellow. I want you to pull my coat so I can pimp some scratch out of her.'

The baboon liked that banana I threw him. He was ready to talk the pimp game.

He said, 'The suckers in Hell want ice water, but it's late for them. They ain't never going to get no ice water. The way you start with a bitch is the way you end with a bitch. You can start pimping hard on a bitch and then sucker out and blow her, but ain't no way you can turn it around and pimp on Pepper after starting with her like a sucker. Forget her and get down on a fresh bitch.'

I said, 'You mean there is no way to get any scratch out of her?'

He said, 'Now you see I didn't say that. I said you couldn't *pimp* any scratch outta her. A foxy cold-blooded stud can always find an angle to cross a broad outta scratch.'

I said, 'I'm not foxy, but I think I could be cold-blooded enough to cross that slick bitch Pepper. Weeping, you are the fox. Lay some game on me and put me to the test. I'll split any scratch I take off right down the middle with you.'

I hadn't noticed it was raining. Now it was raining hard enough so that Weeping had turned to run up the window on his side. He had just raised it and was about to answer my proposition when there was a frantic rapping on his window. It was one of his whores.

Through the closed window of the locked door she said loudly, 'Daddy, open the door! My feet are soaked. Nothing is happening out here tonight, and besides I am hot as Hell. The vice is watching me. It's Costello. He told me to get off the street or he would bust me. Please open the door.'

Weeping was a cold gorilla all right. He sat there for a long moment. His monkey face was tight and hard. He casually opened the wind wing as the rain beat down on his whore. She stuck her nose through it.

Without moving toward the wing, sitting erect in the car seat, he hollered, 'You bullshit Bitch, make something happen. You a whore, you suppose to be hot. Let Costello bust you. He can't make a beef stand up unless he ketches you with a trick. You dumb chicken-hearted bitch, whatta you think I got this ass pocket full of fall scratch for? Now get out there and work. Don't worry about the rain. Walk between the rain drops, Bitch.'

He slammed the wing shut.

Her face was wild and angry through the murky glass. Her dope-rotted teeth were ragged fangs in the dimness as she pressed her face close to the glass.

She screamed, 'You just lost a girl. You had four, now you got three. I'm cutting you loose, Shorty.'

Weeping let his window down and stuck his head out into the rain as she walked away. He was all gorilla now.

He screamed, 'Bitch, I give you odds you won't split. As much of my dope you been shooting, I'm playing ketch up. You rank Bitch, you know if you split I'll find you and stick my knife in your stinking ass and gut you to your breast bone.'

I wondered if he had lost her. He read my mind.

He said, 'She ain't going nowhere, look at this.'

He turned his car engine on and started the windshield wiper so we could see the street. There she was back out there in the rain whistling and waving at the passing cars.

He switched the engine off.

He said, 'That bitch knows I ain't jiving. She'll make me some scratch this morning. Now Youngblood, about Pepper. You don't know anything about her. You ain't long out of the joint. I like you, so my advice is the same I gave you at first. Forget her. Try in another spot.'

What he said about my not knowing her made me curious.

I said, 'Look Weeping, I know you like me, and if you do, run Pepper down for me.'

'Did you know that peckerwood of Pepper's is the bankroll behind the biggest policy wheel in town?'

I said, 'No, but if the old man is flush isn't that good. Why give Pepper up because she's in shape? If you gave me an angle I could get some of that policy scratch.'

'Look Blood, brace yourself. Here is the rest of the rundown. Pepper is a rotten freak broad. You ain't the only stud she freaks off with. I could name a half dozen who ride her. The dangerous one is Dalanski the detective. He is in a bad way over Pepper. If he ever found out you were freaking off with her, Blood, shame on your ass.'

I was shaken by the rundown. Like a sucker I believed that I was the whole show in her love life. I was thinking like the young punk I was.

I said, 'Are you sure there are that many studs laying her?' He said, 'Maybe more.'

I had a belly ache and a worse headache. I felt lousy.

I mumbled, 'Thanks for the advice and the run down, Weeping.'

I got out of the Buick and walked home in the rain. When I got there it was three thirty and Mama was angry, worried and raving. She was right, of course. I was violating my parole to be out after eleven P.M.

I was coming out of the drugstore to make a delivery when I bumped into him on the sidewalk. It was old Party Time.

While doing his year for our caper he had copped a lonely-hearts broad through the mails.

She went his train fare. He finished the bit and went to visit her and made a home.

She had died, and the home went to relatives who threw him out. After five bits, he was still full of crooked inspiration. I liked him, but not enough to join him again in a hustle. I had only been out four and a half months. I cooled it and avoided him in a smooth way.

I hadn't touched Pepper in a week. She had called the drugstore twice just before closing. She had made licking and sucking sounds to get me out to her place. I made excuses and put her off. I wondered at the time why I was so important when she was a douche bag for that mob that was laying it into her.

The day before Weeping brought me a proposition, Dalanski, the roller, came into the drugstore for cigarettes and gave me a thoughtful look.

I was walking home. It was my day off. It was Saturday night around nine. I had been to see a prison movie. It was a grim drama. A young green punk tried a double cross. He was criss-crossed into the joint. He made deadly enemies while doing his long bit.

When he got out, a long black short pulled up and riddled him with a tommy gun.

A big black car was pulling to the curb toward me. There was something familiar about that small pin-head driver. It was Weeping.

He jerked his head and opened the car door. I went over and got in. He was excited. At first I thought because his car was clean.

He told me, 'Blood, put a smile on your face. Old Shorty's got good news for you. How would you like a half a G in your slide?'

I said, 'All right, give me the poison and take me to the baby.'

He said, 'I ain't shucking. It's cream-puff work. In fact Tender Dick, it's what you like to do best. Want the run down?'

'If you are going to tell me some broad is going to lay out five-hundred frog-skins to get her rocks off, say it. I would lay a syphillis patient that died a week ago for that kind of scratch.'

Then he said, 'Pepper is the broad. All you have to do is take her to bed and go through a full circus with her, that's all. Are you game?'

'Yes, if I get a rake off from the bleacher seats,' I said, 'and you tell me who wants the show on.'

His eye brows jitterbugged. He was a slick joker. I should have run from him.

He said, 'No, I can't tell you who. Don't worry about the scratch, it's guaranteed. Are you in?'

I said, 'Yes, but I want to know more. Like why?'

The tale he told me went like this. A fast hustler from New York who specialized in pressure rackets saw a chance to trim Pepper's old man out of a bundle.

The hustler knew that Pepper was a dog and a freak. He also knew that Pepper's old man was hung up on her.

Even though he had met her in a whorehouse and squared

her up, he was dangerously jealous of her and unpredictable if he caught her wrong.

The hustler felt that Pepper would be in a sweet state for pressure if solid evidence could be gotten showing Pepper as the dog she was.

The hustler was sure he could force her to help him in his scheme to trim the old man. He needed clear unfaked photographs.

His plan would be simple. Once he got the club over Pepper's head, he would force her to sneak in phony hit slips against the policy wheel.

The hustler had discovered that for Pepper, from her inside position in the wheel, it would be very simple.

The hustler would pay me five bills after I had brought Pepper to a prearranged setup.

I was all for the scratch, and eager to give Pepper some grief for the way she had used me, and outslicked me.

Weeping told me the trap was set. I was to wait until Pepper itched enough to call me. I was not to call her.

When ever she called, I was to tell her to meet me in the barroom of an old but still elegant hotel on the fringe of the arcade and shooting gallery section of town.

I was then to call him. I was to make sure that at least two hours passed between her call and when I went to the desk and asked for the key to apartment two-fourteen. My name would be Barksdale. That name I'll never forget if I live to get a hundred.

On the third day after I had gotten the rundown on the trap, Pepper called the store. It was eight fifty-five P.M., five minutes before closing. I answered the phone. She was burning blisters for one of our parties.

She invited me to her place as usual. I told her that I had to tidy up the store and also mail an important package at the downtown post office for my boss.

I asked her if she could get dressed and meet me by ten-thirty in the barroom of the hotel. It would be more convenient that way. She agreed.

I called Weeping. He told me to maneuver Pepper's face

toward the head of the bed as much as possible when we got into the act.

I went to the barroom and drank rum and coke until she got there.

I almost felt sorry for her when I saw her coming through the door. She looked so innocent and clean, not at all like the cruddy filly that humped up a funky lather beneath a mob of jockeys.

We took a booth so I could watch the clock. She was Jacqueline the Ripper with a fly, but she had a great gentle touch inside if you know what I mean.

She was a space buff all right. She was checking out my readiness for entry into inner space.

At eleven sharp Mr and Mrs Barksdale picked up the key to their pad. We walked onto the stage.

Wyatt Earp would have gone ape over the pad.

It was overstuffed horse-hair living room. Gleaming brass bed, giant cherubs on the wall, Gideon Bible on the marble top bedroom table. Midget, efficiency kitchen cubicle. So what, we hadn't come to cook.

High on the wall over the bed were the two gold colored cherubs. Their eyes were holes, their mouths popped wide holding the light fixtures.

When we got into the brass bed we got the show on the road.

I was almost sure some steamed up joker in the adjoining room had his gizmo focused on the carnival through a drilled hole peeking from a cherub's empty eye socket.

Pepper let me out of her Hog at one-thirty in the A.M. just two blocks from Weeping's whore stand. I felt good. I was going to collect five fat ones for my pleasant night's work. It was like having a license to steal.

I spotted Weeping's pin-head in his Buick. As I walked toward him, I couldn't stop thinking about that Eastern blackmailer. I thought about that green rain that would fall when Pepper started rolling those phony hits in. I thought about how I could catch a few palms full.

Smooth as silk the pay-off came off. When Weeping handed me my scratch he gave me a funny look.

He said, 'Take it easy Blood, take it easy.'

The next day I went downtown and got clean.

It was the early years for the Nat King Cole Trio. They were playing for a two-buck dance that night at Liberty Hall. Party and I were in the balcony at a table overlooking the crowded dance floor. We were slaving like sand hogs trying to tunnel into the flashy high yellows on our laps. They were almost stoned. Ready for the killing floor.

Party saw him first coming in the front door of the auditorium. He knifed me in the side with his elbow.

Then con style, from the side of his mouth, he whispered, 'Dalanski, the heat.'

The bastard's head was on a swivel. He was looking everywhere at once. I felt mad butterfles with stingers ricocheting in my belly when his eyes spotted me and locked on me. I froze, his eyes were still riveted to me as he walked up the stairway straight for me.

I pretended to ignore him. He walked up behind me and stood there for a long moment. Then he dropped a hand like an anvil on my shoulder.

He said, 'Get up! I want to talk to you.'

My legs were shuddery as I stood in a small alcove with him.

He said, 'Where were you around ten and after last night?'

Relief and courage flooded me. That was easy; I hedged. 'Why?'

He said, 'Look punk, don't get cute. Where were you? Don't answer. I know where you were. You were out on Crystal Road in the night time burglarizing the home of Mr and Mrs Frank Ibbetts. Night-time burglary is five to ten.'

My courage and relief swiftly drained out. Frank Ibbetts was Pepper's old man. He was roughly frisking me now. He ran his hands into my side pockets. With one hand he brought out the three hundred dollars left from my pay-off, plus twenty clean dollars. The other came out with a strange brass door key.

He said, 'Jeez, for a flunky in a drugstore you got a helluva bankroll. Where did you get it and where and what does this key fit?'

I said, 'Officer, that's crap-game money. I have never seen that key before.'

He grabbed me firmly like he had captured Sutton and walked me through the dancers out the door to his short.

He took me down and booked me on suspicion of Grand Theft burglary. He also booked the scratch and key as evidence.

Mama came down bright and early the next morning. She was in a near fainting dither. She was clutching her chest over her heart.

She said, 'Bobby, you are going to kill your mama. You haven't been out six months and now you are back in trouble. What's wrong with you? Are you crazy? You need prayer. Get down on your knees and pray to the good Lord.'

I said, 'I don't need to pray. Mama, believe me there is nothing to worry about. I didn't steal anything from Pepper's house. I am not nuts. Pepper will tell them the truth. Mama, I was with her.'

I got my first nightmare inkling of the cork-screw criss-cross when Mama broke into tears. She rolled her eyes to heaven.

She blubbered, 'Bobby, there's no hope for you. You are going to spend your young life in prisons. Don't you know Son, your mama loves you? You don't have to lie to me.'

'I went out to see her early this morning,' she said 'She told me she hasn't seen you in a week. Mr Dalanski has brought Pepper's spare key down here. That key in your pocket was one you stole when you made a delivery out there.'

Finally, she went down the corridor. Her shoulders were jerking in her sobbing.

It was an iron cross. My public defender went to that hotel to get corroboration for my alibi. The joint had been too crowded, too hectic. None of the employees remembered Pepper and me. At least they said they didn't.

The desk man on that night had been a substitute and wasn't now available. My signature wasn't on the register anyway.

I went into court again with the dirty end of the stick. I

was a parolee arrested at one A.M. with a bottle of whiskey in front of me in a public place.

Pepper looked like a prospect for a convent. She had stripped herself of paint and gee-gaws. She testified that the key found in my slide was hers, and that yes, it was possible that I had stolen it while making deliveries to her home. No, she had not seen me for a week before my arrest.

My defender had gotten a change of venue. I was afraid to go before the judge who had sent me to the reformatory.

I got two years in State Prison for Grand Theft, the amount, five-hundred dollars. My parole was to run concurrently with the new sentence.

Pepper's old man was with her in court. They bought the cross. I couldn't figure who had sold it to them.

Was Dalanski the joker that Weeping worked for? Or had Dalanski heard that I had a wad, and without knowing anything about the hotel affair sold it to Pepper?

For what reason had the old man bought it? Had those hotel employees been bribed or threatened? If Dalanski was the brain, did he want me out of the way for a reason other than Pepper?

Maybe some day I'll find out what really happened. I know if I had had lots of scratch Miss Justice would have smiled on me. She favors the bird with the scratch.

The Waupun State Prison was tough, but in a different way than the reformatory. Here the cons were older. Many of them were murderer's serving life sentences.

These cons would never put up with the kind petty tyranny that was practiced in the reformatory. Here the food was much better. There were industries here. A con could learn a trade if he wanted to.

He could go into the yard during recreation hours and learn other trades and skills. Here the desperate heist men congregated to plot new, more sensational robberies. The fruits and punks lay on the grass in the sun romancing each other.

This was a prison of cliques, of bloody vendettas. I found my level with the soft-spoken smooth Midwestern pimps and stuff players.

Since I was one of the youngest cons in the joint I bunked in a dormitory. It was like a suite in the Waldorf compared to the bug infested tight cells in the reformatory with their odious crap buckets.

It was there in that dormitory that I got the insatiable desire to pimp. I was a member of a clique that talked about nothing except whores and pimping. I began to feel a new slickness and hardness.

I worked in the laundry. I kept my clothing fresh and neat. It was in the laundry that I met the first man from whom I got cunning to balance my hardness.

He was an old Drag man with his bit getting short. He was the first to attempt to teach me to control my emotions.

He would say, 'Always remember whether you be sucker or hustler in the world out there, you've got that vital edge if you can iron-clad your feelings. I picture the human mind as a movie screen. If you're a dopey sucker, you'll just sit and watch all kinds of mind-wrecking, damn fool movies on that screen.'

He said. 'Son, there is no reason except a stupid one for anybody to project on that screen anything that will worry him or dull that vital edge. After all, we are the absolute bosses of that whole theatre and show in our minds. We even write the script. So always write positive, dynamic scripts and show only the best movies for you on that screen whether you are pimp or priest.'

His rundown of his screen theory saved my sanity many years later. He was a twisted wise man and one day when he wasn't looking, a movie flashed on the screen. The title was 'Death For an Old Con.'

He died in his sleep behind the high gray walls. His fate was that that lives like a specter with all cons. The fear of dying in a cell.

I sure missed that convict philosopher. The wisdom he taught me took me successfully through my bit. I was released after twenty-one months. I got three months good time for good conduct.

With good time I was free, hard, slick and bitter. No more

small towns for me. I was going to the city to get my degree in pimping.

The Pepper cross had answered a perplexing question for me. Why did Justice really always wear a blindfold? I knew now. It was because the cunning bitch had dollar signs for eyeballs.

4

A Degree in Pimping

When I got back to Milwaukee, Mama and the street, my mind was straitjacketed into the pimp game. Back in the joint I had dreamed almost nightly. They were cruel playlets.

They were fantastic. I would see myself gigantic and powerful like God Almighty. My clothes would glow. My underwear would be rainbow-hued silk petting my skin.

My suits were spun-gold shot through with precious stones. My shoes would be dazzling silver. The toes were as sharp as daggers. Beautiful whores with piteous eyes groveled at my feet.

Through the dream mist I would see shaped huge stakes. The whores' painted faces would be wild in fear. They would wail and beg me not to murder them on those sharp steel stakes.

I would laugh madly. Springs of scarlet would spurt from their behinds as I joyfully booted them crotch first onto the sharp pikes. They would flop around like dying chickens. They would finally fall away in a welter of blood into two red halves.

When I awoke my ticker would be earthquaking inside me. The hot volley of the savage thrill lay sticky wet between my trembling thighs.

I had other terrible dreams. I would be very tiny. A gargantuan Christ, in a sea of light, would be towering above me. In his anger his eyes would be blazing blue suns. His silky platinum hair would stand on end in his rage.

A shaft of purest white light would shoot from the tip of his index finger. He would point toward a woman. Her back would be turned to me. He would hand me a barbed leather whip.

Like a crash of summer thunder he would command, 'Punish this evil woman. Destroy the devil inside her. The Lord so directs thee.'

Eagerly I would grab the heavy whip in both hands. I would

bring it down with all my force on the woman's back. She would just stand there. The scarlet would drain down from her slashed back. She would be standing to her knees in a river of blood.

She would turn her brown agonized face toward me. It would be Mama. I would be shaking and screaming in my sweat. It was horrible. I could never cut the dream off until its end. It had to run its fearful course. The dreams about Mama came until her death.

For a day or two following them, these dreams would recreate in day-dreams. Sudden dark arrows of depression and regret would stab into that open sore in my mind. I would get high. The narcotics seemed to ward off like armor the stealthy arrows.

After a week of rest and Mama's soulfood, my color and strength came back. On a Saturday night I decked myself out in one of the vines and topcoat I had bought the day before Dalanski busted me.

I remembered the pimp rundowns at the joint. I had learned my first step had to be a fast cop. I needed a whore to hit the city scene. I had to get on that fast track to pimping.

I was only several months away from age twenty. My baby face was gone. I was six feet two. I was as thin as a greyhound on a crash diet. I went into an underworld bar, The 711 Club, crowded with pimps, whores, and thieves.

I stood at the far end of the bar stalling with a coke. I faced the front door. I turned and asked the slightly familiar elephant beside me about Weeping and Party.

He turned his head. His dime-sized eyes got stuck in my fly's zipper as he looked me over head to toe. He remembered me.

He said, 'About a month ago your boon coon Party caught sixty in the county. One of them tight pussies opened his nose wide enough to drive a freight train through. He caught a stud whamming it into her. The stud quite the scene. The broad had to go to a croaker to get Party's shoe outta her ass.'

Then after pausing to thumbnail a ball of snot from his trunk, he said, 'Old Weeping fell dead outside a shooting gallery in Saint Paul. Musta' shot some pure, cause a lookout on the sidewalk heard him mumble before he croaked. "Well kiss my dead mammy's ass if this ain't the best smack I ever shot."'

The elephant again raised his hoof toward his filthy trunk. The sissy barkeep sat a fresh bottle of coke on the log before me. I yanked my eyebrows into a question mark.

He lisped, 'The runty black bitch in the middle of the bar sent you a taste.'

Without taking my eyes off his thin yellow face, I said, 'Sugar, run her down to me. Is the bitch qualified? Is she a whore? Does she have a man?'

The corners of his mouth see-sawed. He slugged his soggy, dirty bar rag against my reflection on the bar top.

He almost whispered, 'The bitch ain't nothing but a young skunk from Saint Louis. She ain't nothing but a jazzy jive whore. I'm more whore than she is. She ain't got no man. She's a come freak. She's Georgied three bullshit pimps since she got here a month ago. If your game is strong you could play a hog outta her ass. She ain't but eighteen.'

I eased a bone from my pocket, put it on the bar for the fresh coke. I frantically remembered those pimp rundowns in the joint.

I said, 'Tell the bitch no dice. I'll take care of the little things, and if she is qualified maybe I'll let her take care of the big things. Give the bitch a drink on me.'

On the juke box Ella Fitzgerald was crying about her 'little yellow basket.'

The bar keep twinkle-toed toward her with the wire and drink. Through the blue mirror I zeroed my eyes in on the target. My ass bone starched on stiff point. Her big peepers were two sexy dancers in the velvet midnight of her cute Pekinese face.

Hot scratch fever streaked through me. I thought, if I could cop her and get a pimp's terms she would be out of pocket poison to all white tricks that pinned her.

Those pimps back in the joint sure knew basic whorology. I was glad my ears had flapped to all those rundowns.

A Degree in Pimping | 57

They had said, 'Chase a whore you get a chump's weak cop. Stalk a whore you get a pimp's strong cop.'

My turn down of her measly first offer had her jumpy. It was a slick sharp hook twisting in the bitch's mind. Her juicy tongue darted out like a red lizard past her ivory teeth. It slithered over the full lips. She wiggled toward me in an uneven race with the bar keep. He was sliding her green drink between me and the elephant.

I heard a low excited trumpeting in the trunk of the elephant. He had dug her flawless props and gourmet rear end. It was rolling inside her glove-tight white dress.

I painted a lukewarm indifferent grin on my face as she perched on the stool. I noticed a roll of scratch wedged deep between the black peaks.

She said, 'Who the hell are you, and what is that off the wall shit you cracked on the bartender?'

My eyes were sub-zero spotlights on her face.

I said, 'Bitch, my name is Blood, and my wire wasn't off the wall. It was real, like me. Bitch, you sure got a filthy, sassy job It could get your ass ruptured.'

The big vein at the temple in the tiny dog face quivered. Her rapper was shrill.

She bleated, 'I ain't no bitch. I'm a mother-fucking lady. The stud ain't been pulled outta his mammy's womb that kicks my ass. Goddamnit, call me Phyllis. Be a gentleman and respect me. I'm a lady.'

The icy blasts busted the thermostat in my spotlights.

I could feel my cool spit on my lips as I roared, 'You stinking black Bitch, you're a fake. There's no such thing as a lady in our world. You either got to be a bitch or a faggot in drag. Now Bitch, which is it? Bitch, I'm not a gentleman, I'm a pimp. I'll kick your funky ass. You gave me first lick. Bitch, you're creaming to eat me up. I'm not a come freak, you are. I'm a freak to scratch.'

My blast had moved her. Those joint rundowns sure worked. I could see those sexy dancers were hot as hell there in the midnight. She was trying to conceal from me the freakish pain-loving bitch inside her.

She was comical like that fire-and-brimstone preacher. He was trying to hide his hard-on from the cute sister in the front pew flashing her cat for him.

The broad was speechless. I had called all the shots. I turned toward the crapper.

As I walked away I bombed her. I said, 'Bitch, I'm splitting when I come out of that crapper. I know your pussy is jumping for me. I know you want me for your man. Some lucky bitch is going to steal me from you. You better toss that bullshit out of your mind. Get straight Bitch, and tell me like it is on my way out. You had your chance. After tonight you don't have any.'

Inside the crapper, I ripped a wad of paper from its holder. I wrapped the saw buck and the four singles around it. What ever happened out there, I had to show a bankroll.

I stood there in the crapper. I was letting the heat seep deep into that bitch out there. Was I going to cop my first whore? My crotch was fluttery at the thought of it.

I walked out of the crapper. She was outside the door. I almost trampled her. I ignored her. I walked to the bar to pay my light tab. She was peering over my shoulder. I peeled the saw buck off.

I told the barkeep, 'Steal the change and cop a Hog.'

His bedroom gray eyes sparkled. His delicate pinkie scooted the saw buck back to me across the log.

He said, 'Sweetie, it's on me. Come back at two and cop a real girl.'

She tugged at my sleeve as I turned from the bar. She looked up at me. Those dancers had stripped.

I looked down at the hot runt and said, 'Well Bitch, it's your move. Do I cut you loose?'

She grabbed my shoulder. She pulled me down toward her. I could feel her hot breath on the side of my head. She popped that lizard tongue into my ear almost to my eardrum. It sent hot shivers through me. I stayed cool. I turned my head and knifed my teeth into the side of her neck. I don't know why she didn't bleed. She just moaned.

Then she whispered, 'You cold-blooded sweet mother-fucker, I go for you. Let's go to my pad and rap.'

We walked to the slammer. I glanced back. The elephant was staring at us. His tongue was frenching his chops. His trunk was twitching for a party.

On the sidewalk she handed me the key to her yellow thirty-six Ford. I was lucky. I had been taught to drive the laundry truck back in the joint. The Ford's motor sang a fine tune. It wasn't a pimp's wheels, but it sure would make the trip to the city track.

I drove to her pad. On the way she played on me. She was setting me up for the Georgia. That lizard thought my ear was a speedway. It did a hundred laps inside it. I was still green. I shouldn't have let her touch me.

Her pad was a trap for suckers all right. She had pasted luminous white stars on the hotel room's blue ceiling. There was one blue light. It glowed sexily from behind a three foot plaster copy of Rodin's 'The Kiss.'

There was a mirror over the bed. There were mirrors on the walls flanking the bed. There was a polar-bear rug gleaming whitely in front of a blue chaise lounge.

I sat on the lounge. She flipped on the portable record player. Ellington rippled out 'Mood Indigo.'

She slipped into a cell-sized bathroom. Its door was half shut. The peke was digging a washcloth into her armpits and cat. She was nude. She sure was panting to swindle me out of my youth. I wondered if and where she had stashed that roll of scratch.

She came out belly dancing to the Indigo sex booster. She was a runt Watusi princess. Her curvy black body had the sheen of seal skin. I had one bitch of a time remembering the dialogue that covered this kind of a situation.

What had the pimps in the joint said: 'You gotta' back up from them fabulous pussies. You gotta' make like you don't have a swipe. You gotta' keep your mind on the scratch.'

'Stay cold and brutal. Cop your scratch first. Don't let 'em Georgia you. They'll laugh at you. They'll cut you loose like a trick after they've flim-flammed you. Your scratch cop is the only way to put a hook in their stinking asses.'

She danced toward the head of the bed. She stooped over and raised the edge of the red carpet. Her rear end swayed to the Indigo. It was grinning at me. It was theatre in the round for sure.

She danced toward me. She had two thin reefers in her hand. That box at the side of the bed had rejected and Indigo was encoring.

She stood between my legs. Even through the trouser cloth I could feel the hot dampness of her outer thighs. The inner surface of my knee caps tingled under the heat.

She quivered and rolled her jet satin belly under my nose. Her humming of the Indigo was low and throaty. She sure qualified as the package the pimps had warned about. My twenty-one month cherry was aching to chunk out.

She took a lighter off the cocktail table. She ran the sticks in and out of her mouth to get an even burn. She lit them and handed me one.

She said, 'Daddy, this is light green pot from chili gut country. It will make us mellow. Why don't you take your clothes off?'

I took a deep pull on the stick of reefer. I looked up into the sultry dreamy eyes.

I parroted, 'Bitch, don't put shit in the game. Business always comes before pleasure in my book. I'll take my clothes off when I know I'm taking them off with my whore. I don't sucker for the Georgia. Jar loose from respectable scratch, Bitch.'

I had heard it verbatim in the joint. It worked like a lie detector. The motor in her belly threw a rod. Her eyes had a faraway look.

She was busy tailoring the con for me. She collapsed to a yogi squat on the polar bear rug. Her moon was winking at me. Her voice was bullshit sweet.

She warbled, 'Sweetheart Daddy, you already shot me down. I'm your sweet bitch. I got a C note coming from a trick with his nose open for me. He'll spring for it tomorrow night. It's yours, but you got to wait. Now come on and put your freak baby to bed.'

My system had been clean. The reefer was powerful. She didn't know how desperately I needed to pimp. She couldn't know she was the first. I couldn't let her escape.

I had to have a whore. That reefer was sending currents of anger and hatred through me in time with Indigo. My mortal enemy squatted on that white rug.

I thought, 'I'm going to murder this runt black bitch if she don't give me that scratch she had in her bosom.'

Like a brute cop giving a heist man a last chance to confess, I said, 'Bitch, give me that scratch you had between your tiddies.'

Her peepers ballooned in surprise and anger.

She gritted, 'You're pimping too hard skinny ass nigger. I have changed my mind. Get your lid and benny and split.'

The Indigo was on a torrid upbeat. Like brown-skin lightning I leaped erect from the chaise. I flung my right leg back.

I could feel the tendons at my hip socket straining. My eyes sighted for a heart shot. My needle-toed eleven triple-A shoe rocketed toward her.

The lucky runt turned a fraction of a second in time. The leather bomb exploded into her left shoulder blade. It knocked her flat on her belly. She lay there groaning.

Then like in the dreams in the joint, I kicked her rear end until my leg cramped. Through it all she just moaned and sobbed. I was soaked in sweat. Panting, I lay on the bear-skin beside her. I thrust my mouth against her ear.

In an icy whisper I said, 'Bitch, do I have to kill you to make you my whore? Get up and give me that scratch.'

She turned her head and looked into my eyes. There was no anger in them now, only fear and strange passion. Her tremulous mouth opened to speak. For a long moment nothing came out.

Then she whispered, 'You got a whore Blood. Please don't kick me any more. I'm your little dog. I'll do anything you say. I love you, Pretty Daddy.'

Her talons stabbed into the back of my neck as she

tried to suck my tongue from its roots. I could taste her salty tears.

She wobbled to the record player. She lifted a corner of it. She slid that wad of scratch from beneath it. She rejected Indigo. She put another platter on the turntable.

Lady Day was singing a sad lament. 'My man don't love me, treats me awful mean. He's the meanest man that I ever seen.'

I was standing on the bear skin. She came toward me with the scratch in her hand. She laid it in my palm. I riffled it in a fast count. It was respectable. It had to be over two bills. I was ready to let that cherry pop.

I scooped the ninety-pound runt up into my arms. I bit her hard on the tip of her chin. I carried her to the side of the bed. I hurled her onto it. She bounced and lay there on her back. She was breathing hard. Her legs were a wide pyramid.

I got out of my clothes fast. I snatched the top sheet off. I ripped it into four narrow strips. I tied her hands to the bed posts. I spread eagled her legs. With the longer strips, I tied her legs to the top of the springs at the sides of the bed.

She lay there a prisoner. I put her through the nerve shredding routines Pepper had taught me. She blacked out four times. She couldn't pull back from the thrilling, awful torture.

Finally, I took a straight ride home. On the way I tried to smash the track. I reached my destination. The blast of hate was big enough to spawn a million embryo black pimps.

I untied her. We lay there in the dim blueness. The fake white stars glowed down on us. Lady Day still moaned her troubles.

I said, 'Bitch, I want you to hump like Hell in these streets for a week. We're going to the big track in the city. Oh yes, this week we got to get that title to the Ford changed. I don't drive no bitch's wheels. It's got to be in my name, understand?'

She said, 'Yes, Daddy, anything you say. Daddy, don't get angry, but I was bullshitting about that C note trick.'

I said, 'Bitch, I knew that. Don't ever try to con me again.'

I got up and put my clothes on. I peeled a fin off the scratch and put it on the dresser.

I said, 'I want you in the street at six tonight. Stay out of the bars. Work the area around Seventh and Apple.'

'I'll come through some time tonight. You be there when I show. If you get busted your name is Mary Jones. If you forget it I can't raise you fast. Have some scratch whenever I show.'

I went down to the street. I got into my Ford. It roared to life. I drove toward Mama's. I felt good. I wasn't doing bad for a black boy just out of the joint.

I shuddered when I thought, what if I hadn't kept my ears flapping back there in the joint? I would be a boot black or porter for the rest of my life in the high walled white world. My black whore was a cinch to get piles of white scratch from that forbidden white world.

Mama was pressing a young customer's hair. She saw me get out of the Ford in front of the shop. She called me inside with a waggle of the pressing comb.

She said, 'I have been worried. Where have you been all night? Where did you get the pretty little car? Did you find a job?'

I said, 'A friend of mine let me borrow it. Maybe he'll sell it to me. I stayed with him all night. He's got a hundred-and-three fever. I'll try to find a job tomorrow.'

She said, 'There's a roast in the oven. Shut the gas off and eat. I hope, Son, you haven't been with Pepper.'

I looked down at the nut brown, shapely girl getting her hair pressed.

I said, 'Pepper? She's too old for me. I like young pretty brown-skin girls. Pepper's too yellow for me.'

The young broad flashed her eyes up at me. She smiled. I winked and ran my tongue over my lips. She dug it. She blushed. I put her on file.

I turned and walked to the sidewalk. I went upstairs and attacked the roast.

I took a long nap. At five-thirty P.M. I went down and got into the Ford. I drove to Seventh and Apple. I parked.

At five minutes to six I saw Phyllis coming toward me. She was a block away. I fired the engine and pulled away.

It sure looked like I had copped a whore. I went back at midnight. She looked mussed up and tired. She got into the car.

I said, 'Well, how goes it, Baby?'

She dug in her bosom and handed me a damp wad of bills. I counted it. It was a fin over half a C.

She said, 'I'm tired and nasty, and my shoulder and ass ache. Can I stop now, Daddy? I would like a pastrami and coffee and a bath. You know how you kicked me last night.'

I said, 'Bitch, the track closes at two. I'll take you to the sandwich and coffee. The bath will have to wait until the two o'clock breakdown. You needed your ass kicked.'

She sighed and said, 'All right, Daddy, anything you say.'

I drove her to an open-air kosher joint. She kept squirming on the hard wooden bench. Her butt must have been giving her fits. She was silent until she finished the sandwich and coffee.

Then she said, 'Daddy, please don't misunderstand me. I like a little slapping around before my man does it to me. Please don't be as cruel as you were last night. You might kill me.'

I said, 'Baby, never horse around with my scratch or try to play con on me. You blew my stack last night. You don't have to worry so long as you never violate my rules. I will never hurt you more than to turn you on.'

I drove her back to the track. She got out of the car. As soon as she hit the sidewalk, two white tricks almost had a wreck pulling to the curb for her. She was a black money-tree all right.

The next day I took her to a notary. In ten minutes we walked out. She gave me the three bills back that I had paid her for the Ford.

It was legal now. She wasn't beefing. Her bruises were healing and she was ripe for another prisoner of love scene. She finished the week in great humping style. I had a seven-bill bankroll.

Sunday evening I packed the runt's bearskin and other things into the trunk of the Ford.

A Degree in Pimping | 65

I parked around the corner from Mama's. I went up to get my things together. Mama caught me packing. Tears flooded her eyes. She grabbed me and held me tightly against her. Her sobbing was strangling her.

She sobbed, 'Son, don't you love your Mama any more? Where are you going? Why do you want to leave the nice home I fixed for you? I just know if you leave I'll never see you again. We don't have anybody but each other. Please don't leave me. Don't break my heart, Son.'

I heard her words. I was too far gone for her grief to register. I kept thinking about that freak, black money-tree in the Ford. I was eager to get to that fast pimp track in the city.

I said, 'Mama, you know I love you. I got a fine clerk's job in a men's store in the city. Everybody in this town knows I'm an ex-con. I have to leave. I love you for making a home for me. You have been an angel to stick by me through those prison bits. You'll see me again. I'll be back to visit you. Honest, Mama, I will.'

I had to wrestle out of her arms. I picked up my bags and hit the stairs. When I reached the sidewalk, I looked up at the front window. Mama was gnawing her knuckles and crying her heart out. My shirt front was wet with her tears.

5

The Jungle Fauna

The yellow Ford ran like an escaped con. We got to Chicago
in two hours. We checked into a hotel in a slum neighborhood,
around Twenty-ninth and State Streets. We took our stuff out
of the Ford's trunk.

It was ten P.M. I threw some water on my face. I told the runt
to cool it. I went out and cruised around to case the city.

I turned the wipers on. A late March snowfall was starting. About a mile from the hotel I saw whores working
the streets.

I parked and went into a bar in the heart of the action. It
stank like a son-of-a-bitch. It was a junkie joint. I sat sipping
on a bottle of suds; I couldn't trust the glasses.

A cannon with a tired horse face took the vacant stool in my
right. His stall took the one on the left. The stall had a yellow
fox face. Out of the corner of my eye I saw him pinning me.
He snapped his fingers. I jerked my head toward him.

He said, 'Brother, you are lucky as a shit-house rat. What
size benny and vine you wear? I'm Dress 'em up Red. Stand
up brother so I can dig your size. I got a pile of crazy vines
dirt cheap.'

I stood up facing him. He ran his eyes up and down me.
He unbuttoned my top coat. He pulled my vine's lapels. He
shoved me back toward Horseface. I stumbled, half turned to
apologize to Horseface. There was a streaking blur behind me.
It was so fast I couldn't have sworn I had seen it. I found out
later what it had been.

Horseface showed his choppers, got off the stool and trotted
through the slammer. I faced the stall.

I said, 'Jim, you got my size? Do you have any black
mohairs?'

The stall smiled crookedly at me. He straightened my tie.

He said, 'Slim, I got blue and black mohair, I can fit you

like Saville Row in London. You want the blue too? The bite is two for fifty slats.'

I said, 'Man, let's go. I am ready to cop.'

His brow telescoped like I was going to open a door and catch his mother crapping in my hat. He started oozing toward the slammer.

He said, 'Brother, I don't know you well enough to trust you. I got to protect my stash. Wouldn't it be a bitch if you went with me and copped? What if you came back later and beat me?'

'No, Slim, cool it. I'll be back in twenty minutes with the vines. Here's a slat. Get a taste on Dress 'em up Red.'

I ordered another beer. I was trying to stall that twenty minutes out. I sure needed those vines.

After an hour I figured Dress 'em up Red got busted or something.

I asked the fat broad tending bar where the swank joints were. She named a few, and gave me directions. My bill was eighty cents. I left a twenty-cent tip and walked to the Ford.

The wind wing on the street side gaped open. It had been jimmied. The car door had been unlocked through it.

I got in. I remembered the runt's costume jewelry had been locked in the glove compartment. I unlocked it. Some slick bastard had slit the cardboard bottom from underneath. There wasn't even an earring left.

I started the motor and turned the lights on. The snow had stopped falling. My headlights beamed on a squatting junkie whore with a Dracula face peeing in the gutter. She grinned toothlessly into the glare like maybe she was a starlet taking bows at a movie premiere.

I thundered the motor. She stood up wide legged. Her cat was a mangy red slash. She was holding up the bottom front of her dress with her rusty elbows. Her long black fingers were pulling her snare wide open to stop me.

As I shot by her, she shouted, 'Come back here Nigger! It ain't but a buck.'

I drove through the snow-slushed streets. The street lights were dim halos in the murk.

I thought, 'I can't put the runt down in a spot like back there. I have to find somebody to give me a rundown.'

I drove a hundred blocks. Suddenly a huge red neon sign glittered through the gloom. It read 'Devil's Roost.' It was one of the joints the fat broad at the hype bar had told me about.

Gaudy Hogs and Lincolns were bumper to bumper. They pigged the parking spaces on the Roost's side of the street. I parked across the street. I got out of the Ford and crossed the street.

I started walking down the sidewalk toward the Roost. The Bird, Eckstein and Sarah sent a crazy medley of soul sounds from the rib and chicken joint's loudspeakers. The street was as busy as a black anthill. Studs and broads in sharp clothes paraded the block.

The hickory-smoked chicken and rib odors watered my mouth. I was at the point of stepping into one for a fast feast. The sign said 'Creole Fat's Rib Heaven.' I didn't make it.

A long, stooped shadow stood in my way. He was chanting at me like a voodoo doctor. He pointed toward a store front. It's window was blacked out with blue paint.

He sang, 'Shootin' 'em up inside, heavy and good. Scratch piled up like cords of wood. Geez you look lucky, Jack. Seven, eleven point right back. That's sure you, Jack. Go in fast. Come out quicker. Lady Luck is a bitch but you can stick her.'

His topcoat was a threadbare green-checked antique. The tops of his shabby black shoes had criss-cross holes snipped out. His bulging corns were humps pressing through the vents. He stank like a bootlegger's garbage. There was something ghostly familiar in the banana yellow, Basset-Hound face.

I said, 'Jim, I'm not in the mood to whale the craps. Say, don't I know you?'

His transient eyes jerked their bags. They moved over my shoulder, searching down the sidewalk for a fresh prospect. His bald head glistened like a tiny yellow lake under the street lamp.

He said, 'Jack, I can't put a pistol on you. I can't force you to go inside and collect your scratch. Kid, you too young to know me. You might a heard of me. I'm Pretty Preston. I gave the whores blues in the night when I was pimping at my peak. Who are you?'

His name triggered my clear memory of him. He had driven a gleaming black La Salle car. I had shined his shoes back in the pressing shop days.

Then he had been sleek and handsome like a yellow Valentino. I remembered his diamonds. They had winked and sparkled brightly on his fingers, in his shirt cuffs, even on his shirt front.

I thought, 'Could this really be the same dandy? What had happened to him?'

I said, 'Preston, I know you. I'm the kid who used to shine your Stacy's back on Main Street. Remember me? I'm pimping myself now. You sure pimped up a storm when I was a kid. What happened? Why are you steering for this craps joint?'

He had a dreamy, far-away look in his dull brown eyes. He was probably remembering his long ago flashy pimp days. He sighed and put his arms around my shoulders. I walked with him through the door of the craps trap.

The raw stink of gamblers' sweat punched up into my nose. We sat on a battered sofa in the almost dark front of the joint. Through a partition I could hear the tinkle of silver coins. I heard the flat cackle of the bone dice laughing at the cursing shooters begging for a natural.

He said, 'Sure, Kid, I remember you. Christ, you got tall. I gotta be getting old. What's your name? Kid, I been getting funky breaks since I came to this raggity city twelve years ago. I'm just steering for a pal who runs the joint.

'Hell, he needs me more than I need him. I'm gonna catch a hot number, or a wild daily double. Old Preston's name will ring again. How many girls you got?'

I said, 'Slim Lancaster, but they call me Young Blood. Blood for short. I only got one now, but with all the whores here I'll have boo-koos in a month. I just got in town tonight. I want to put my girl to work. Give me a rundown on some streets after I dash next door for a slab of ribs. I haven't dirtied a plate since noon. Anything I can get you?'

He said, 'Blood, if you must do something, get me a half pint of Old Taylor at the corner liquor store. I'll rundown for you, but you ain't going to like my tail-end rundown at all.'

It felt good to step out into the fresh, chilly air. I stopped in the rib joint and put my order in. I saw the front of the Roost on my way to the corner.

I tiptoed and peeked through the bottom of the window blind. The joint was jumping. Pimps, whores, and white men crowded the circular bar.

Some skinny joker with scald burns on his face was fronting a combo. He tried to ape the Bird's phrasing and tone. His tan face had turned black. He was choking on his horn.

Mixed couples danced to 'Stomping at the Savoy' on a carpet-sized dance floor in the rear. Silk broads itching for forbidden fruit sat in booths lining the walls.

Their faces glowed starkly in the red dimness. Their long hair flopped around their shoulders as they threw their heads back. They laughed drunkenly with their black lovers.

I took my peepers out of the slot. I walked toward the corner to cop the bottle for Preston. I made a skull note to pop into the Roost after Preston's rundown.

I was fifty feet from the corner when I saw him. He was in the center of a small crowd. His high crown white hat was bobbing a foot above it. He was a nut brown giant.

As I drew closer I could see his snow-white teeth. His heavy lips were drawn back in a snarl. His wide shoulders jiggled. He was stomping on something. It was like maybe he was a sharply togged fire dancer or maybe a dapper grape crusher from Sicily.

I squeezed through the crowd for a ringside view. He was grunting. His labor was yanking the sweat out of him. The crowd stood tittering and excited like a Salem mob watching the execution of a witch.

The witch was black. She had the slant eyes and doll features of a Geisha girl.

The chill breeze whipped back the bottom of his benny. The giant's thigh muscles rippled inside the pants leg of his two-hundred-dollar vine.

The Jungle Fauna | 71

Again and again he slammed his size-thirteen shoe down on the witch's belly and chest. She was out cold. Her jaw hinge was awry and red frothy bubbles bunched at the corners of her crooked mouth.

At last he scooped her from the pavement. She looked like an infant in his arms. His eyes were strangely damp. He wedged through the crowd to a purple Hog at the curb. He looked down into her unconscious face.

He muttered, 'Baby, why, why do you make me do you like this? Why don't you hump and stop lushing and bullshitting with the tricks?'

Still holding her tenderly, he stooped and opened the front door of the Hog. He placed her on the front seat. He shut the door and walked around the Hog to the driver's side. He got in and the Hog roared away into the night.

The crowd was scattering. I turned to a fellow about my age. His eyes were glazed. He was sucking a stick of gangster.

I said, 'That stud would have gotten busted sure as Hell if the heat had made the scene.'

He stepped back and looked at me like I was fresh in town from a monastery in Tibet.

He said, 'You must be that square, Rip Van Winkle, I heard about. He's heat. He's vice heat. They call him Poison. He's got nine whores. He's a pimp. That broad is one of 'em. She got drunk with a trick.'

I went into the liquor store. It was five-after-twelve. I ordered the half pint. The clerk put it on the counter. I swung my topcoat away to get my hide in my hip pocket. I had two hundred in fives and tens in it. I had five C notes pinned to my shorts in a tobacco sack between my legs.

My fingers touched the bottom of the pocket. My right hip pocket was empty. I was sure my hide had been on that side. I dug my left hand into the left pocket. Empty!

Within seconds both my sweaty hands had darted in and explored all my pockets a half-dozen times. The clerk just stood there amused watching the show. His hairy paw slid the half pint back toward him away from foul territory.

He said, 'Whatsa matter, Buddy, some broad ram it into you for your poke or did you leave it in your other Strides?'

My mind was ferreting. It back pedalled, tore apart the scenes and moves I had made. I was a confused, jazzy punk.

I said, 'Jack, your score is zero. I'm not a vic. I just remembered I got my scratch on Mars. I'll be back when I get back.'

He was shaking his head when I walked out. I crossed the street. I was headed toward the Ford. I wasn't going there to look for my hide on the seat. I was going there to peel off one of those C notes next to my balls.

I had remembered the scene back in the hype joint. I saw that rattlesnake lightning again. For the first time I saw the thrill of the cop on the face of the Horse. The Fox had sure held my balls in the fire for Horseface.

I thought, 'As slick as those two bastards are they can't miss making a million or getting croaked.'

From that day to this one almost thirty years later no scratch has ever been in my hide.

I copped the bottle. I was hurrying to pick up my rib order. Old Preston was back out there bird-dogging suckers. I saw him point a joker into the joint. He slapped the balking sucker on the rump. The vic went inside. He saw me and hobbled toward me. For the first time I saw his crippled walk. He grinned when I laid the bottle on him.

He said, 'Thanks Kid, want first suck?'

I said, 'Jack, it's all yours. After I get my ribs I'll duck back in the joint and rap with you.'

Preston had his bad dogs propped on a chair when I got back. I stumbled over his make-shift sandals beside the sofa. I sat down. His feet stank like a terminal cancer victim. Even a budding pimp has to have a cast iron belly. I unwrapped and started to gobble the ribs.

He said, 'I guess you saw pimping Poison hanging that whore on the corner. He's number two mack man in town.'

Through the peppery grease I burbled, 'Yeh, she looked dead to me. I guess he checked her into the morgue. How does he cut the double action? Who, as strong as he is, could top him?'

He tilted the bottle straight up and drained it. He said, 'She ain't croaked. She'll be back out before daylight humping her ass off. He's the top Nigger vice roller in town. His pimping don't faze the white brass just so he don't kick no white asses. Poison is a nice sweet stud compared to Sweet Jones. Sweet's the top spade pimp in the country.'

I said, 'Preston, I want to be great like Sweet. I want my name to ring like his. I want to be slick enough to handle a hundred whores. Can you pull my coat so I can cut into Sweet and get down right and really do the thing.'

In the half darkness I saw his yellow jaw pop loose. His hound face was twisting sideways in quizzical amazement. His face jig-sawed like maybe I had asked him to let me knock him up. He starched like a corpse on the sofa.

He said, 'Kid, you bang a cap of smack or something? Sweet's crazy as a flock of loons. Your bell ain't never gonna clang that loud, unless you go crazy too. He's killed four studs. He ain't human. He's got every Nigger in town scared shitless. His whores call him Mr Jones.

'He hates young punks. I can't cut you into him. Kid, I like you. You're good looking. You conned me that you're intelligent. I am going to give you some advice. Take it or leave it.

'I came to this town twelve years ago. I was so pretty just my ass would have made you a Sunday face. I brought five whores with me. I had been one hell of a pimp back in the sticks. I was only twenty-eight when I got here.

'Just like you, I had to cut into Sweet. It was easy for me. I was yellow and pretty. I also had three beautiful white whores in my stable. I didn't know Sweet hated yellow Niggers and white men.

'He grinned that gold-toothed smile for a year. He conned me that he loved me. He was a hype even then. He started to rib me, called me a square. I tried hard to be like him, so I got hooked on H.

'My habit screwed my mind up. All I wanted to do was bang H and coast. Like a real pal he kept my stable humping. At first his angle was Uncle Sweet to my whores. In six weeks he was giving me and my whores orders. He tore my image down before my whores. He copped my stable.

'One morning, I was puking sick. Sweet was torturing me. He hadn't brought me my stuff in twenty-four hours. I was cold as ice wrapped in a blanket, then red hot. I was naked, crawling on the floor, nailing my body bloody when he came in. He stood over me flashing that gold in his jib.

'Sweet said, "Easy now you pretty yellow bastard. There's been a panic. Until this morning I couldn't cop any stuff. I copped you a sixteenth in Spic town. You know I gotta' love your stinking junkie ass to stick my neck out like that. Ain't that a bitch, I just noticed when you sick you almost black as me.

'"I wish that bastard white father of yours could see you down there on your knees begging this black Nigger to stop your misery."

'Sweet held the tiny cellophane pack out to me. I was too weak to take it.

'I said, "Please Sweet, cook it for me and load my outfit. It's inside the candy-striped tie in the closet. Sweet if you don't hurry, I'm sure to croak."

'I was one big ache and cramp. He walked slowly to the closet. He fumbled past the striped tie on the rack. He was getting his kicks making the yellow Nigger suffer.

'I screamed, "Sweet you had your mitt on the right one. It's there! Right there?"

'Sweet finally got the spike out of the tie lining. I was too weak to shoot the H when he got it cooked. I held my arm flat on the carpet. My eyes begged him to tie me up and bang me.

'He pulled my belt from my trousers on a chair. He tightened the belt around my arm above the elbow. My veins stood out like blue rope. He stabbed the needle into a vein in the hollow. The glass tube turned red. I lay there freezing to death waiting for the smack to slug the sickness and pain out of me.'

Preston stopped for breath. Bubbles of sweat had popped out on his bald head. While running down Sweet's double cross, he had really relived it.

I licked the hot sauce off my hands. I crushed the greasy

sack into a ball and sailed it into a paper box at my end of the sofa. I fished my handkerchief out and wiped my mouth and hands.

Those dice the house was using had a Ph.D. Every ten minutes a chump would shuffle from the rear with a tapped-out look on his face.

I said, 'Christ, Sweet's slick and cold blooded. What happened after that?'

Preston said, 'That shot took the fever and pain away. I wasn't ready to go a fast fifteen with Joe Louis. I felt better. Sweet stood in the middle of the floor watching me. My legs were weak when I finally stood up. I stood there naked.

'I said, "Sweet, I know you have stolen my stable. I know I have been a prize sucker, I demand that you lay a grand or so on me. I got to kick this habit you conned me into. I won't give you any headaches. You got to loan me that G."

'Sweet just stood there like a black Buddha for a long moment. For a second I thought he was going to put his foot in my ass like I was a whore. He grinned. He pulled my robe from the foot of the bed. He draped it around my shoulders.

'Then he said, "Sweetheart, I ain't stole no whores from you. Them whores would have blew to the wind if it don't be for me. You got me. I'm just like your whore. Wouldn't you rather I had them whores than some bastard you couldn't cop a favor from? Course I'm going to give you the grand. I'm even going to give you back that buck-toothed yellow whore you had. I want you to straighten up. Sweetheart, I love you."

'I said, "Sweet when do I get the grand? I got to know it's coming at a certain time."

'Sweet said, "Look Sweetheart, you get it no later than tomorrow morning. I'll bring the buck-toothed bitch with me. Today before noon I'll send you a quarter piece. You got no reason to sweat. Sweet's in your corner, Sweetheart."

'He chucked me under the chin and walked out. The runner came with the quarter piece at eleven o'clock. I was beginning to think Sweet was only half rat.

'At noon two rollers broke the door down. I was coasting.

I was draped in my PJ's. They found the H and booked me for possession. I got a fin. I kicked the habit cold turkey in city jail. I did three years, nine months in the State Joint.

'I left my hair, teeth, and looks in the joint. A con ran a shiv into my plumbing. That's why I limp and pee out of this tube in my side. I ain't had a whore since.'

Preston had choked up.

He said, 'Kid, you still want to try this track, and cut into Sweet?'

I turned my face from him. He was mopping his tears away with his sleeve. I was sure a lost, stupid punk. After a rundown like that, I was still itching to take my crack at the fast track.

The rundown had only boosted my desire to meet the slick, icy Sweet. If I had been smart I would have jumped in that Ford and rushed back to the sticks.

I thought, 'Sweet hates yellow and white. I am black like him. The runt is black. Sweet won't have a black whore. I have no reason to fear him. I have nothing that he wants. I have to find him and pick his brain. I got to take that short cut to become a great pimp.'

I said, 'To hell with the Sweet cut-in. I'm not bats, but I got to try this track. Yeh, Preston, you sure got the hurt put to you. Man, I feel for you. When I start pimping a zillion, I'll do something big for you. You are over due for a break. Now tell me the best spot to down my package.'

He said, 'You gotta' get your head bumped, huh? What kind of package you got?'

I said, 'Black, eighteen, cute, stacked, and three way.'

He said, 'Blood, we are sitting on the best street in town for a package like that. Only drawback is this street is crawling with fast, whore-hungry pimps.

'You would also be playing your girl against a half-dozen strong, jasper whores on this stem. They pimping tough as studs.

'They got some fancy con to lay on a fine young whore. If your game ain't tight, you'll blow your girl fast. How long you had her? What kind of wheels you got?'

I said, 'About a week, but I got her up tight. The Bitch loves me. Nobody can steal her. Temporarily I got a Ford.'

He threw his head back and started laughing. I thought he had flipped his cork. He died laughing for a full minute. The tears were rolling down his cheeks when he stopped.

He said, 'Blood Lancaster, Slim Young, Dizzy Willie, or whatever your name is, don't get down in this town. If you ain't hip that a pimp don't never have a whore tight. Do you believe any whore can love a pimp?

'You ain't no pimp. These slick Niggers will steal that young bitch as soon as you down her. The bartenders and bell hops on this fast track are better pimps than the best in the hinterlands.

'You ain't got no front and flash. Some of these bootblacks got Hogs. You'll get that young bitch dazzled out from under you. Get out of town and be a good pimp in a chump town. Go to the West Coast. Believe me, you ain't ready for this one.'

He stopped rapping. He sat there just looking at me like I should bolt out the door and head for suckerville. He sure thought he had spooked me. His ribbing had me hot as a Bull Run musket.

I thought, 'What did this crippled flunky think I came here for? I knew I was slow. I sure didn't intend to stay slow. I was determined to maybe get as fast and slick as Sweet Jones, the boss pimp. If I blew the runt it wouldn't be the end of the world. This poor cry baby had let Sweet's cross destroy him.'

I said, 'Look Preston, I got lots of heart. I'm not a pussy. I been to the joint twice. I did tough bits, but I didn't fall apart. I believe my whore loves me in her freak way. I believe I got her.

'If I'm wrong, and I blow her, so what. I won't give up no matter what happens. If I go stone blind, I'm still going to pimp. If my props get cut off I'll wheel myself on a wagon looking for a whore. I'm going to pimp or die.

'I'm not going to be a flunky in this white man's world. You can't convince me I can't pimp here. I know I can get my share of pussies to peddle. I'm going to get hip to what I don't know.

I'm not afraid of Sweet. I'm going to cut into him and pick his brain like a buzzard.'

A heavy-set Greek with a carny face came in the door. I dummied up. He walked by us, then went through the small door in the partition. Preston started to put his shoes on. He looked nervous.

I asked, 'Who's the big stud? Is he heat?'

He said, 'Oh, he's the owner of the joint, come to check the bankroll and cut box.'

'Then you and your pal are flunkies for the Greek?'

Before he could answer the Greek came out. Preston was slipping into his topcoat. The Greek paused and glared at him.

He said, 'I ain't payin you a fin a night to sit on your keister. I can get a hundred boys to jump for that fin and the cot in the back. Your ass will grow icicles in the alleys if you don't get on the ball. Get out on the midway and dump some suckers into the joint.'

Preston said, 'Yes, Sir, Mr Nick, but I wasn't setting there but a minute before you showed. You know nobody can pull a mark better than me.'

I avoided Preston's eyes when we got on the sidewalk. I knew what I'd see there. I felt sorry for him. I pulled a saw buck from my pocket. I folded it and dropped it into his ragged coat pocket. He took it out and put it in his short pocket.

He said, 'Thanks Blood, maybe I was wrong about you. Maybe you got the guts for the fast track. You'll need all you got. Good luck, Kid.'

I said, 'Preston, thanks for the rundown. In six months you'll have to anchor your eyeballs. I'm getting down right on this stem tomorrow night. You can't stop a stepper. Don't worry if the Greek boots you out, I'll cop you a pad.'

I peeped into my skull file and saw that Roost note. My Mickey Mouse read one-thirty A.M. I headed toward the Roost. I had been in town only three-and-a-half hours. It had cost me only two-hundred and twelve slats to find out how little I knew. It's easy for a half-wise punk to lock his mind. Just this was worth a fortune.

I thought, 'I have to keep my mind like a sponge. I'll use my eyes and ears like suction cups. I have to know everything about crosses and whores.

'Fast, I got to find out the secrets of pimping. I don't want to be a half-ass gigolo lover like the white pimps. I really want to control the whole whore. I want to be the boss of her life, even her thoughts. I got to con them that Lincoln never freed the slaves.'

The Roost was still jumping. I copped the one open stool at the middle of the bar. A Mexican broad in a red satin cocktail dress brought me a pink Planter's Punch.

The combo was speed-riffing 'Tea For Two.' Through the bar-length mirror I could see a black ugly stud playing stink finger with an angel-faced white broad in a booth behind me. He was playing pocket pool with his other hand. The broad had her eyes closed. Her rhinestone tiara looked like a phony halo. She was biting her bottom lip like maybe she was taking a heavenly trip right there in the booth.

My ear cups started sucking. The dapper joker on my right was rapping to the stud on the other side of him.

He was saying, 'I want my three bills back. That pretty bitch ain't turned three tricks since you sold her to me. The bitch is dying. She's falling apart. She can't walk the street.'

The seller said, 'Jack, I sold you the package as is. I ain't responsible for divine acts.'

The buyer said, 'Divine my ass. You knew that dog was rotten inside and needed a grand's worth of carving. Give me a yard and a half and take the bitch back.'

The seller said, 'You a stick up man? The bitch was whole when I sold her. Maybe you trying to play con on me. Maybe you stomped on the package. Maybe you put the bitch in bad shape. I ain't buying her back even if you only wanted a slat for her.'

The buyer said, 'Ain't this a bitch? I went for the okee doke. I'm out three bills for a black dog with a foot in the grave.'

The seller said, 'I'm pimping for myself, Jack. I ain't got no time to pimp for you. Just to get you off my ass, I'm going to rundown for you.

'There's a whore house up state with all Spic trade. They don't spend but a fin, but there's a zillion of 'em. On weekends they line up on the sidewalk.

'All you gotta do is cop some pills. Patch the bitch up and take her up there. Up there, ain't no walking. She can flat back and so long as she keeps breathing you can get some scratch. Jack, she may even last long enough so you can invest the scratch to overhaul her, and still show a profit.

'The bitch is black and pretty. She ain't got much mileage on her. Them Spics are wild for black broads. Jim, I been running down the out for you. If you go for it call me at noon.

'In the meantime I'll contact the joint. Me and the house broad are tight. It's a cinch you can place your grief tomorrow.'

The buyer said, 'Jack, you know I deserve some cooperation. I'll try anything to break even on that dog. I'll call you at noon. I ain't salty with you now. Let's split and make the scene at the lair. I'll pop for a coupla rounds.'

The buyer stood up. He knocked his knuckles against the log. The cute Mexican broad came toward him to check him out. She stood before him. She was smiling.

The seller drained his glass and stood. He leaned across the log staring into her bosom. I was digging the action from that trap door in the corner of my eye.

She said, 'Both tabs come to twelve dollars. Yours is seven. Your friend's is five.'

The buyer said, 'I've got 'em both. Here's a double saw. Keep the change Miss "Bet I Get You." Say Girl, was that bum your father who brought you in when you started to work here last night? Ain't you afraid I'll salt and pepper you and eat you raw?'

She said, 'No, not my father, my husband. He's no bum. He had on his work clothes. People are not good to eat. It's not nice to eat people. Thanks for the tip. Come back soon.'

The buyer hurled his beak toward the ceiling and laughed. Flakes of grayish white dust clung to the hairs in his nostrils. He had snorted and loaded his skull with H.

Her mouth was still smiling. Her big black eyes had slitted in

Latin fury. She turned away toward the register. She punched it. She came back. She stood staring at the buyer. She had a fin and three slats in her hand. She was crushing them into a missile. In the mirror I saw the seller shaking his head as he walked out the door.

The buyer was looking at her like the eight slats had made her his indentured slave. The four-carat stone on his left hand flashed like a neon as he caressed his fly.

He said, 'If that tramp was your man I'm stealing you. Shit, I should kidnap you right now. You ain't got no business juggling suds. Bitch, You got a mint between your big hairy legs. I'm gonna show you how to make a grand a week. I ain't never wanted nothing and didn't get it. Bitch, I'm gonna get you. I'll be back at four to pick you up.'

A massive black bulk with a face like a rabid bull dog had come on the scene. It had to be the joint bouncer. He was standing several feet behind the buyer, grinning like a starved croc. He was hunching his shoulders. The Mexican broad was shaking. She fired the missile. It struck the buyer on the tip of his beak. He threw his hands across his face.

She shouted, 'You stupid ugly filth. You insane Nigger bastard. Do you think I'd let you touch me? I wouldn't shit in your mouth to save your slimy life. If you ever look at me again I'll cut your heart out!'

The bouncer streaked toward the buyer like a howitzer shell. His feet clickety-clacked like the wheels of an express train against the parquet floor. He vised the buyer's rear end through the tail split in his topcoat.

He seized the scrawny neck with his other giant paw. The buyer was almost airborne. The tips of his shoes did a tap dance against the floor on his way to the door. The joint was silent. The buyer swiveled his head back toward the angry tamale.

Just before he skidded toward the sidewalk he screamed, 'You square-ass greasy chili-gut bitch. I'm gonna triple-cross you.'

The joint got back on jump time. The combo started to riff 'Mood Indigo.'

I thought about the runt. The Mexican broad had her hands

on her hips. She was looking at me. She wanted me to say the buyer was a no-good bastard. She didn't know I was up as a pledge in his club.

I put a deuce on the log and walked out. It was two-thirty in the A.M. I walked to the corner. Preston had been right. Poison's black whore was standing in front of the liquor store. She hit on me. That terrible beating she had taken sure hadn't cured her bad habit.

She said, 'Hi Slim, give me ten and sock it in. I won't put the rush on you handsome. Cop a jug and let's go freak off.'

I jerked my head away from the sight of her like she was Medusa. I put my dogs in high gear and crossed the street. I had a quick vision of Poison's thirteens giving me a butt ache.

I got into the Ford and made a U-turn. I was going to the runt and some doss. I caught Preston in my headlights on the turn. He was still out there trying to make the Greek richer. He waved. I honked.

The mercury had fallen. The icy streets were like a ski run.

Less than a mile from the Roost, I saw a clean front of a hotel. The blue neon sparkled out 'Blue Haven Hotel.' I went into the blue-and-red lobby. A broad was on the desk. She had a razor slash on her tan cheek. She had the build and rapper of a heavyweight wrestler.

She said, 'You want something permanent or just for the night?'

I said, 'How much are the permanent pads? I want the best you got. Whatever it is, it's got to be on the front with a view.'

She said, 'The best single rooms are thirty-two fifty a week. The best three-room apartments are a hundred a week.'

She got up and went to a red board behind her. She took several keys off and gave them to me.

The elevator operator was an old stud reading a wild Maggie and Jiggs comic book. He was whistling 'When the Saints go Marching In.' His peepers were glued to it like maybe he had found the map to the 'Lost Dutchman.' I got off on the third floor.

I looked at two single rooms. The carpets in them were

stained and the furniture was battered. This was an underworld hotel all right. I could smell the odor of gangster grass in the hallways.

I took the stairs to the fourth floor. I looked into two apartments. I went for the second one. It was freshly decorated in gold and black paint. The furniture was blond and new.

It was spotless and flashy. The gold-draped front window gave a wide view of the stem. The pad was perfect for now. It would do until I hit the big time with a big stable.

I went to the elevator and pressed the down button. The floor indicator dial was stuck between floor number two and three.

I took the stairs down. I figured the antics of Maggie and Jiggs had put a lot of pressure on the old joker. Some whore in the hotel was probably down there with the old coot. They were maybe using the comic book as a guide.

I went to the desk. I registered and paid a week's rent in advance. I put the key in my pocket and went to the Ford. I drove toward the runt. I saw a black whore leading a white man into the front door of the Martin Hotel, a hundred yards from the Haven. The runt could take her good tricks there.

It was four A.M. when I got there. I parked and went up the hotel stairs. An elevated train shook the stairway as it passed. Its shadow leaped through the second floor window and plunged like a rattling, speeding ghost across the wall.

I turned left to number twenty. I twisted my key in the lock and stepped inside. The runt was wide eyed. She leaped from the bed. She had on red baby-doll pajamas. She squeezed herself hard against me. She acted like I had been gone a year.

She said, 'Oh Daddy, I am so glad you're back. I was worried like hell. Where have you been? Do you love me as much as I love you? Did you miss me? I'd die if anything ever happens to you.'

A heart-aching montage tornadoed through my skull. I gritted my teeth. I felt my fingernails ice-picking into my palms. The runt's love con had resurrected sad old scenes.

I saw poor black Henry. He was on his knees blubbering

his love for Mama. I saw his pitiful eyes begging Mama not to break his heart.

I saw Mama kicking herself free of his clutching arms. I saw that terrible look of scorn and triumph on Mama's face. I thought about the worms that had devoured his flesh, in his lonely grave.

I shuddered and punched the runt with all my might against the left temple. On impact, needles of pain threaded to my elbow. She moaned and shot backward onto the bed. She bounced like she was on a trampoline. There was a crunching, pulpy thud on the second bounce. She'd crashed face first on the steel edge at the foot of the bed.

She just lay there breathing hard. I moved to the foot of the bed. I grabbed a fist full of hair. I turned her face toward me. Her eyes were closed and there was a bloody gash just above her right eyebrow.

I went to the face bowl and drew a pitcher of cold water. I doused her full in the face. Her eyes flickered open. She just lay looking up at me. A scarlet trickle ran down her cheek across her chin.

She stroked the side of her face. She saw the blood. Her eyes full-mooned. Her mouth was open. I stood looking down at her. The guts in my scrotum were twisting. I could feel hot currents firing up that generator at the base of my weapon.

Then she said, 'Why Daddy? What did I say to get my ass whipped? Are you high or what?'

I said, 'Bitch, if I have you a hundred years don't ever ask me where I been. Don't ever try to play that bullshit love con on me. We're not squares. I'm a pimp and you're a whore. Now get up and keep a cold towel on that eyebrow.'

She got up and stood at the washbowl washing the blood off. Her big eyes were staring at me through the mirror. I didn't know she had started to keep a revenge score in her skull. Seven years later she would tally up and happily cross me into prison.

She sat on the side of the bed pressing a towel against the wound. I got in the sack in the raw. In fifteen minutes the leak had stopped. It was now only a small puckered slash.

She crawled in beside me. She nibbled at my ear. That lizard did cross-country laps and then took the boss trek around the world. I lay there silently. I was trying to figure the real reason why I had slugged her. I couldn't find the answer. My thoughts were ham strung by the razor-edge of conscience.

She whispered, 'Daddy, do you feel like tying me down? Please. I want you to.'

I said, 'Bitch, you got a one track mind. I'm gonna tie you down like a sow in a slaughter house. After you get your rocks off I'm gonna give you the rundown on that stem you're working tonight. Get on your back. Stretch your legs out and put your arms above your head. That's right you sweet freak bitch.'

6

Drilling for Oil

That thunderbolt El train had trembled the room a half dozen times. Dawn had broken through a smeary sky. Fingers of pale gray light poked through the frayed window shades.

She was lying in my arms. I saw flakes of brown blood beneath her chin. Her heart against my side was sprinting like a wildcat's facing the hounds. I could hear the clip-clop of an ice-huckster's horse. The creaking wagon wheels were in rhythm to his pitch.

He sang, 'Ice Man! Ice! A hundred for twenty, fifty for a dime. Keep your watermelon cold and your poke chops fine. 'vite Old Joe up to chitlins just any old time. Ice Man! Ice!'

I thought, 'Even the ice man is starving down here. I gotta' get down up there on that stem. Off Preston's rundown, that stem must be a sonuvabitch. I gotta' down her there. It's where the scratch is.

'When I rundown to her I have to be cool and confident. I can't falter and tip her I'm still going to school. I gotta really remember the 'get down' rundown I hustled from those pimps in the joint.'

I said, 'Phyllis, Daddy's been out there casing those streets. It's like walking in a river of tricky crap. If I had any other bitch but you I would say she couldn't go out there and get me some scratch. Baby, I got a lot of confidence in you.

'I know no stud or con bitch can sell you a pig in a poke. In fact I would stand in the Halls of Congress and swear that you would be too busy getting scratch to even listen to bullshit. Am I right so far about you, or have I overrated you?'

She said, 'Daddy, I'm a big girl now. No nickel-slick bastard can steal me from you. I you-know-what you, and always will. Honey, I just want to be your little dog and make you a million dollars.

'When we get rich maybe you won't mind if Gay, my

daughter, lives with us. She's only two. She's so cute and friendly. You'd be crazy about her. My aunt in Saint Louis takes care of her.'

I thought, 'I was sure a sap making like a pimp. Here I'd had her a week and I was flat-footed. I hadn't heard about a crumb crusher. Worse, I hadn't given her a deep quiz. I really knew nothing about her. It had been the one rundown from the joint I'd goofed. I had been satisfied with the shallow rundown from that sissy barkeep.'

The pimps in the joint had said, 'There ain't nothing more important than what makes a new bitch tick and why. You gotta scrape her brain. Find out whether the first joker who layed her was her father or who. Make her tell you her life story.

'If she can remember back in her mammy's ass, good! Fit all the pieces together. Maybe then you'll know if she's a two-day package or a two-year package. Don't try to play 'em in the dark. Quiz 'em into a crack-up if you have to. Wake 'em up from a dead sleep. Check the answers you got with what you get.'

I said, 'Girl, your rap is right on the scratch. It's you and me against the world. I'm gonna' make a star out of you. We are going to get rich as cream. You gotta hump your ass off in those streets, Baby. As soon as we get a big bundle you go cop the kid. Now forget about her until we get in shape. I don't want anything in your skull but those tricks out there.

'Now listen carefully. I want you to work nothing but the street. Stay out of the bars. Don't drink, smoke gangster, or use anything while you're working. Your skull has got to be sharp and clear out there. Otherwise you could lose your life, and almost as bad, my scratch.

'Believe me, I am not yeasting it. I want you to memorize everything that happens while you're working. I want a rundown every night after you knock off. Maybe some stuff player will set you up like tonight and take you off tomorrow night.

'Keep those crack-wise Niggers out of your face. If I see you rapping to a jasper broad I'm gonna put my foot in your ass.

Play for cruising white tricks. Spade tricks are trouble. They all want to make a home.

'You're black and beautiful. They can't resist you. They are the freaks and they got the scratch. Ask them for a hundred and take ten. You can go down on a price. You can't go up. Don't go to nobody's pad. For a double saw or over take 'em to the Martin down the street from where we are gonna move. Flip out of wheels as much as possible. Flip 'em fast and crack more scratch for overtime.

'Your name is Mary Jones. I got enough B.R. to raise you fast. You're not a thief. I don't need a bondsman or a lip now. You don't have a sheet. You see a young girl out there, square or whore, pull her. Be friendly to her. Build me up. You know, tell her how smart and sweet I am. Don't let no bitch pull you. This family needs some whores. Don't bring no junkie bitch to me. Now is there anything you don't understand?'

She said, 'No Daddy, I dig everything. You can wire me if something turns up I don't dig. Daddy, I am so proud of you. You are so clever and strong. I feel so safe being your girl. I'm gonna be a star for you.'

I had told her all I knew. It was just pimp garbage. What the ninety percent know to tell a whore. What she really needed to protect herself in those terrible streets were daily rundowns for as long as she was my woman. How could I rundown the thousand crosses she'd face?

All I knew I'd gotten from the pimps in the joint. They were only fair pimps from small towns. None of them had the guts or savvy for this rapid track. The runt and me were a pure case of the blind leading the blind. I was bone tired. I had to be fresh for our debut.

I said, 'Sugar, let's cop some doss. We got a hectic night coming up. Oh! I forgot, some louse put the heist on your slum. Don't worry, with what you got to offer, I'll have enough scratch soon to score for the real thing. This is our last day in this flophouse. I copped us a jazzy little pad uptown. Sleep tight baby puppy.'

She said, 'All right, Daddy. I'm going to sleep. I wonder how Gay is doing?'

When I woke up I thought the runt had scalded me with hot grease. I was in a flaming sweat. My ticker was smashing inside my chest like a wrecker's demolition ball. That cunning joker playing God had conned me again. I had whipped my poor mama again. The runt's frightened big eyes almost touched mine. That puckered gash looked like she had grown an extra cat.

She was saying, 'Daddy, Daddy, you all right? It's your baby, Phyllis. Damn, you had a bitch-kitty nightmare. Was the heat chasing you or something?'

I said, 'No Baby, as a matter of fact, you were in trouble. You had done a stupid thing in the street. You let a Nigger pimp con you into his Hog. It turned out he was a crazy gorilla. He was trying to cut your throat. I saved you before he croaked you. Dreams often carry warnings. So Bitch, stay out of those pimp's Hogs.'

She said, 'Daddy, I'm looking for white tricks in Hogs. That's where the long scratch is. Ain't no Nigger pimp going to put my ass in a sling. I'm too slick for that okee doke. You not going to get salty with me about a dream I hope. Daddy, I ain't going to bullshit out there.'

It was five-twenty. By seven o'clock we had moved to the Blue Haven. The runt went for the pad. First thing she lifted the phone off the hook to see if it works.

I said, 'Tell your tricks to call you here.'

She laid the bearskin and freaked the joint off with her lights and other crap. Except for the fake stars it was a fair mock-up of her pad where I had copped her. She went to the street to get down at eight.

I had told her to work just the block where we padded for a week or so. I went to the front window. Ten minutes after she got down she broke luck. A white trick in a 'thirty-seven Buick picked her up. I timed her. She had racehorse speed. She was back on the track in nine and a half minutes.

A black pretty broad could sure scratch a white man's itch fast. I watched her scratch three. I showered and got as pretty as I could. I made an urgent skull note to cop a hot vine connection. I also needed a gangster and cocaine contact. I

got the elevator. I left the key at the desk. I had told the runt
to check her scratch past forty slats into the toe of my tan
Stetsons.

I got into the Ford. I waved to the runt on my way to
the Roost. It sure was a thrill to have a young fine bitch
humping for me.

I parked across the street from the Roost. I dabbed a
sponge into the box of Sun Glow face powder in the glove
compartment. I made my face up into an even, glowing tan.
I got out and crossed the street toward the Roost.

It was ten-thirty. The sky was a fresh, bright bitch. This first
April night had gone sucker and gifted her with a shimmering
bracelet of diamond stars. The fat moon lurked like an evil
yellow eye staring down at the pimps, hustlers, and whores
hawk-eyeing for a mark, a cop.

I felt the raw tenderness of first April winds lashing at the
hem of my white alligator. I felt the birth stirrings of that
poisonous pimp's rapture. I felt powerful and beautiful.

I thought, 'I am still black in the white man's world. My hope
to be important and admired can be realized even behind this
black stockade. It's simple, just pimp my ass off and get a ton
of scratch. Everybody in both worlds kisses your ass black and
blue if you got flash and front.'

I was six store fronts away from the Roost. He stood in the
center of the sidewalk. I looked down at him. He was a foot
shorter than the runt. He looked like a black baby who had
taken ugly pills. His head was the size of a giant pumpkin. His
voice was a squeal like a clappy joker makes when the croaker
rams a sound down his dingus.

He squealed, 'Shine 'em up, Hot Shot. If I had your hand
I'd throw mine away. Get on bigtime. Shines ain't but a dime.
Shine 'em up.'

I looked down at my Stomps. They could stand a gloss all
right. I followed the pointing, gnarled finger to the dwarf's
open-air stand. It sat at the mouth of a gangway between two
buildings. The red fringes of its tattered canvas top rippled in
the breeze.

I climbed into the chair. The dwarf was slapping polish on

my Stetsons. A thin stud with at least a half a grand in threads on his back took the other chair. He was wearing silver nail polish. He was reeking with perfume.

A gleaming black custom Duesenberg eased into the curb in front of me. The top was down. My peepers did a triple take.

A huge stud was sitting in the back seat. He had an ocelot in his lap dozing against his chest. The cat was wearing a stone-studded collar. A gold chain was strung to it.

He was sitting between two spectacular high-yellow whores. His diamonds were blazing under the street light. Three gorgeous white whores were in the front seat. He looked exactly like Boris Karloff in 'Black-face.'

He was rapping something. All five of those whores were turned toward him. They were listening and paying attention like he was God giving them a pass to Heaven. He could have been running down a safe place to hide because the world was coming to an end.

I said, 'Who is that?'

The dwarf said, 'You gotta be from outta town. That Sweet Jones. He's the greatest Nigger pimp in the world.'

The thin joker said, 'That spotted cat, Miss Peaches, is the only bitch he cares lives or croaks. Shit, them whores you pinning ain't but half the stable. If they got Nigger pimps in outer space, he's the best of them, too. He's gonna take them whores into the Roost and pop some. He's lugging twenty Gs in his raise. Ain't no heist man crazy enough to stick him up though. He croaks Niggers for his recreation.'

I couldn't believe what I saw. This was only nineteen thirty-eight. Those Duesenbergs cost a fortune. He must have been the only black pimp in the country who owned one. My peepers jacked off just watching him and those high powered whores. It was as exciting as maybe Christ making his encore.

The dwarf had shined my Stomps. I gave him a buck. I sat there and watched Sweet Jones and those whores get out of the Duesenberg and walk toward the Roost. The black-spotted cat slinked beside him.

I thought, 'Tonight I got to cut into him. I got to be careful so I don't blow him. The cut in has to be in the Roost. I'll go in and cook up something in there.'

I got off the stand. I passed Poison's problem whore. She was sitting beside a joker in a red Hog. She had a bottle of gin in her jib turned straight up. As I neared the Roost I saw old Preston trying to shoo two marks into the Greek's joint. Just as I turned into the Roost he bucked his eyes and jerked his thumb at me. He was tipping me Sweet was in the Roost. I nodded my head, and went in.

It was an off night for the combo. The juke box was grinding out 'Pennies From Heaven'. The joint hadn't crowded yet. There were maybe a half dozen couples in the booths. Sweet Jones and his whores were the only people at the log. They were in the center. The cat was licking her paws beneath Sweet's stool. I sat at the log near the front door facing him and the stable. The pretty Mexican broad was standing in front of him.

Sweet was buying the house a drink. She served his party. She glanced at me. She remembered my drink. She brought me a Planter's Punch on Sweet. The floor waitress loaded a tray from the log and served the couples in the booths all on Sweet.

I sat there studying Sweet. He had to be six feet six. His face was like a black steel mask. Not a flicker of emotion played over it. He kept smashing the heels of his brute-sized hands together like he was crushing an invisible throat.

Even at a distance it made me edgy. I guess it kept his whores on the brink of peeing on themselves. If he had smiled maybe they would have dropped dead from shock. He sure proved pimping wasn't a charm contest.

Those whores lit his cigarette. They took turns feeding him sips of his Coke. They fought to ram their noses up his ass.

I froze; one of the white broads was whispering in his ear. Those unearthly gray eyes of his in the ebony sockets were staring at me. I could hear the thud of those meat sledges.

I thought, 'Christ Almighty! Mama darling, I hope my double hasn't put the muscle on this broad for some snatch or scratch. Please don't let this broad bum-finger me!'

He slid his terrible pearl-gray peepers off me. I saw him pound the bottom of his glass against the log. The Mexican broad expressed to him. He was rapping to her. She was nodding her head and looking down the log at me.

My Stetsons on the stool rung were slamming together like the heels of a Flamenco Dancer. The juke box was sobbing Lady Day's beef about her mean but sweet man. I wondered if I'd see the runt again, and if not how soon she'd get another ass kicker.

The couples in the booths were bug-eying the arena. It was maybe like the Circus Maximus. The doomed Christian, me, pitted against the king of beasts, him, plus the ocelot.

The Mexican broad came slowly toward me. Her face was tight and serious as she stood before me. She had pity in her peepers. She hated capital punishment.

She said, 'Mr Jones wants you to come to him pronto.'

She turned and walked away. I staggered to my feet. I started hoofing that thousand miles to Mr Jones. On the way I dusted off the hundred-and-seventy-five I.Q. in my skull.

I got to him. The cat snarled under the stool. It pasted its yellow eyes on me. I jerked my eyes from the cat and kept them riveted to the floor. I was afraid to look into Sweet's glowing peepers up close. I knew I'd crap in my pants.

He whirled around on his stool, his back to the log. I glued my peepers to the tapping tips of his needle-toed patent leather stomps. I flinched at each crash of his huge hooks.

He whispered, 'Nigger, you know who I am? Look at me when I'm spieling to you.'

That teletype in my skull hammered out the escape hatch.

It read, 'For this maniac you gotta be just like a Mississippi Nigger. You gotta pretend he's a white lynch-mob leader. You gotta con him, but be careful, don't get cute. Keep your nose square in his ass. Jeff it out all the way.'

I said, 'Sure I know who you are Mr Jones. You're the black God of the sporting world. Ain't a Nigger alive, unless he's stupid and deaf, that ain't heard your fame and name ring. The reason I don't look at you is because I remember what happened to that sucker in the Bible that snitched a peep.'

His whores broke out into gales of laughter. Miss Peaches wasn't a lady. She broke wind and grinned. Those patent-leather toes stopped tapping. Could I be selling it?

He reached out and grabbed my chin. He held my head up and cupped it in his giant hook. I flexed my belly to take up the slack in my bowels. Those deadly gray slits almost slugged me into a dead faint. When he opened his Jib I saw spidery webs of spit for an instant bridge his fat lips.

He said, 'Little Nigger, who are you and where you from? You kinda look like me. Maybe I layed your Mammy, huh?'

I neatly side-stepped his booby trap.

I said, 'Mr Jones, I'm nobody trying in your world to be somebody. I was born right here in your town. Could be my Mammy went for you. What bitch wouldn't? If I was a bitch I'd give you some scratch to get some.'

He said, 'Nigger, you like fine white pussy? This dog of mine wants you to lay her. I give my whores what they want. You going to lay her for a double saw?'

My skull raced out the warning, 'Fool! Watch your ass!'

I said, 'Mr Jones, I don't want no kind of a pussy unless it hangs on my own whore. Mr Jones, I'm a pimp, like you. I don't want nothing but some pimp scratch. My principles won't let me turn no reverse trick.

'Mr Jones, I ain't no party freak. I want to be great like you. I ain't never going to amount to anything if I screw up the rules of the pimp game. You the greatest pimp on Earth. You got great pimping by the rules. Would you want a poor dumb pimp like me to chump out at the start?'

His freak white woman pouted at his side. She begged Nero to flip his thumbs down.

She said, 'Mr Jones, make this pretty punk freak off with your baby. You don't let nobody say no to you. Since he's dreaming he's a pimp it will be wild kicks for me. Force him, Daddy, force him. Show him who's boss. Sic Miss Peaches on him.'

He shoved her aside. The boa constrictor uncoiled from around my chest. I saw contempt paint over the skull and crossed bones in his peepers. I drew a deep breath.

He roared, 'You little pissy, green-ass Nigger. You a pimp?

You can't spell pimp. You couldn't make a pimple on a pimp's ass. Nigger, I'll blow your head off through that ceiling. Don't let the word pimp come outta your jib in my presence. Now get outta my face, Pussy. I oughta stick my swipe in your jib.'

The cat slithered from under the stool. She crouched on her belly and stared up at me.

I wasn't David. Good thing I wasn't. I was sure mad at the kooky bastard. I grinned and fished a fin out. I tossed it on the log and dragged tail out the door to the street. I was glad I hadn't stacked that sling-shot switch blade in my pocket against that thirty-eight magnum stuck beneath Goliath's belt.

The door smacked Preston a hard shot in the forehead. He had been peeping through a slat in the door blind. He rubbed his head. He looked scared.

He said, 'Kid, I told you he's nuts. You keep it up, a ground hog will be your mailman. To play it safe you better give me your Mama's address. I gotta know where to ship your corpse. Where you going now?'

I said, 'Look Preston, I didn't cut into him. He cut into me. Hell, I ain't no head-shrinker. I couldn't handle the maniac. I'm splitting to the Ford to think.'

He was clucking his jib when I walked away from him. I collapsed onto the Ford's seat. I was stinking from the fear-sweat in the bar. My pants were soggy.

I saw the white broad that was burning to freak off with me. She was holding the Roost door open. Sweet filed out. His whores strutted out behind him. They walked behind him to the Duesenberg.

A tall brown-skin joker with a gleaming head of processed hair got out of a red Hog. He was the gutty stud I saw pouring that gin down Poison's girl.

Sweet's stable had gotten into the Duesenberg. The shiny-topped joker and Sweet were rapping on the sidewalk. They pounded each other on the back. They looked like boon buddies. Miss Peaches stood lashing her tail at Sweet's side.

I almost leaped out of my hide. It was Preston banging on the car window. I unlocked the door. He slid in. His peepers were ballooning, looking past me to Sweet on the other side of the street.

He was sucking air like a mackerel on the beach. He was shoving a rusty owl-head twenty-two pistol across the seat. He was trembling like the zero second had come to assassinate maybe F.D.R.

He said, 'Kid, you sitting here hating him, ain't you? You despise his guts. I saw the way you was looking at him. A bastard like him ain't got a right to live on God's green Earth.

'Do yourself and the world a favor, Kid. Take this rod and walk sneaky like down that sidewalk while he's rapping to Glass Top. Stick the barrel in his ear and pull the trigger. Then quick, blow the cat's brains out. It's easy, Kid. You can do it.

'Every Nigger in the country will love you. Kid, it's your chance to get great. Go on, Kid, do it now. You ain't never gonna get a choicer chance.'

I said. 'Preston, I'm not hip to the murder game. I don't want to get hip to it. I don't want to blow his brains out on that sidewalk and waste them. I want his brains to work inside my skull. You getting old, Preston. You can't even dent the mustard. He screwed you around a thousand times worse than me.

'You can't lose for winning. Why don't you be the hero and croak him. Look Preston, take that tommy gun and split. I like you, but give me a break, huh? I've had a funky night and my skull needs a change.'

He said, 'Kid, you think I ain't got the guts? He ruined me, Kid. He destroyed me. He's just another Nigger. He ain't no bear, and that cat ain't no tiger. I'm going over there right now and cash them out.'

Old Preston sprang out of the car. I watched him all the way. That game leg had him tilting from side to side. He looked like one of those doughty Spirit of Seventy-Six jokers on the posters around the Fourth of July.

I wondered if he was tanked up with enough rot-gut moxie to really fold Sweet's dukes for good across his chest. Preston was on the other side of the street only twenty feet from Sweet and Glass Top. His mitt was rammed into his benny pocket keeping the rod warm and ready. Preston's shoulders and back were stiff and straight. Sweet's back was toward me. He was facing the sidewalk.

I thought, 'The old Dingbat may do it. He sure had reasons. Sweet put the hurt to him all right. Will there be much gore? Will Sweet croak right away or flop around on the street like a chicken with its head wrung off? Will Miss Peaches leap up and cut Preston's throat?

'If Preston croaks him I'll have to cut into Poison. I'll bleed his skull. He will be top pimp. Maybe a couple of those ten whores Sweet's got will go for me. I'd be some kind of sonuvabitching young pimp in a Duesenberg.'

Preston came abreast of Sweet. He had slowed to an amble. I could see his yellow mitt easing out of his pocket. He got maybe three feet past Sweet and stopped. He was going to do it! He was coming back for a fatal flank sneak.

At that instant Sweet turned his buffalo head and looked down at Preston. Miss Peaches stiffened. I saw a black cavern open in Preston's toothless yellow face. The chicken-hearted bastard had been chilled by those awful gray orbs and the cat. He was grinning at Sweet. He scooted his empty hand out of his pocket.

Preston might have made it if Sweet hadn't turned those lights on him. Old Preston bowed his bald head. He walked toward the Greek's joint. His shoulders were sagging. His back was a stooped slouch. Old Preston had missed his choice chance at glory.

I just sat watching Sweet and trying to plot a way to cut into him. It looked hopeless. Finally, Sweet got in the rear seat of his Duesenberg. The cat leaped into his lap. One of the white broads roared it away. I saw Glass Top pat his greasy dome as he turned into the Roost.

I thought, 'That glossy-top stud with a face like a pretty whore's might be the tunnel to Sweet.'

I took my sponge out and freshened my makeup. I got out of the Ford and walked to the Roost. The joint was getting crowded. I was lucky. There was an empty stool in the middle of the log.

The beautiful joker was on a stool next to it. The memory of that four-slat tip out of the fin sent the tamale skidding to me. I sipped my Planter's Punch. I drummed my Stetsons against the stool legs. Hamp's 'Flying Home' was rocking the joint.

A pack of white broads had a booth behind me. They looked like they had been to a P. T. A. meeting. Their perfume sent a medley of sexy odors through the joint. They were flirting their cans off. I guess they were writers. They were maybe doing urgent research on the 'Sexual Habits of the Black Male.'

I wasted no time. I was afraid the pretty joker might split. I snatched my eyes from the excited pack in the mirror. I turned my head toward him and touched him lightly on the sleeve.

He was sure a wrongdoer all right. He frogged at least three inches off his stool. It was like I'd stabbed him in the butt with a red-hot poker. He turned his shocked face toward mine. His silky long-lashed eyes were popped wide in alarm. He had panicked like maybe a cute nun caught naked in the Priest's bedroom by the Mother Superior.

I said, 'Jeez, excuse me, Jim. I didn't know you were in deep thought. I'm sorry I hit on you like a square. My name is Young Blood. I'm a friend of Preston's. You must be the fabulous Glass Top. It would be a boss honor to buy you a taste.'

He patted his shiny mop and said, 'Yeah, Man, I'm Glass Top. What's your stupid story? You young studs sure ain't got no finesse. It drags me to get hit on like that. When somebody touches me I like to be digging it and facing the stud, you know?

'I ain't salty. I dig you ain't nothing but a punk that needs his coat pulled to social polish and class. I ain't no lush. You can spring for a Coke if you want. Tell her to sugar it heavy.'

The Mexican broad spooned sugar into a glass and brought his Coke. He stirred it with a straw. He raised the glass to drink. I noticed ugly black tracks tracing the veins on his light-brown mitt. He was a junkie for sure. He would know where to cop C, and probably gangster for the runt. He was also a pal of Sweet's. Maybe I could make a two-bird killing here.

He said, 'So, you know Preston? What's your racket? You a till tapper or maybe a burglar, huh?'

I said, 'I been knowing Preston since I was a kid. I used to buff his stomps when he was pimping. I'm no till tapper or burglar. I'm a pimp. You must be a pimp yourself. I saw you rapping to the best pimp there is.'

He said, 'You a pimp? I ain't never heard of you. Where you been pimping, in Siberia? Sweet ain't the best pimp there is. I am. Pimps are just like cars. The best known ain't no real yardstick to the best car. It's like I'm a Duesenberg and Sweet's a Ford. I got all the quality and beauty. He's got all the advertising and all the luck.

'Sweet's got ten whores, I got five. These whores in town ain't hip to how great I am yet. When they wake up to me I'll have to fight 'em off with a baseball bat. How many girls you got?'

I said, 'I only got one girl now. I just got out of the joint, but I'm going to have ten in a year. This town will hear about me. I was thinking about cutting into some top pimp like Sweet. I'm not stupid enough to think I don't need to learn a thousand times more about pimping than I know. I also need connections like for girl and gangster. I'm just a kid in darkness waiting for some brain to help light the way.'

He said, 'Stay cool, Blood. I just remembered I left my kitty's slammer open. I'll be back after I lock it.'

I looked in the mirror and saw him go out. He turned left towards the Greek's joint. I knew he was going to Preston to check me out. When he walked out that panting pack behind me turned as one. It was like Cary Grant had walked out.

The juke box was moaning gut-bucket blues. Some joker was singing 'Going down slow; Don't send no Doctor; Doctor sure can't do no good; Please write my mother, tell her the shape I'm in; I'm going down slow.'

I remembered, it had been my father's favorite record. He had kept it spinning on the rich Victrola. I remembered his shocked face there in the doorway when he discovered it and everything else gone. I wondered if he were alive and still in town. If I ran into him I sure wouldn't know what to say to him after all these years.

I saw the silk chicks crane their necks toward the door. I

switched my eyes left in the mirror. I saw Glass Top coming in. Those chickens were clucking when he sat down.

I said, 'Jack, aren't you afraid those silk broads behind us will rape you?'

He said, 'Shit, if you stripped and searched all of 'em you wouldn't find a C note. They ain't nothing but square housewives. They sick of that half-ass screwing at home. They laying to swindle chump Niggers outta their youth.

'They know enough on each other to keep all their jibs sealed. Ain't a chance for their husbands to tumble to what's going on. So what if some white joker who knows 'em made this scene and saw 'em? Everyone of 'em is just slumming, out with the girls. Jack, what they got is a secret sex club.'

I said, 'Top, I'm frayed. I sure wish I had a snort of girl. Can you score?'

He told me, 'Blood, I believe you are a down young stud. I got news for you. You can score right with me. I got the best girl and boy in town. Even my reefer is dynamite. Blood, I love you. You got heart. How much stuff you want?'

I said, 'What's the bite for girl?'

'A fin a number-five cap. A sixteenth for a C. A piece for a grand. I got a cozy pad around the corner. There you can fly to the moon, Pimping Buddy.'

I said, 'Top, let's split to your pad. If your girl is mellow I'll maybe go for a C note.'

I threw a fin on the log. The Mexican showed me her choppers like I was her dentist. Three square black studs were standing rapping to the purring pack in the booth.

We went out and got in Glass Top's Hog. My foot struck a bottle. I looked down. It was the dead gin soldier Poison's whore had sucked dry. The Hog shot from the curb like a red torpedo. Eckstein's syrupy 'Cottage For Sale' oozed from the Hog's radio.

I thought, 'I sure gotta hurry and get my ass into a Hog at least. I'll cop a Duesenberg in maybe a year. Geez, it must be one-thirty. I shoulda checked on the runt. My luck is changing though. This glossy-top joker is my in to Sweet.'

He lived in a plush apartment building. It had all the jazz.

Technicolored lights spotlighted the exterior. Fake rubber plants stood tall in the foyer.

We took a chrome-and-brass elevator to his second-floor pad. Thick red broadloom carpet wall to wall in the hall. Fresh black and gold paint sparkled the walls and ceilings.

A Polynesian-type dream took our bennies and my lid in a small silver-mirrored entrance hall. My feet sank into the soft lavender carpet. I could hear the deep-throated boom of a console phonograph. The Ink Spots' lead tenor was parfaiting 'Whispering Grass'.

I followed Top and the olive-tinted beauty into the womb-like living room. Double heavy lavender drapes covered the windows. Not a beam of street light or sunshine could violate this pimp's lair.

Top and I sat on a long gray sofa. It had cost him a big buck to lower the ceiling with the silver lame fabric. The only light came from the glass-topped cocktail table. It gurgled and flashed a pale blue light.

A score of yellow, red, and orange tropical fish streaked inside the aquarium built six inches below the table top. Two gray rubber hoses at each end of the tank ran down into the lavender carpet. It was a slick drain off and fresh water gimmick.

The broad was almost naked. She stood wide legged in front of us like a bellhop waiting for orders. The table's blue light behind her silhouetted her Coca Cola bottle curves inside the flame red shortie gown. I saw a four inch cone of jet hair between her thighs. She had a rare cat with that extra dimension. I unglued my eyes and looked into her face. She had the dreamy eyes of a freakish Mona Lisa.

He said, 'Bitch, bring a coupla outfits and some caps of girl and boy. Oh yeah, Blood, this is Radell.'

That awesome round butt of hers jiggled as she wiggled past me. The big white phonograph in the corner was booming out a novelty tune. 'When your pipes get dry then you know you're high. Everything is dandy. You truck on down to the candy store but you don't get no peppermint candy. Then you know your body's sent, you don't care if you don't pay rent. Light a tea and let it be if you're a viper.'

'This pretty gowster is sure pimping his ass off,' I thought.

'He's a crazy gowster if he thinks he'll con me into banging any H. I'm not even sure about shooting the girl. Of course, I can't come off like a hayseed either.'

I said, 'Jim, you sure ain't jiving. Your layout is a sonuvabitch.'

He said, 'I got five bedrooms here. These whores on this fast track dig front and flash. You can't pimp here unless you got 'em. Jack, this C I got ain't going to let you split for a while. You may as well shed your threads and get in the groove.'

The broad brought the outfits, a spoon and a dozen white and brown caps. She put them on the cocktail table. She slid it closer to us. The water tidal-waved in the tank. The fish darted in a frenzy. She stooped and started unlacing Top's shoes. I reached into my pocket for a C note. I had peeled it off from my crotch stash before leaving the Haven.

He said, 'This flight is on me. It's a sample. You can cop what you want later.'

We stripped our clothes off to our shorts. His were candy-striped silk. I felt like a bum in my white cotton jocks.

The broad draped our clothes on each arm of the gray over-stuffed chair across the room. She didn't have any of my scratch in her mitt when she came away. She stood next to me. The phone on the end table beside him jangled. He uncradled it.

He said, 'Castle of Joy, what's your desire? Oh yeah, Angelo, she's here. Hell no she ain't dossing. She's on her way.'

He hung up and said, 'Bitch, just slip your benny on and get downtown to that head bellboy at the Franklin Arms. Dimples and the other girls are getting more action than they can turn. Take the key to the kitty and get there fast.'

The broad zipped out of there in less than three minutes. She sure liked getting her man some money. Those tricks at the Franklin were going to give their swipes a treat all right.

I thought, 'I gotta make the runt cultivate her cat like that broad's.'

He said, 'That's a good young bitch I got there. I copped her in Hawaii a year ago. There are twenty-thousand white suckers in town for a convention. They got a double saw in one hand and their swipes in the other.

'Radell ain't had no sleep in thirty-six hours. My other four whores been humping at the Franklin since early this morning. I can't miss a five G score for the three days even with Angelo's thirty percent off the top. Ain't but a C a day for a girl in oil for the heat.'

He got up and whistled our belts through the loops in our pants. He walked back and started to coil my belt around my arm just above the elbow hollow.

'Look Top, I'm not a square,' I said, 'but I ain't shooting no H. I'm game to bang some C. I've been curious to try it like that.'

He said, 'Kid, I ain't squeezing your balls to hip you that after Mink comes Sable. Ain't nothing a greater blast than horse. It's your privilege to wake up slow if you want. Horse is what puts the ice in a pimp's game.'

He upended a cap of girl into the spoon and stuck an eye dropper into the fish tank. He pressed the bulb and drew the dropper full. He emptied it into the spoon. He held the yellow flame of a table lighter beneath the spoon and took a tiny wad of cotton from an ash tray. He tossed it into the bowl of the spoon and then wrapped a thin piece of cellophane around the tip of the dropper. He fitted the needle on it. He stuck the hollow end of the needle into the cotton and drew the dropper full.

I felt my blood smashing against the tight coils of the belt. I saw the veins balloon in the throbbing hollow. I smelled the sharp sickly-sweet odor of the cocaine. My palms were dripping sweat. He had the spike in his right hand. He grabbed my forearm with his left hand. I turned my head and closed my eyes. I bit down on my bottom lip waiting for the stabbing plunge of the needle.

He said, 'Damn! You got some beautiful lines.'

I shivered when it daggered in. I opened my eyes and looked. My blood had shot up into the dropper. He was pressing the bulb. I saw the blood-streaked liquid draining into me. It was like a ton of nitro exploded inside me. My ticker went beserk. I could feel it clawing up my throat. It was like I had a million swipes in every pore from head to toe. It was like they were all popping off together in a nerve-shredding climax.

I was quivering like a joker in the hot seat at the first jolt. I tried to open my talc-dry mouth. I couldn't. I was paralyzed. I could feel a hot ball of puke racing up from my careening guts. I saw the green, stinking puke rope arch into the black mouth of the waste basket. I felt the cool metal against my chest. I saw Top's manicured fingers pressing it close to me.

He was saying, 'You'll be all right in a minute, Kid. You thought I was bullshitting when I told you I had the best stuff in town.'

I still couldn't say anything. I felt like the top of my skull had been crushed in. It was like I had been blown apart and all that was left were my eyes. Then tiny prickly feet of ecstasy started dancing through me. I heard melodious bells tolling softly inside my skull.

I looked down at my hands and thighs. A thrill shot through me. Surely they were the most beautiful in the Universe. I felt a superman's surge of power.

I thought, 'It was a cinch that any stud as beautiful and clever as me would become the greatest pimp in history. What bitch could resist me? I turned and stared at the ugly stud beside me.'

He said, 'Did you hear those chapel bells? Ain't they a bitch, Kid?'

'Yeah man, I heard 'em loud and clear. Right now I'd like to see the bitch I couldn't make. It's sure wild to bang girl. The only time I'll snort after this is when I'm in the street between bangs.'

He said, 'Blood, you sure know what to say. Just don't forget where to cop. The more you buy, the cheaper I'll make it. I love you, Blood. We gonna be tight.'

He had a time trying to bang himself. He was only around thirty-two, but most of his veins had folded. He finally hit pay clay in his inner right thigh. He kept the needle in pumping the horse into the vein then drawing it out.

I said, 'Jack, why the hell do you screw around like that?' He said, 'Man, you ain't hip? That's where the thrill is. When I jack this joint off the horse kicks my ass groovy.'

I lost tally of time while we sat on the sofa and banged stuff. After the second cap I started banging myself. After that first bang the thrill wasn't as good and sharp. Top was coasting. There were three caps of H still on the table top. There was no girl. I had banged five caps of girl. I looked at my Mickey. It was five A.M. I went to my clothes and started to dress. My ticker was speeding inside my frosty chest.

I said, 'Top, I gotta split. I want a sixteenth of girl and a can of reefer. Here's a C note and twenty slats.'

He pulled up from the sofa. He took the scratch and went into a bedroom. He came out and handed me a tobacco can sealed with rubber bands.

He said, 'Kid, I put a coupla yellows in your bag so you can come down and get some doss. Where you padding? You don't wanta walk through the street with that package of sizzle on you. I'll call a cab.'

I said, 'Thanks Top. I'm padding at the Blue Haven, but my wheels are just around the corner across from the Roost. I'll hoof it there. The fresh air will be a kick.'

I stood at the living room doorway to the entrance hall. He was uncapping a thing of horse.

I thought, 'Now's the time to crack on him to sew up the cut into Sweet. I gotta phrase it right. This joker envies Sweet.'

I said, 'Top, I was thinking how much more common sense and cool you got than your pal Sweet.'

His hands froze. His eyes beat his mouth to the question. I knew Preston hadn't told him about my clash with Sweet. I guess Preston's chicken act had blocked Sweet out of his mind.

Top said, 'You know Sweet personally?'

'I met him last night in the Roost. That tall blonde of his wanted me to freak off with her. Sweet offered me a double saw to do the job. I stood on pimp principle and turned him down. He flipped his cork. He forced me to split. He told me he'd blow my head through the ceiling. I figured he might do it.

'I guess now I have blown my chance to get acquainted with him. I don't suppose anybody in town is strong enough with him to square me and cut me into him. As foxy as you are Top, I wouldn't be shocked if you couldn't cut it. After all the man is complicated. Come to think about it, Top, I don't have a real need to meet him since I met you.

'My main reason now is I don't want a crazy enemy like that. So if you tell me it's over your head, I'll forget it, stay out of his way and take my chances. I love you Top, and I wouldn't want anythign to happen to you on my account.'

He gobbled it raw and whole. He flung his girlish head back and rolled off the sofa to the floor. He held his elbows against his belly and laughed like I'd told the funniest joke human ears had ever heard. He was gasping when he finally stopped. He patted his mop.

'Sweet ain't dangerous, sucker,' he began. 'He ain't never croaked anything but yellow Niggers. He's croaked four of them in the last twenty years. He ain't croaked nobody in over two years. He's ninety percent Bull scare. He don't kill nobody unless they bad mouth him or muscle his whores.

'But he sure hates white folks. He pimps awful tough on white whores. When he puts his foot in their asses he's really doing it to the white man. He says he's paying 'em back for what they done and are doing to black people. His brain is rotted from hate.

'Shit, he probably wouldn't know you if he saw you again. He wasn't salty with you for turning down the freak-off. He was playing strong con on his white whore. He's got his whores thinking he's God. Even a square from Delaware should know God ain't going to kiss your ass when you tell him no, you poor boob.

'I tell you what. I gotta take him some stuff this weekend. I'll buzz your crib to let you know just when. I'll stop on the way and pick you up. I'll take you with me to his pad. He ain't nothing but a big ugly Nigger with a filthy loud mouth.'

I said, 'I pad in four-twenty under the name of Lancaster. Top, you gotta overlook my dumbness. I told you I was just a kid in darkness needing some brain to light the way. Top, I sure appreciate your coat-pulling. See you later, Pal.'

He said, 'All right, Kid, keep that sizzle in your mitt so you can down it in a hurry. Oh yeah, you can cop a spike at any drugstore. You gotta crack for insulin with it.'

I walked into the entrance hall. I flicked my sponge across my greasy face in the silver mirror. I went out the door to the elevator. It opened on the ground floor. I flinched before the stark morning light.

Out on the sidewalk, I saw Glass Top's red Hog pulling to the curb. It was his five whores back from the Franklin Arms salt mines.

I thought as I walked to the Ford, 'How about it? Those five whores are probably checking in a coupla grand for a night's work. Why couldn't it be me up there in that crazy pad with my mitt out for all those frog skins?'

The night people had vanished from the street. Knots of squares on the way to work bunched at the street-car stops. I got in the Ford and U-turned toward the Haven.

I saw an all-night drugstore and pulled into the parking lot. I copped a saw buck pair of binoculars, and at the drug counter, I got the insulin and copped spikes and eyedroppers. Five minutes later I got to the Haven. I parked on the street.

I glanced up at our apartment window. I saw the drapes flutter. I got a flash of the runt's dark face pulling back. I walked through the lobby to the elevator. The joint sure looked shabby after Top's joint.

I thought as I got on the elevator, 'If the runt is shitty and tries to third degree me this morning I'll bury my foot in her ass.'

I got off on the fourth floor. I walked down the hall to four-twenty. I slid the rubber bands off the top of the tobacco can. I opened the top and took my packet of girl out. It was wrapped in tin foil inside a penny balloon. I shoved it into my watch pocket. I took a yellow from the top of the loose reefer and dry-swallowed it.

I knocked on the door. I waited a full minute. I knocked again, harder. Finally the runt opened it. She was stretching and massaging her eyes with her fists, conning me she had been fast asleep. She jumped into bed. She turned her back and pulled the covers to her ears.

I put the can of reefer on the dresser. I saw a tiny pile of bills on it. I heeled them apart. It was only forty slats. I went to the closet and checked the toes of the tan Stetsons. Empty! I stashed the binoculars in a coat pocket with my C and bang outfit. I saw smoke spiraling from a cigarette lying on the base of the plaster copy of 'The Kiss' near the front window.

I said, 'Bitch, what did you do break your leg, or knock off as soon as you saw me split? Is this tonight's take? Turn over so I can see that black mug of yours.'

I was standing at the side of the bed. My right hand was resting on the closed plastic lid of the record player. The tips of my fingers were touching the back of it near the motor. It was warm. I raised the lid. Lady Day's whimper about that 'mean man' was on the turn table. The runt turned slowly. I looked down into her face. Her eyes were narrow. Her jib was puffed out. She and Lady Day had been dragging me through the mud all night. The whore was acting like an outraged housewife.

She said, 'Ain't I never going to be nothing but a bitch to you? Call me Phyllis the whore, or Runt the fool. You'd never believe it but I'm human. That scratch I made tonight ain't bad. These streets are new to me. I gotta feel my way and get hip to the tricks.'

That cocaine was blowing a frosty blizzard through my skull.

I said, 'Bitch, when your funky black ass is in the grave you'll still be a bitch. Bitch, one of these brights you're going to shoot your jib off, I'll curtsy and call you Runt the Corpse. You stinking bitch I'm hip you're human. You're a human black slop-bucket for those peckerwood swipes.

'You gutless idiot, I'm going to throw you out that window if you don't get the kinks outta your ass an hustle some real scratch. Don't get hip to the tricks, Bitch. Get hip to what I'm rapping. If you don't stop your bullshit, I'm gonna kick your heart out and stomp on it. Now don't crack your jib unless I rap to you, Bitch.'

I started to take my clothes off. She just lay there staring at me. Her eyes were gleaming like a crazy Voodoo Doctor's. I got into bed. I turned my back to her. I could feel the freak inching toward me.

She stroked the back of my neck. I felt the hot tip of the lizard on the back of my neck. I felt the scab on her brow scrape the tip of my ear. I pulled away toward the edge of the bed.

She said, 'Daddy, I'm sorry I bugged you. I love you. Please forgive me.'

The bed creaked when I rattlesnaked to strike. I hooked my right heel under the bed springs. I raised myself on my right elbow. I drew my ved left arm back so the back of my left fist touched my right cheek. I grunted for velocity and blackjacked my left elbow into her gut-button. She groaned and wrapped and unwrapped her legs. She chattered her teeth like she was freezing to death.

I could feel that yellow drawing a heavy black curtain inside my dome. Just before I went under I thought, 'I wonder if the runt can lug a hundred and fifty pounds to that window.'

7

Melody Off Key

The blast of the phone woke me. The pad was dark as hell. I flung my left hand out for the runt. She wasn't there. I fumbled the receiver to my ear.

I said, 'Hello, this is Mary's brother.'

He said, 'I wanta speak to Mary. Put her on, yeah?'

I said, 'She just went out. She's taking a walk.'

He hung up. I cradled the phone on the bedside table. I switched the table lamp on. I checked Mickey. It was seven-thirty P.M. I wondered if I had blown the runt.

I got up and checked the closet. Her clothes were still there. I went to the dresser. I checked the forty slats. Two were missing. There was a note beside the scratch.

It read, 'Daddy, I took a deuce for the street. I'm gonna hump my ass off. Please try to be a little sweet to your little bitch dog, huh?'

I thought, 'I'm stumbling upon some pimp answers. It looks like the tougher a stud is the more a whore goes for him. I'll sure be glad when those four days pass and I go with Top to the Sweet cut in. I gotta watch that the runt don't get hip I'm banging stuff. Gee, I'm starved. I gotta eat before I bang some girl.'

I went to the phone. The broad who should have been a wrestler picked up.

I said, 'Anybody down there to get me bacon and eggs?'

She said, 'Wait a second, I'll let you talk to Silas, the elevator man.'

The old Maggie and Jiggs fan said, 'Yeah, Big Timer, what is it?'

I said, 'Silas, can I get bacon with eggs over light, and toast?'

He said, 'Yeah, there's a greasy spoon right across the street. I'm going now.'

I hung up and went to the closet. I got the spy piece. I went to the window. I saw the old jink hobble across the street toward the Busy Bee Cafe.

I made a sweep up and down the street to spot the runt. I didn't see her. I zeroed the spy into the greasy joint. The runt was draining a cup of coffee at the counter. She came out. Her eyes flashed whitely up at our window.

She walked down the street twisting her rear end at the passing cars. I saw her round black ass hook a white trick in a black Hog. He skidded to the curb. She got in. I wondered if it was the same joker that called.

I ducked into the shower. I was toweling off when I heard a rap on the door. I saronged the towel. On the way to the door I scooped the can of gangster off the dresser and stuck it behind the mirror.

I heard Silas outside the door whistling 'When the Saints Go Marching In.' I opened the door. He had a tray in his hands. I took it. A paper napkin fluttered to the floor. He stooped for it.

I looked into the big brown eyes of a pretty yellow broad coming out of the door across the hall. The scarfaced stud who tooted at the Roost had walked out in front of her. He had a saxophone case under his arm.

She rolled her lustrous eyes at me. They rocketed to that lump on the sarong. Her sly hot smile made a flat statement. 'Please, try it for size.'

I skull noted her. Silas finally tore his eyes from her rear end floating down the hall. He had squeezed the paper napkin into a damp ball.

He said, 'That's a buck.'

I put the tray on the dresser. I took three slats to the door and gave them to him.

I said, 'Silas, that's quite a package with Mr Hyde. Give me a rundown, huh?'

He said, 'Yeah, she's stacked tough enough to make a preacher lay his Bible down. The horn blower ain't had her but a coupla years. She's done rammed her cat scent up his nose and got him hooked. She was a whore until he squared her up.

'He's got it bad. He don't allow her outta his sight. Any club he plays she hasta be right there stuck in his ass. If I was thirty years younger I'd steal her.

'Thanks, Big Timer, for the deuce. Any time you want something, call old Silas. Sit the tray outside your door when you finish.'

I sat on the side of the bed and wolfed down the bacon and eggs. I felt better. I wanted to feel wonderful. I put together everything for bang time. I held the end of a necktie in my teeth. I coiled it and tightened it around my arm. On first stab I hit a perfect bullseye. I did Top's jackoff bit. I threw up. I just made it to the john. The kick was greater than the one at Top's.

I thought, 'What if my black face like magic turned white. Shit, I could go out that hotel front door and sneak through the barbed-wire stockade. I'd be like a wolf turned loose on a flock of sheep. That white world wouldn't tumble that I'm a Nigger. I could pay 'em all back in spades, the Dummy, the White Bull, that bastard judge that crucified me on my first rap. Once I escape this black hell I'll find a way all right. Well Nigger, you're pretty, but a bleach cream will never be invented that will make you white. So, pimp your ass off and be somebody with what you got. It could be worse, you could be an ugly Nigger.'

I dressed and powdered my face. That sure was one pretty sonuvabitch in that mirror. I saw a roach scouting the tray's rim. I shoved the tray out into the hall.

I thought, 'I gotta start stalking that fine bitch across the hall. Maybe I'll decoy the runt to get past that scarfaced watchdog. I guess I'll take a walk. Maybe I can cop my second whore. I feel hard and lucky as a horseshoe.'

I put the can of reefer and the other sizzle into a paper bag. I locked the door and went down the hall toward the elevator. On the way, I stopped at the porter's broom closet. It was unlocked. I tip-toed and shoved the bag of sizzle behind some junk on a shelf.

The cocaine had me froggy. I saw the floor indicator stop at floor number two. I took the stairway to the lobby. I dropped the key on the desk and glided to the street. The cocaine had fitted wings on my feet. I felt cool, breathless, and magnificent. It was a balmy eighty degrees. I was glad I'd left the benny.

I walked toward a rainbow bouquet of neon maybe ten blocks away. My senses screamed on the razor-edge of cocaine. It was like walking through a battlefield. The streaking head-lights of the car arcing the night were giant tracer bullets. The rattling crashing street-cars were army tanks. The frightened, hopeless black faces of the passengers peered through the grimy windows. They were battle-shocked soldiers doomed forever to the front trenches.

I passed beneath an El train bridge. A terrified, glowing face loomed toward me in the tunnel's gloom. It was an elderly white man trapped behind enemy lines. A train furied by overhead. It bombed and strafed the street. The shrapnel fell in gritty clouds.

I was too nervous for the combat zone. I whistled a general in a yellow staff car to halt. He whisked me to that oasis of neon. It turned out he was a mercenary. He shafted me a slat and a quarter for the evacuation.

I got out and mothed toward a dazzling flash. The Fun House. It was a bar. I opened the door and stepped inside. It almost busted the gaskets in my bowels. A phosphorescent green skeleton popped up out of the floor in front of me. It screeched a hollow howl and then dived back into the floor through a trap door.

I just stood there shaking. I couldn't figure why those crazy jokers at the bar were yukking like pickaninnys. To stay with the program I mastered a King Fish grin. I went to the bar and sat between Amos and Andy.

I saw a tall stud with a Frankenstein mask on behind the log. He darted his hand in a sneaky way under the log. There was a wooshing noise like a tire going flat. My stool descended beneath me. I looked up at Amos. My nose was an inch from the log. Amos was grinning down at me.

Amos said, 'You sho nuff ain't been here befo, is you Slim? You frum de big-foot country?'

Andy said, 'Wait til he ketch his win. He gonna buy us a

pitchuh suds. We gonna lurn ole home boy bout dis big city rigamaro.'

Everybody at the crowded log yukked in a deep South accent. Frankenstein pushed his mercy button. I felt the stool stretching up. With the cocaine kangarooing me, and this booby-trapped nest of low-life suckers I stumbled into I had more than a frantic yearning for maybe four-twenty at the Haven.

He walked down the log to me.

He said, 'It's all in fun. Welcome to the Fun House. What'll it be?'

I ignored him. I got off the stool. I looked down at it. Its metal legs were tubular and anchored to the floor. It had to be a compressed air gizmo. I stepped back and looked at the two ex-cotton pickers. I twitched my nose. I looked down and around them, then the length of the log. I fingered the button on that sling shot in my raise.

I King-Fished, 'Holy mackul, boys. You smell dat? I'se wunder iffen some po stupid Nigger's funky-ass, nappy-head Southern Mammy ain't done shit out anuther square-ass, ugly bastard turd?'

Amos and Andy dropped their jibs like plantation idiots. They shot an anguished look at the white joker behind the log. I walked out the door. They didn't dig my humor. Maybe it was too in.

I slammed into a perfumed line-backer. In reflex, I threw my arms around her soft shoulders. She had the flawless face of Olivia de Haviland. She was bigger and prettier. I felt the fabric of her tailored black suit petal stroke across my finger tips. She was the finest broad I'd seen since my last movie. I wondered if she was a whore. I decided to hit on her.

I said, 'I'm sorry. Ain't it a bitch, baby the first time we meet it had to be in a collision like two-square? Sugar, were you going into this tramp joint? Believe me there's no action inside for a package like you. I just stopped in to make a call. My name is Blood. What's yours?'

Her big curvy legs were wide tracked. I saw the fabulous shadow of her rear end on the sidewalk. Through the filmy orange blouse I saw a pink mole on her milk-white midriff. She brushed back a wayward lock of silky black hair from one of the big electric blue eyes. Her even choppers gleamed like rare china. Her crimson tongue doodled across the cupid bow lips. She was doing a bit that would have shook up a eunuch.

She said, 'Blood! How quaint. Your idiom is fascinating. My name is Melody. I don't drink in bars. Occasionally I go to a supper club. I am not looking for action. As a matter of fact my car is disabled. I was going inside to call for help when our heavenly bodies collided. Is it possible that you're not oblivious to the esoteric aspects of car repair? Mine is there at the curb.'

My eyes followed her manicured finger to the sparkling new Lincoln sedan. Everything about her hollered class and affluence.

I thought, 'This beautiful white bitch has class. She sounds like an egghead. With wheels like that she's probably got a bundle in the damer! Maybe she's got some rich sucker in her web. I'll nut roll on her. I'll stay outta the pimp role until I case her. I'll go Sweet William on her. Maybe I can string her out and get all that scratch she's got, then make a whore outta her. With her rear end, this bitch is sitting on a mint.'

I said, 'Darling, I'm not a mechanic. I did learn a little about cars from a buddy in a prep school I just finished. You get in. I'll raise the hood and have a look.'

She got in. I raised the hood. I spotted the trouble right away. A battery cable had jarred loose. I put it back on. I looked around the hood and signaled for the starter try. She did and smiled happily when the engine throbbed to life. She waved me to her. I stuck my head through the open window.

She said, 'Are you driving? If not I should love to take you wherever you want to go.'

I said, 'Honey, I'm not driving and it's a long sad story. You don't want to hear my troubles. If you drop me off at some nice bar, I promise not to bore you with it.'

I got in. She pulled out into traffic. We cruised along. For two minutes we were silent. I was busy trying to think of the opener for that long sad story. I had read a cell-house full of books. I knew I could rise to a smooth pitch. That old philosopher convict had told me I should forget the pimp game and be a con man.

I said, 'Melody, doesn't fate puppeteer humans in a weird way? There I was coming out of that joint. I had just called a garage a hundred miles away. The engine of my car burnt up on my way here from Saint Louis a week ago. I was depressed, lonely, and hopeless in a big, friendless city.

'The mechanic had just dropped the bad news. The charge to get the car is a hundred and fifty dollars. I have fifty. I was blind with worry when I came out that door.

'My elderly mother has to have a pancreas operation. I came here to work for a contractor in the suburbs. I'm a talented carpenter. I need my car to get to work. I'm committed to start work the first of next week. Mama's going to die sure as the sun rises in the East unless I get that money for her operation.

'The strange wonderful thing is, Darling, with all these problems I feel so good. See those garbage cans glittering between the tenements. To me they are giant jewels. I want to climb up on those roof tops and cry out to the stars, I have met, I have found the beautiful Melody. Surely I'm the luckiest black man alive. Convince me you're real. Don't evaporate like a beautiful mirage. I'd die if you did.'

Out of the side scope in my eye I saw those awesome thighs quivering. She almost crashed the Lincoln into the rear end of the gray Studebaker ahead of us.

She cut in sharply and grated the Lincoln's wheels against the curb. She shut the motor off and turned toward me. Her eyes were blue bonfires of passion. The pulse on the satin throat was maniacing. She slid close to me. She zippered her scarlet mouth to mine. That confection tongue flooded my mouth with sugar. Her nails dug into my thighs. She gazed at me.

She said, 'Blood, you sweet black poetic panther. Does that prove I'm real. No, I know I don't want to evaporate, ever. Please, don't let's go to a bar. You can't solve your problems with alcohol. My parents are out of the city until tomorrow noon. Settle for coffee and conversation at my place. Will you,

Blood? Perhaps we can find solutions to your problems there. Besides I'm expecting Mother to call me at home later this evening.'

I said, 'Angel of mercy, I'm putting myself in your tender hands.'

She lived a long way from the black concentration camp. She drove for almost an hour. I could smell the pungent odors of early April plant life. This white world was like leaving Hell and riding through Heaven. The neat rows of plush houses shone in the moonlight. The streets were quiet as maybe the Cathedral in Rheims.

I thought, 'Ain't it a bitch? Ninety-eight percent of the black people back there in Hell will be born and die and never know the joys of this earthly Heaven. There ain't but two passports the white folks honor. A white skin, or a bale of scratch. I sure got to pimp good and cop my scratch passport. Well at least I get a Cinderella crack at Heaven. This is good. It's hipping me to what I'm missing.'

We turned into her driveway. I saw the soft glow of a table lamp behind blue drapes in the front room. She parked the Lincoln in a pink stucco garage that matched the house. The garage was connected to the house. We went through the back door. We passed through the kitchen. Even in the dimness it sparkled.

We moved like burglars through the half-darkened house. We walked on deep-pile carpet up a stairway. We got to the top. She stopped.

She whispered, 'Blood, I was born in this house. Everybody in the block knows me. If some friend passed and knew someone was at home, we might get an unwelcome visitor. We'll go to my bedroom in the rear.'

I followed to her bedroom. She flipped on a tiny blue light over a mirrored dressing table. The bedroom was done in pale blue and off-white. The queen-sized bed had a blue satin canopy over it. I sat down on a white silk chaise next to the dressing table. She switched on an ivory radio. Debussy's 'Clare de la Lune' sweet-noted gently through the room.

She kicked off her tiny black calfskin shoes. She was even

more beautiful here than she had been in the street. She stroked my ear lobes with her fingertips.

She said, 'Mommy's pretty black panther don't run away now. I'm going downstairs and make coffee.'

She went down the stairs.

I thought, 'I'm gonna crack on her for scratch. She should be good for a C note at least. A C note ain't bad to break the ice with. If she springs for it, I'll tie her to that bed and put my Pepper-specialty on her. It's certain to flip a young broad like her who's lived in Heaven all her life! Besides, I ain't never sloughed around in a bed with a canopy. Especially one in Heaven.'

I heard the faint bounce of her tiny feet on the stairway. She came into the bedroom with a silver service. We were going to have coffee in style. She set the gleaming tray on the dressing-table top.

She said, 'Blood, pour us a cup. I'm going to get out of these clothes. Then we can chat.'

I poured two and left them black. I sipped mine. She stepped into a walk-in closet. She stepped out a moment later. All she had on were black panties and the red top of a transparent shortie nightgown. Her small, but sculptured bosom straight-jutted against the red gauze. She sat on the foot of the bed facing me and crossed her legs. I handed her the cup of black.

She said, 'So, you're going to stay in town for a while?'

I said, 'Baby, if I get strong enough encouragement I'll stay all my life. Baby, it's a pity I had to meet you when I'm in bad shape. I want to be good company, but that car problem and Mama won't let my mind stay on a pleasant track.'

Her fingers snapped 'Eureka.'

She got off the bed and went to the dresser across the room. She opened the top drawer and took out a bank book. She came back and sat on the bed. She tapped the red nail of her left index finger against her white teeth. She studied the book's figures. I saw a frown hedgerow her brow. She got up and went to the dresser and threw the book into the open drawer and banged it shut.

I thought, 'This broad has over drawn. She's gonna try the check con on me.'

She stooped and opened the bottom drawer. She brought out a foot-long, foot-tall metal pig. She walked to the dressing table and put the porker on the table beside me.

She said, 'Blood, this is the best I can do to help you now. I don't get my allowance for a week. I have less than a hundred dollars in my account. Cheer up, there must be at least a hundred dollars in quarters and halves in this bank. Believe me, I can vividly imagine what it's like to be colored and faced with your problems. Let's say it's a loan.'

I hefted the poker for a moment to check its gross weight. It was heavy all right. It felt a C note heavy. I reached out and took her hand. I guided her to my side on the chaise. I put my arms around her. I kissed her and sucked at that sugary tongue like a suicidal diabetic. I leaned back from her. I looked into the heart of the blue fire.

I said, 'Baby, it's a wonderful secret that you've discovered. Not many people know it's better to give than to receive. Maybe it sounds crazy, but I wish you weren't so beautiful and generous, so perfect. I don't see how you can miss capturing my foolish heart. You're a cinch to make me yours forever. Baby, I'm just a poor black country boy. Please don't hurt my heart.'

She sure had an appetite for the Jeff con. The blue fire softened. Her eyes were misty and serious. She held my head between her dove-soft palms.

She said, 'Blood baby, I'm white, but I have been more unhappy than any black person all my life. My parents have never understood me. When my whole being cried out for love and understanding, they gave me shiny things to stop my tears.

'Non-whites are like dirt to them. They are narrow and cold. If they found out you had been here they would disown me before they dropped dead. There's a sweet warmth that you have. I know that you can make me happy. I am so desperate for love and understanding. Please give it to me.'

I said, 'Baby, you can dump all your money on the

black horse to win. I'm gonna win 'em all for you, beautiful.'

She said, 'Blood, you're a black panther; I'm a white lamb. I know nothing can stop that panther from taking the lamb, soul and body. The lamb will bide her time to take the panther. The lamb needs and wants it that way. Now listen carefully and please catch the clue of my tragedy so nothing will shock you in my bed.

'Blood, perhaps you are aware of the structural flaws built into the columns of the world's most famous building. It's the Parthenon. The flaw is called entasis. This contrived flaw is necessary so that the fickle human eye sees only perfection. I am a lot like those columns. I am not old, but I am beautiful. My tragedy is that unlike the entasis that gives perfection to the columns, my entasis must be concealed to protect my perfection. Can you understand?'

I thought, 'What the hell, so this broad's got a prematurely-gray cat. Maybe it's a little off-center. If it's odd it will be a novelty kick for me. She's so beautiful the tricks won't notice a tiny irregularity after I've turned her out.'

I said, 'Baby Melody, you haven't opened the door to a square. As fine as you are I wish you had two heads. Now get on that bed on your back. I'm gonna make love to you black panther style. You got some long towels?'

She went to the hall linen closet. She gave me four long slender ones. She slipped off the red top and panties. She lay on her back in bed. I saw her flaw. Was this her entasis? I saw no crotch hair. She looked completely bald downstairs. I tied both her legs to the posts at the foot of the bed. I tied her left arm to a post at the head. The phone jangled on a night stand at her side. She picked up the receiver with her free right hand.

She said, 'Hi Mother, I'm fine. Are you and Dad still having fun? Mother, I miss you both so terribly. Are you coming home tomorrow as planned? Oh good, I'll be at the airport on time. I've gone to bed. I've gotten out that *Anthology of Africa*. I'm going to have a wild time researching the Watusi Warrior. Good night, Mother. Oh, tell Dad to bring me some of that heavenly Miami beach wear. I'll be a sensation here on the beach this summer.'

I had taken my clothes off when she hung up. I lashed her free arm to the fourth bed post. I looked down at her. Her eyes were pleading.

She said, 'Remember Blood darling, you are not an unsophisticated bumpkin. You are not prone to shock states. I know you are going to find my entasis as sweet and desirable as the rest of me.'

I wondered why she still worried about her entasis. She knew I saw she was hairless downstairs. I put my knee on the bed. I stroked her belly. I felt cloth. I took a close look. A custom flesh-colored jock belt bandled her crotch. I ripped the elastic top down over her round hips. I jumped back. My rear end bounced on the floor. I struggled to my feet.

I shouted, 'You stinking sissy sonuvabitch!'

His real entasis had popped up pink and stiff. It was a foot long and as thick as the head of a cobra.

He was crying like I had put a lighted match to his entasis.

He sobbed, 'You promised to understand. Please, Blood, keep your promise. You don't know what you're missing. It's delicious you fool.'

I said, 'Look man, I made my promises to a broad, not a stud. I'm a pimp, not a faggot. I'm getting the hell out of here. I'm charging you the porker for my time and your bullshit.'

He lay there blubbering. I speed dressed. I took the porker off the table and stuck it under my arm. I walked toward the stairway. I looked back. His beautiful face was ugly in anger and hate.

He screamed, 'You dirty Nigger liar, thief! Untie me you Coon Bastard! Oh, how I wish I had your black ass tied here on your belly!'

I said, 'Man, as slick as you are you'll untie yourself before long. Yeah, that entasis could murder me all right.'

I walked down the stairway. I went through the house to the back door. I walked down the driveway to the street. I walked for an hour before I got out of the residential sprawl.

I was lucky to hail a Yellow Cab as soon as I got to a busy intersection.

When it got me to the Haven, the meter read fourteen-thirty. I gave the cabbie a fin and a saw buck. I looked up at my window. The runt was at it. It was two A.M. It had been like a nightmare Halloween all the way. All trick and no treat. I was icy sober.

Then it struck me riding up on the elevator. That white faggot could cross me. What if he couldn't free himself by the time his folks got home? He was a cinch to cover himself. He'd say a Nigger burglar or holdup man had robbed him and trussed him up.

I was a two-time loser. Five to ten would stick to me like flypaper. Even if he untied himself right away he might be mad enough to frame me. I remembered the Dalanski-Pepper cross. I was sweating salt balls when I retrieved my stash in the broom closet.

I went to my watch pocket with the cocaine. I knocked on four-twenty. The runt opened the door. She was grinning.

She said, 'Hello, Daddy-angel. Your dog bitch bumped her black ass off tonight. Gotta piggy bank, huh?'

I said, 'So whatta you want, bitch, a medal for doing your whore duty?'

I didn't answer her question. I looked down to see if she'd sprouted an entasis. She was buck naked. I stepped inside and bolted the door. There were seventy slats on the dresser. I turned and lowered my face. She kissed me. I put the porker on the base of 'The Kiss' statue.

I gave her the can of grass. She sat on the bed. She shook some grass out of the can onto a newspaper in her lap. She started rolling a joint. I took my clothes off. I went into the bathroom to shower and scrub the sissy taste out of my jib. The piercing heavy odor of the gangster wafted to me.

Over the roar of the shower I shouted, 'Girl, there's a gap under that slammer. Chink it up with a rag or something. Torch a coupla sticks of incense.'

I came out of the bathroom and got into bed beside her. She handed me a joint. I lit it and sucked it into a roach. I squeezed tobacco from the tip of a cigarette. I stuck the butt of gangster into the empty tip. I twisted the end and lit it. It was a good reefer.

I could feel my skull go into a dreamy float. I got one brilliant thought after another. The trouble was each one I tried to hold long enough so I could put a saddle on it stampeded. It was maybe like the painful irritation a drunk wrangler suffers trying to corral a herd of greased mustangs.

Gangster was sure a whore's high. That reefer confusion was no good for a pimp's skull. That beautiful sissy had buried a hot seed in my guts. The wild flower blossomed. I dreamily drifted into the runt. I rolled sleepily out of the warm churning tunnel. I wouldn't need a yellow tonight.

8

Grinning Slim

I opened my eyes. I saw glinting stars of dust whirling like a golden hurricane through a bright shaft of noon sun. I looked through the open bedroom door. I saw the runt sitting at the livingroom window. She was doing her nails. She lifted her eyes from her nails. She looked into the bedroom.

I said, 'Good morning, li'l freak puppy. I'm gonna call Silas to run across the street for ham and eggs. Are you hungry?'

She said, 'Yeah, I'm hungry, but the way he moves around it would take him a week to cop. I'll slip on something and go myself.'

She went to the closet and slipped on her blue poplin rain-or-shine coat. She took a fin off the dresser and held it up for my consent. I nodded my head. I heard the door shut when she went out.

I lit a cigarette. I thought, 'I wonder if Melody has the heat looking for me. I've only got a day or so left before Glass Top takes me to Sweet Jones. I'm gonna cool it. I won't go out at all. I'll stay right here in the hotel until Top calls me.'

The phone rang just as the runt came through the bedroom door. She put the plates wrapped in wax paper on the dresser. She picked up the receiver. I got up, took my plate and started to eat with a plastic fork.

She said, 'Hello. Oh, Chuck, how are you, sweetie? I was just thinking about you, lover. No, I can't. I wish I could come out for a few drinks, but my brother won't be home from work until six. Mama's not well at all. I have to stay here during the day to take care of her. I could slip out around seven. Yeah, I could do that until eight for twenty. Bye, bye, sugar blue eyes.'

She hung up the phone and her coat. She sat naked on the side of the bed eating.

I said, 'Bitch, I got an idea for that cat of yours. You gotta take a stiff brush and brush the hair straight down every time you think about it. Put some hair grower on it until you got maybe a four-inch cone. Your tricks will pant to bury their beaks in it. It will make your cat unique with that extra dimension.'

She mumbled, 'Where on Earth did you get a jazzy idea like that?'

I said, 'Bitch, ain't you hip yet? I'm a pimp with great imagination, that's all.'

She finished her flapjacks. She got up and gathered up an armful of our soiled clothing. She went into the bathroom. I heard the water sloshing in the bowl. She was doing our laundry. I turned my back to the sunlight. I felt old Morpheus slugging his velvet hammer against my eyelids.

I woke up in darkness. I looked at the front-room window. The street lights were on. I turned the nightstand lamp on. Mickey said seven-ten. The runt was gone. She was breaking her luck with Chuck.

I thought, 'Jesus, I sure needed rest, all right. That fast track I've been blundering on sure took the juice out of me.'

I got up and went into the bathroom to brush my teeth. I had made several brush strokes when the phone rang. I picked it up. He rapped before I could open my mouth.

He said, 'Kid, this is Glass Top. The plans have changed. I'm in a hurry. Be outside your joint in fifteen minutes. You got that?'

I said, 'Yeah, but . . .'

He had hung up. I dressed even faster than I had at the sissy's pad. I rushed down the hall. I stopped at the broom-closet stash. I hurled the sizzle into the corner on the shelf. I took the stairs three at a time to the lobby. I sailed the key to the desk top. I bolted out the door.

Top was parked in front of the joint in the red Hog. He had his hand over the horn when he saw me. I got in. The Hog squealed from the curb. Top was sure in a hurry. I could hear the harsh whisper of the Hog's tires against the pavement. We passed that neon bouquet. I looked back and saw the Fun House sign flashing. I wondered if Melody was out here somewhere booby trapping with his entasis.

I said, 'Jack, I didn't expect your call for a coupla days. What happened?'

He said, 'There's a big boxing match tonight. All the biggest pimps and whores in the country are gonna be at Sweet's after the fight. Kinda like a party. All of 'em use stuff. Even with Sweet as the middleman I should take off a coupla grand for my end.'

'Sweet never goes to fights. He can't stand big crowds, and besides they won't let Miss Peaches into fights. Sweet's gnawing his nails waiting for this stuff. He ain't got none for himself and he's anxious to cop some stuff for those birds coming from the fight.'

I said, 'Have you cracked anything about me to him?'

He said, 'Kid, you ain't hip I'm a genius? He called and I rapped to him this morning. I played you off as my punk nephew from Kansas City. You got wild ideas you wanta be a pimp. I've tried to chill you back to K.C. to maybe hustle pool or even be a broom mechanic. You're a stupid, stubborn punk. I've told you a thousand times you ain't got it to pimp. You gotta pimp.

'You would eat ten yards of Sweet's crap. You think he's God. You won't believe your uncle is tight with God. I'm Glass Top. I gotta save face even for a snot-nosed punk. Maybe if you hang around the inside of the fast track for a hot minute you'll get scared. You'll wise up, get outta my ass and run your ass back to K.C. Now Kid, don't shoot your jib off at his pad. If he don't remember you from the Roost, don't wake him up.'

I said, 'Don't worry Top. I won't rank us. I'll never forget you, Pal, for the cut in. That was sure some beautiful stuff you played for Sweet.'

He caressed his patent-leather hair. He erected his wide shoulders inside his blue mohair jacket. His pretty, bitch face wore that terrible conceit and awful pride maybe of a cute mass murderer who never gets her victims' blood on her. The full moon through the windshield shone flush on his face.

He said, 'Kid, you ain't heard nothing yet. Shit, I done

drove three whores screaming crazy with this brain. They in the boob box upstate right now babbling about Pretty Glass Top. Even Sweet ain't shipped but two up there. He's been pimping almost twice as long as me.'

I said, 'Christ, Top, I don't get it. Why drive a whore nuts if she's still humping out the scratch. A stud would have to be slick as grease to plant bats in the skull of a bitch that was sane. I can't dig how a stud could do it. I ain't hip to it.'

He said, 'Sucker, what you don't dig, and ain't hip to would make a book bigger than this Hog. Now you take Sweet, the two he crossed were young white broads with small mileage. He's sick in the head. He's got an insane hate for the whole white race.

'He was a crumb crusher of seven down in Georgia when the white folks first poisoned his skull. His mammy was jet black and beautiful. The peckerwoods for miles around were aching to lay her. The son of the wealthy plantation owner that Sweet's old man share-cropped for way-laid her on the way to a spring. He punched her out, tore her clothes off and socked it into her. She was naked and crying when she got back to her shack.

'The peckerwood pig hid out in the woods. Sweet's old man came in from the fields and found his wife clawed and bawling. He was close to seven feet and weighed three hundred. Sweet still remembers how his old man hollered and butted his head against the door of the shack. The hinges ripped loose.

'He knew the woods like a fox. He found the white boy. He left him for dead. He covered him with brush. He slipped back to his shack. Sweet remembers the white boy's blood on his old man, even on his old man's bare feet. He had stomped the white boy to a red pulp out there in the lonely woods. The old man figured he was safe. The white folks would never find the corpse in those thick woods. He cleaned himself, repaired the shack door, and waited.

'He hadn't croaked the white boy. He had only maimed and paralyzed him. That night a white man out possum hunting with his dogs heard the kid bleating under the brush. He was out of his skull. It was midnight before the kid's raving made sense to the white folks.

'Sweet heard the mob's horses galloping toward the shack. He hid in the loft just as the crazy gang came through the shack slammer. Sweet peeped through a crack and watched them beat his old man's head bloody. They dragged him outside. Sweet saw the whole mob rape his mother.

'Finally all was quiet except for his mother whimpering on the bed. He sneaked out of the loft. Through the open door he saw his old man swinging in the moonlight from a peach tree in front of the shack.

'His mammy went to the funny farm. Sweet was taken in by a share cropper on the same plantation. He worked the fields until he got seventeen. He ran away and caught a freight train North. He was eighteen when he got his first whore. She was a white girl. He drove her to suicide before he got nineteen. Sweet's gotta be sixty now.'

He paused. He steered the Hog with one hand. He took a cigarette from his jacket pocket. He punched in the dash-board lighter.

I thought, 'No wonder Sweet's off his rocker. I wonder why Top really gave me that tight rundown on Sweet?'

The lighter popped. Top lit his cigarette. He sucked hard. He blew out a white cloud against the windshield that for an instant blotted out the moon.

He said, 'I ain't insane like Sweet. My skull is clear and cool. I ain't no mixed-up Southern Nigger. I was born in the North, I grew up with white kids. I don't hate white people or any other people. I ain't no black brute. I'm a pretty brown-skin lover. I love people.

'When I was a square, I was even engaged to marry a white girl. Her parents and friends put pressure on her and she chickened out. I guess I loved her. Right after we quit I went to a hospital for my nerves. I ain't had nothing but whores since. It's like I told you when I met you. Sweet's a Ford and I'm a Duesenberg. He's just an ugly lucky nut.'

I said, 'But Top you cracked your booby-box score was

higher than Sweet's. Those three gibbering bitches upstate sure don't show no love for whore people.'

He said, 'There you go, fool. A young chump is just like a dumb bitch. He can't figure nothing out himself. He's gotta have a rundown on everything. Of course I drove those whores crazy, but for a sane reason, sucker.

'A pimp cops a whore. He cons her maybe if she stays in his corner humping his pockets fat, at the end of the rainbow she's got a husband and a soft easy chair. To hold her beak to the grindstone, he pumps air castles into her skull.

'She takes all the stable grief. She humps her ass into a cramp to outshine the other whores in the family. At first, it's easy for the bitch to star. As she gets older and uglier her competition gets younger and prettier.

'She don't have to be no brain to wake up there ain't no easy chair at the end. She gets hip there ain't never even been a rainbow. She gets larceny in her heart. She bullshits herself that if she can drive all those young pretty whores away from the pimp that rainbow might come true after all. If it don't, she'll get her revenge anyway.

'It's a violation of the pimp book to quit a whore. A bitch like that is a ticking bomb. Every day, her value to the pimp drops to the zero line. She's old, tired, and dangerous. She can rattle a pimp into goofing his whole game. If the pimp is a sucker he'll try to drive her away with his foot in her ass. She's almost a cinch to croak him or cross him into the joint.

'I'm a genius. I'm hip that after a bitch has had maybe ten-thousand tricks drill her she ain't too steady, skullwise. I don't tip her I'm salty and disgusted. I talk like a sweet head-shrinker to her. Indeed of air castles, I pump her full of H.

'Her skull starts to jelly. I'll be worried as hell about her. I'll start sneaking slugs of morphine or chloral hydrate into her shots. While she's out, I'll maybe douse her with chicken blood. She comes to, I'll tell her I brought her in from the street. I tell her I hope you didn't croak anybody while you were sleep-walking.

'I got a thousand ways to drive 'em goofy. That last broad

I flipped, I hung her out a fifth floor window. I had given her a jolt of pure cocaine so she'd wake up outside that window. I was holding her by both wrists. Her feet were dangling in the air. She opened her eyes. When she looked down she screamed like a scared baby. She was screaming when they came to get her. You see, kid, I'm all business. I ain't got an ounce of hate in me.'

He had been driving for at least an hour. I had lost track of time and space. I saw no black faces in the streets around us. I saw tall gleaming apartment houses. Some so tall they seemed welded to the night sky.

I said, 'Yeah Top, you're a cold clever stud all right. I'm sure glad you're yanking my coat. Jesus, Sweet must live in a white neighborhood.'

He said, 'Yeah, Kid, he lives just around that next corner, in a penthouse. Like I told you he's lucky as a shit-house rat. It's a million-dollar building. The old white broad that owns it is Sweet's freak white dog.'

I said, 'But don't the white tenants blow the roof because Sweet lives there?'

He said, 'Sweet's old white broad owns the building, but Sweet runs it. At least he runs it through a old ex-pimp pal. Sweet stuck him into a pad on the ground floor. Patch Eye, the old stud collects the rents and keeps the porters and other flunkys on their toes. All the tenants are white gamblers and hustlers. Sweet is got the old ex-pimp running book wide open. The action a day just from the tenants runs two or three grand. I'll say it a thousand times Sweet is a lucky old stud.'

He turned the corner. He eased the Hog into the curb in front of a snow-white apartment building. A moss-green canvas canopy ran from the edge of the curb twenty-five yards to the kleig-lighted fancy front of the building. A gaunt white stud in a green monkey suit was standing in stooped attention at the curb. We got out. Top walked around the Hog to the doorman.

The doorman said, 'Good evening, gentlemen.'

Top said, 'Hello Jack, do me a favor. When you take my wheels to the back see that it's parked close to an exit. When

I come out, I don't wanna hassle outta there. Here's a fin, Buster.'

The doorman said, 'Thank you, Sir. I'll relay your wish to Smitty.'

We walked into the green-painted, black-marbled foyer. I was trembling like maybe a hick virgin on a casting couch. We walked up the half-dozen marble steps to an almost invisible glass door.

A Boston Coffee-colored broad slid it open. We stepped into the green-and-pearl lobby. A tan broad as flashy as a Cotton Club pony sat behind a blond desk. We walked across the quicksand pearl carpet to the front of it. She flashed two perfect dozen of the thirty-two. Her voice was contralto silk.

She said, 'Good evening, may I help you?'

Top said, 'Stewart and Lancaster to see Mr Jones.'

She turned to an elderly black broad sitting before a switchboard beside her.

She told her, 'Penthouse, Misters Stewart and Lancaster.'

The old broad shifted her earphones from round her wrinkled neck to her horns. She plugged in and started batting her chops together. After a moment she nodded to the pony. We got the ivory flash again.

The pony said, 'Thank you so much for waiting. Mr Jones is at home and will see you.'

I followed Top to the elevators. A pretty brown-skin broad in a tight green uniform zipped us to the fifteenth floor. The brass door opened. We stepped out onto a gold-carpeted entrance hall. It was larger than Top's living room.

A skinny Filipino in a gold lame outfit came toward us. He was grinning and bowing his head. His lank hair flopped across his skull like the wings of a wounded raven. The crystal chandelier overhead glittered his gold suit. He took my lid. He put it on the limb of a mock mother-of-pearl tree.

He said, 'Good evening. Follow, please.'

We followed him to the brink of a sunken living room. It was like a Pasha's passion pit. A green light inside the gurgling bowl of a huge fountain beamed on the vulgar face of a stone woman squatting over it. She was nude and big as a baby elephant. The red light inside her skull blazed, her eyes staring straight ahead. Her giant hands pressed the tips of her long breasts into each corner of her wide open mouth. She was peeing serenely and endlessly into the fountain bowl.

We stepped down to the champagne, oriental carpet. Sweet was sitting across the dim room on a white velour couch. He was wearing a white satin smoking jacket. He looked like a huge black fly in a bucket of milk. Miss Peaches was curled at his side. She was resting her black spotted head on a silk turquoise pillow. Sweet was stroking her back. She purred and locked her yellow eyes on us. I got a whiff of her raw animal odor.

Sweet said, 'Sit your black asses down. Sweetheart, you been dangling me. What happened? Did that raggedy nickel Hog break down? So this is your square country nephew?'

Top sat on a couch beside Miss Peaches. I sat in a blue velour chair several yards to the side of Top. Sweet's gray eyes were flicking up and down me. I was nervous. I grinned at him.

I jerked my eyes away to a large picture on the wall over the couch. A naked white broad was on her hands and knees. A Great Dane with his red tongue lolling out was astraddle her back. He had his paws hooked under her breasts. Her blonde head was turned looking back at him. Her blue eyes were popped wide open.

Top said, 'Man, that Hog ain't no plane. I got here quick as I could. You know I don't play no games on you, Honey.'

I said, 'Thank you, Mr Jones, for letting me come up with unc.'

My voice triggered the Roost memory. He stiffened and glared at me. He smashed his hooks together. It sounded like pistol shots. Peaches growled and sneered.

He said, 'Ain't you the little shit-ball I chased outta the Roost?'

I said, 'Yeah, I'm one and the same. I want to beg your pardon for making you salty that night. Maybe I coulda gotten a pass if I had told you I'm your pal's nephew. I ain't got no sense, Mr Jones. I took after my idiot father.'

Sweet said, 'Top, this punk ain't hopeless. He's silly as a

bitch grinning all the time, but dig how he butters out the con to keep his balls outta the fire. He sure ain't got no tender dick to turn down my pretty big-ass Mimi. Kid, I love black boys with the urge to pimp. Ain't no surer way to amount to something. Your uncle ain't but a good pimp. I'm the greatest in the world. He wired me he's hoping you'll fold on this track and split back to the sticks.

'You got one whore he tells me. You could have the makings. This joint is going to be crawling with fast whores in a coupla hours. I'm gonna be pinning you. I'm gonna watch how you handle yourself. Maybe I'm gonna make you my protege. You gotta be icy; understand, Kid, icy, icy? You gotta stop that grinning. Freeze your map and keep it that way. Maybe I'm gonna prove to your half-ass pimp uncle that I can train even a mule to win the Kentucky Derby.'

Top said, 'Shit, Honey, you didn't have to tip him I'm pulling for his split. I love the kid. I just don't think he can cut the pimp game. The kid raps good. I ain't denying it. He should be maybe a Murphy player or even a mitt man. His ticker ain't icy enough to pimp on this track.'

I thought 'Top pads in a pig sty compared to this layout. It looks like I'm in.'

Sweet said, 'Sweetheart, let's go in a bedroom and cap up and bag that stuff for those jokers. I'm gonna have old Patch Eye come up here and deal it off. I ain't no dope peddler. I'm a pimp. Kid, you can cool it. Have the Filipino bring you a taste. If you want, get it yourself from the bar over there.'

They went around a hand-painted gold silk screen through a doorway. Peaches padded behind them. I saw a bronze bell on a table beside the couch. I decided to get my own taste. I walked across the room to a turquoise bar. I went behind it. I took a tall crystal glass off the mirrored shelf on the wall. I mixed creme de menthe and bubbly water.

I took my green, cool drink and walked toward the floor-to-ceiling glass door. I slid it open and stepped up into the patio. I looked up; the April zephyrs were balleting the burnt-orange and pale-green Japanese lanterns. They danced on glowing jade cords strung high above the lime floor.

The ice-cream-yellow moon seemed close enough to lick. I walked to the pearl parapet. I looked out at a brilliant sea of emerald and ruby neon bursting pastel skyrockets toward the cobalt blue sky bejeweled with sapphire stars.

I thought, 'Sweet sure has caught lightning in a thimble. He came out of the white man's cotton fields. He's pimped himself up to this. He's living high in the sky like a black God in heaven with the white people. He ain't no Nigger doctor. He ain't no hot-sheet Nigger preacher but he's here.

'He pimped up his scratch passport. That barbed-wire stockade is a million miles away. I got more education, I'm better looking, and younger than he is. I know I can do it too.'

I remembered Henry and how religious he was. Look what happened to him. I remembered how I used to kneel every night by the side of the bed to pray. I really believed in God then. I knew he existed. Now I wasn't so sure. I guess the first prison rap started to hack away at my belief in him.

I often wondered in the cell how, if he existed, he could let the Dummy destroy Oscar who loved him. I told myself at the time, maybe he's got complicated long-range plans. Maybe even he's got divine reasons for letting the white folks butcher black people down South.

Maybe some morning about dawn all the black folks will sing Hallelujah! God's white board of directors will untie the red tape. God will roll up his sleeves. He'll smash down the invisible stockades. He'll kill all the rats in the black ghettos. Fill all the black bellies and con all the white folks that Niggers are his children, too.

Now I couldn't wait. If he were up there or not I had to go with the odds. I stared into the sky. It was the first time I'd prayed since Steve, the tramp. I know now it was more fearful alibi than anything else.

I said, 'Lord, if you're up there, you know I'm black and you know my thoughts. Lord, if the Bible is really your divine book then I know it's a sin to pimp. If you're up there and listening you know I'm not trying to con you.

'Lord, I'm not asking you to bless my pimping. I ain't that

stupid. Lord, I know you ain't black. Surely you know, if you're up there, what it's like to be black down here. These white folks are doing all the fine living and sucking up all the gravy. I gotta have some of that living and some of that gravy.

'I don't wanta be a stickup man or a dope peddler. I sure as hell won't be a porter or dishwasher. I just wanta pimp that's all. It's not too bad, because whores are rotten. Besides I ain't going to croak them or drive them crazy. I'm just going to pimp some real white-type living out of them.

'So Lord, if you're up there listening, do one thing for me. Please don't let me croak before I live some and get to be somebody down here in the white man's world. I don't care what happens after that.'

I looked down over the parapet. I wondered if the undertaker had been born yet who was slick enough to paste a sucker's ass together after a Brodie fifteen-stories down. I heard Tuxedo Junction pulsing behind me. I had pitched my pipes dry. I upended my drink.

I turned and walked toward the glass door. I saw the Japanese lanterns splashing color on the polished alabaster-topped tables. The Filipino had sure been busy flopping his mop. I slid the door open to a chorus of profanity. The whore scent flared my nostrils. There must have been thirty yapping pimps and whores lounging around the spacious pit.

I stepped down and slid the door shut. An ebony satin-skinned pimp was sprawled in the blue velour chair. A tawny tan tigress was kneeling before him between his legs. She had her chin rammed into his crotch. She clutched him around the waist like a humping two-dollar trick in an alley.

Her dreamy maroon eyes rolled toward the top of her long skull. She was staring at his fat blue lips. It was maybe she expected him to whistle the 'Lost Chord'. The rock on his finger exploded blue-white, frozen fireworks. He raised his glass to curse all square bitches. He was con-toasting all whores. The room got silent. Somebody had strangled the gold phonograph in the corner.

He toasted:

Before I'd touch a square bitch's slit,
I'd suck a thousand clappy pricks and swim through
    liquid shit.
They got green puke between their rotten toes and snot
    runs from their funky noses.
I hope all square bitches become syphilitic wrecks.
I hope they fall through their own ass-holes and
    break their mother-fucking necks.

It was the first time I'd heard it. It was the first time for the
crowd, too. They roared and begged him to do it again. He
looked toward the hand-painted Chinese screen.

All eyes turned to Top and Sweet coming into the room.
An old black stud wearing a white silk patch over his right eye
trailed behind them. Peaches followed him. He looked like a
vulture decked out in a gray mohair vine. Peaches stood before
the white velour couch and bared her fangs.

The three pimps sitting on it scattered off it like quail under
a double-barreled shotgun. They thumped their rear ends to
the carpet. Sweet, Top, and Peaches sat on the couch.

I sat on a satin pillow in the corner near the glass door. I
watched the show. I saw Patch Eye go and sit behind the bar.
Everybody was in a big half-circle around the couch. It was
like the couch was a stage, and Sweet the star. Sweet said, 'Well
how did you silly bastards like the fight. Did the Nigger murder
that peckerwood or did his black ass turn shit yellow?'

A Southern white whore with a wide face and a sultry voice
like Bankhead's drawled, 'Mistah Jones, Ahm happy to repoat
thet the Niggah run the white stud back intu his mammy's ass
in thu fust round.'

Everybody laughed except Sweet. He was crashing together
his mitts. I wondered what madness bubbled in his skull as he
stared at her. A high-ass yellow broad flicked life back into the
phonograph. 'Gloomy Sunday', the suicide's favorite, dirged
through the room. She stared at me as she came away.

Sweet said, 'All right you freakish pigs. Patch Eye's got
outfits and bags of poison. You got the go sign to croak
yourselves.'

They started rising from the satin pillows and velour ottomans. They clustered around Patch Eye at the bar.

The high-ass yellow broad came to me. She stooped in front of me. I saw black tracks on her inner thighs. The inside of her gaping cat was beef-steak red. She had a shiv slash on the right side of her face. It was a livid gully from her cheekbone to the corner of her twisted mouth. Smallpox craters covered her face. I caught the glint of a pearl-handled switch-blade in her bosom. Her gray eyes were whirling in her skull. She was high.

I was careful. I grinned. Sweet was digging us. He was shaking his head in disgust. I wondered if he thought I oughta slug her in the jib and maybe take that shiv in the gut.

She said, 'Let me see that pretty dick, handsome.'

I said, 'I don't show my swipe to strange bitches. I got a whore to pamper my swipe.'

She said, 'Nigger, you ain't heard of me? I'm Red Cora from Detroit. That red is for blood. You ain't hip I'm a thieving bitch that croaked two studs? Now I said show that dick. Call me Cora, little bullshit Nigger. Ain't you a bitch with one whore? You gonna starve to death, Nigger, if she's a chump flat-backer. Nigger, you better get hip and cop a thief.'

A big husky broad with a spike in one hand and pack of stuff in the other took me off the hook. She kneed Cora's spine.

She said, 'Bitch, I'm gonna shoot this dope. You want some? You can Georgia this skinny Nigger later.'

I watched Cora's rear end twist away from me. She and the husky broad went to the bar and got a spoon and a glass of water. I looked at Sweet. He was giving me a cold stare.

I thought, 'This track is too fast. I can't protect myself. With young soft bitches like the runt I'm a champ. These old, hard bitches, I gotta solve. I gotta be careful and not blow Sweet. If I sucker out any more tonight he'll freeze and boot me.'

I sat in the corner bug-eyed for two hours. My ears flapped to the super-slick dialogue. I was excited by the fast-paced, smooth byplay between these wizards of pimpdom.

Red Cora kept me edgy. She went to the patio several times. She was H-ed out of her skull. Each time she passed she cracked on me. She was sure panting to view my swipe.

Several of Sweet's whores came in. None of them had been at the Roost with him that first time I saw him. All of them were fine with low mileage. One of them was yellow and beautiful. She couldn't have been more than seventeen.

There was a giant black pimp from the Apple. He had three of his whores with him. He had been boasting about how he had his swipe trained. He was one of the three at the party that didn't bang stuff. I had watched him snort girl and down a few mixed drinks. He had a glass in his hand standing over Sweet and Top on the couch.

He said, 'Sweet, ain't a bitch living can pop me off unless I want her to. I don't care if she's got velvet suction cups in her cat. Her jib can have a college degree, she ain't gonna make me pop against my will. I got the toughest swipe in the world. I got a C note to back my crack.'

Sweet said, 'Sucker, I got a young bitch I turned out six months ago that could blow that tender sucker swipe of yours in five minutes. I ain't going to teach you no lesson for a measly C note. If that C note ain't all you got, put five bills in Top's mitt and you got a bet.'

The big joker snatched a roll from his side pocket. He plunked five C notes into Top's palm. Sweet eased a bale of C notes from the pocket of his smoking jacket. He covered the bet in Top's hand.

Sweet snapped his fingers. The beautiful yellow broad kneeled before the standing giant. She started to perform before the cheering audience. Within less than three minutes she had won the bet for Sweet.

The big joker stood there for a long moment with his eyes closed. He had a goofy grin on his face. One of his whores snickered. He slapped her hard against the jaw. He went to the bar.

I thought, 'She sure has a head for business. Pepper was great, but she couldn't hold this broad's douche bag.'

I got up and went behind the Chinese screen through the door. I went down a long hall. I passed three way-out bedrooms. I went into a mirrored john. It was as big as a bedroom. I pushed the door shut. I should have locked it.

I walked to the stool. I raised the lid. That tough bitch Red Cora darted in. She was licking out her red tongue. Her gray eyes were voodooing in her skull. She was hot as hell for my relative innocence and youth. She was a double murderess with a skull load of H and a hot jib.

I stood there before the deadly bitch. I searched the thin catalogue in my skull. I didn't know the right crack for a situation like this. I mumbled a plaintive pitch.

I said, 'Now listen girl, you haven't given me a nickel. I'm not your man.'

It was like trying to stand off a starving leopard with a broom straw. She snaked that shiv out of her bosom and popped the gleaming blade open. She clawed my fly open with the other hand. I heard buttons bounce on the tile floor. My ticker was doing a fox trot.

She said, 'You jiving pretty sonuvabitch. You ain't no pimp. I'm gonna eat your sweet ass up or chop off your dick.'

I backed up to the wall beside the stool. I could feel the wet throbbing tips of my fingers against the cool tile. She was grabbing inside when Sweet bulled in. He seized a fistful of her long hair. She squealed in pain. He jerked her away from me toward the door. He cussed her as he drove his needle-toed shoe into her wide caboose several times.

He said, 'Bull-shit bitch, this chump is in my school. I ain't gonna let you Georgia him. Now nix, bitch, nix.'

I heard her high heels staccato against the tile as she fled. He turned toward me. His black face was gray with fury. Maybe Sweet would forget I wasn't yellow. I remembered what Top had told me about those four murders.

He thrust his flat black nose against mine. I could feel a spray of spit strike my lips as he cursed me. He twisted the collar of my vine like a garrote around my throat. He had snatched me six feet from the wall.

He shouted, 'Listen you stupid little motherfucker. You know why that bitch screwed you around? You always grinning like a Cheshire Cat. What's funny? Can't I get the sucker outta you? I can't make a pimp outta a pussy like you.

'I told you once, do I have to tell you a thousand times? Green-ass Nigger, to be a good pimp, you gotta be icy, cold like the inside of a dead-whore's pussy. Now if you a bitch, a sissy, or something let me know. I'll put you in drag and you can whore for me. Stay outta my face Nigger, until you freeze up and stop that sucker grinning.'

I heard his ground grippers skid against the floor as he hurled me against the wall. The back of my skull torpedoed into it. Through a drowsy fog of pain I saw him float away.

My back snailed down the wall. I laughed at the funny way the shoe tips turned in as the long legs glided across the tile. I sat there on the cool floor gazing at the weird comical legs stretched out before me.

I saw a pair of blue mohair legs right angle the flat ones. I looked up. It was Top. He bent over to help me up.

He said, 'Kid, now you believe the ugly bastard is insane? Take this key to my Hog. Get it outta the lot in back. Park in the block and cool it. I'm getting outta here myself as soon as I cop my end of the smack scratch.'

I riveted my eyes to the champagne carpet. I zigzagged through the snickering whores and pimps. I made it across the pit to the elevator. The Filipino was standing beside it. He was pressing the down button.

He looked like a friendly brown snake sausaged in gold foil. He reached up and stroked my jacket collar down flat from around my ears. He took my lid off the pearl tree. He stuck it on my skull and snapped the brim. I felt the sweat band needle the aching boil. I adjusted my lid.

He said, 'Good night, Sir. Sammee hopes you had fine time.'

I said, 'Sammee pal, it's been a wild night. I'll never forget it.'

I got a whiff of crotch as the elevator plunged to the lobby. I wondered if the pretty brown-skin jockey whored a little bit as a side line.

I stepped out of the gilded cage into the lobby. I saw a

winking red-arrowed sign in the rear. I walked to the glass door below it. I went down the white stone steps to the parking lot.

I spotted Top's red Hog in the ocean of cars. I went to it, unlocked it and got in. A big white Buick was parked in front of it. A grinning brown-skin joker in white overalls came toward the Buick.

I saw Smitty blue-stitched across his breast pocket. He pulled the Buick out. I keyed the Hog and scooted it out of the lot. I whipped around the corner and coasted to the curb fifty feet from the entrance of Sweet's apartment building.

I shut the motor off. I lowered the driver's side window. I put my lid on the seat. I threw my head back on the top of the seat. I closed my eyes. I dozed. Something was crushing my jaw. A blinding spot light burned into my eyeballs. I heard a fog-horn voice.

It blasted, 'Police officers! Nigger, what the hell you doing. What's your name? Show us your identification.'

I couldn't answer with my jaw crushed in a vise. I was dazed. I lowered my eyes below the inferno of light. I saw a white brutish wrist. Thick black hair bristled on it. I saw muscles cord and ripple across it as the vise tightened around my jaw bone. I wondered if the copper was Satan and I had croaked in the Hog and was being checked into Hell. Hell or not, Satan wanted identification. I remembered the Fox and the Horse. I didn't even have a hide.

Satan swung the Hog door open. The door frame black-jacked the top of my skull as Satan yanked me from the Hog. He released my jaw and slammed me across the hood of the Hog. My wet palms skidded on the top of it.

Satan's fellow demon was punch-frisking me from breast to shoe soles. He poked an index finger inside my shoe. I felt a tickle in the arch of my instep.

I said, 'My name is Albert Thomas. Hell, I wasn't doing anything officers. I was just waiting for my uncle. I lost my wal—.'

I didn't finish. A galaxy of shooting stars orbited my skull. It was like a flame-hot poker was imbedded in that sore bump at the back of my skull.

I heard the tinkle of glass against the hood. I puked and nose dived to the hood. I felt the warm stinking mess against my cheek as I lay across the hood gasping.

Glass splinters sparkled on the hood. Satan had slugged his flashlight against my skull. I saw the fellow demon's shadow bobbing inside the Hog. He was frisking it, too.

Satan said, 'Nigger, you got a sheet downtown? Whatta you do for a living?'

I whispered, 'I've never been in trouble. I'm an entertainer. I'm a dancer.'

He said, 'You black, conning bastard. How in the fuck do you know what a sheet is? You been mugged, Nigger. Stand up straight. I'm gonna take you downtown. You can jig a few steps on the show up stage.'

I struggled off the hood. I turned and faced him. I looked up into the red, puffy face. Top came around the back of the Hog and stood between us.

He said, 'What's the beef, officer. This is my nephew and my Cadillac. The kid was waiting for me. He's clean. We been to a party at Sweet's. You know who he is. We're personal friends of his, you dig?'

Satan's puffy face creased into a hyena grin. He rapped on the windshield. I saw the demon's starch-white face peer over the rear seat. Satan waved him from the Hog. He clambered out and stood beside Satan.

Satan said, 'Looks like we made a slight mistake, Johnnie. These gentlemen are pals of Mr Jones. Mister, all your nephew had to do to beat the roust was mention a name.

'Christ, we have to do our job. There's a cat burglar operating in this district. The lieutenant is riding our asses to nab him. Sorry about the whole thing gentlemen.'

The rollers walked across the street. They got into a black Chevrolet and gunned it away. I took a handkerchief from my back pocket, and wiped my face.

I wiped the bits of loose glass and most of the puke off the hood. I threw the rag in the gutter. I got in the Hog. Top u-turned and headed back to Black Town. I touched the bump on my skull. I felt a spot of sticky ooze. My skull had only a tiny split. I wiped my fingers on the end of my lapel pocket handkerchief.

I thought, 'If it gets any rougher on this track, I'll be punchy before long. Maybe I better take Preston's advice and go back to the sticks.'

I said, 'Jeez, Sweet Jones sure has got pull. It was like magic when you cracked his name.'

Top said, 'Magic your black ass. The only magic is in that C note a week Sweet lays on 'em. Every copper in the district from Captain down greases his mitts in that lard bucket in Sweet's pocket.

'Mary, mammy of Jesus, you stink. You musta shit in your pants. You sure getting funky breaks, Kid. Too bad you couldn't handle Red Cora. She's one of the fastest thieves in the country.'

I said, 'Look Top if that crazy, pocked-face bitch had a tunnel straight into Fort Knox, I wouldn't fart in her jib. I hate old hard-leg whores.'

He said, 'That's a chump crack. After you get hip to the pimp game you'll take scratch from a gold-toothed, three-legged bulldog with two heads. Say listen, Kid, don't ever forget to keep that rundown on Sweet under your lid. I'm the only stud he told. He'd twist my skull off and play soccer with it.'

I said, 'Now Top, that's a helluva crack to make. Do I look like the kind of rat square that would cross a pal?'

I was glad when I saw the Haven's blue sign. Top parked across the street from it. I got out. I had crossed to the middle of the street. Top blew the horn. I turned back to the side of the Hog. Top had my lid and a small square of paper in his hand. I took them.

He said, 'Kid, here's my phone number in case you wanta ring me for something. Take it easy now.'

I passed through the lobby. The indicator pointed out the elevator was at the fourth floor. I took the stairs and picked up the sizzle from the broom closet. The runt let me in after the first knock. I walked by her to the bedroom and stuck the sizzle in a coat pocket in the closet. I started taking my stinking clothes off. She was standing in the doorway. I tossed them in a pile in the corner.

She said, 'Daddy, when you passed me you smelled like you'd been dunked in a garbage truck. What happened?'

I headed for the bathroom. I was standing over the stool. She followed me. She stood in the bathroom doorway. I looked over my shoulder at her.

I said, 'Bitch, some white rollers busted me tonight. They got the wire I'm in town to pimp. They took me down and beat the puke outta me. Baby, they wanted me to finger you. They wanted to know where you worked. Shit, I was too pure in heart to put a finger on you, baby. I'm not feeling worth a damn, so go on the dummy, okay?'

I flushed the toilet. I turned the shower on. I gave her a hard look and frowned. She turned and got into bed. I took Mickey off. It was four A.M. I showered and toweled off. I fell into bed without checking the scratch on the dresser. I went to sleep wondering what to do to solve the fast track.

9

The Butterfly

I woke up. The sun was noon bright. I heard a squad of rats or something in the direction of the closet. I turned and looked. It was the runt. She was on her knees in the closet scraping and pulling suitcases and shoes around. The back of my skull was sore and throbbing, I touched it. I felt a crusty cap over the bump.

I thought as I watched the runt's rear end, 'What the hell is she doing?'

I said, 'Damn, Bitch, can't you put a damper on that racket? I gotta aching skull. I wake up, the first living thing I pin is the rusty black ass of a dizzy whore. She's digging a ditch in the closet. Now there's gotta be a prettier way to start a day.'

She snapped her head around and said, 'I'm looking for the reefer. I feel low. Where did you stash it? I couldn't find it last night when I came in.'

I got up and went to the closet. I ran my hand into the coat pocket stash. I separated my stuff from the reefer inside the pocket. I gave her the can. I saw two lonely saw bucks on the dresser. I went back and got into bed.

I said, 'Bitch, I take an outside stash, where else?' I don't wanta come home some night and greet a roller. Wouldn't it be a bitch if he had that can of one to two in the penitentiary in his mitt?

'Christ, your scratch for last night is shitty. What happened? Some joker stick you up? That reefer ain't making you lazy is it? A double saw take for a young freak bitch is outrageous. Shit, you broke your luck for the double saw with the lover, Sugar Blue Eyes.

'You musta shot a blank the rest of the night. I'll murder you, bitch, if I find out you freak off all night with your tricks for a double saw.'

She was licking at the sides of the joint she had rolled. She sat on the side of the bed next to me. She rolled her sassy eyes at me.

She said, 'Daddy, I'm your girl. If I ever stop loving you, I'm gonna quit whoring for you. If you don't croak me I'll get another black man when we're washed up. Right now I'm in your corner all the way.

'White tricks don't move me. I want to vomit when they paw and slobber over me. I baby talk them, but I hate them. Daddy, I just want their scratch. I get a thrill with them all right. It knocks me out that here I am, a black Nigger bitch, taking their scratch.

'A lot of them are clean-cut high muckty mucks in the white world. Some of them show me pictures of beautiful wives and cute children. It makes me feel greater than those white bitches living in soft luxury. Those white broads got Nigger maids they laugh at. They think we ain't good for nothing but clowning and cleaning. It would give them a stroke to see their trick husbands moaning and groaning and licking between a black whore's thighs.

'I know I ain't got no silky hair and white skin. I'm damn sure hip those white men ain't leaving Heaven to come to Hell every night just for the drive. They coming because those cold-ass white broads in Heaven ain't got what these black whores in Hell got between their legs. Black and low as I am, I got secrets with their white men those high-class white bitches ain't hip to.

'Now, Daddy, we rap so little I got carried away. I ain't nobody's fool but yours. I wanted to rundown to you this morning about last night. You put me on the dummy remember? After I turned Chuck at the Martin, I got a roust. Two white vice coppers picked me up. They rode me around and felt over me. One of them was a mean, nasty bastard. The other, blond nice one, was sorry for me.

'Nasty said, "I know this black bitch is a cinch ringer for those eight larceny from the person beefs. We oughta take her down and put her on a Show Up or two. What the hell, Carl, we know she's a whore."

'Blondie said, "But Max, she ain't no hard leg. She's just

a beautiful young sexy kid with a mother to support. You know how tough it is for Boots to get three squares and a roof in this town. Let's give her a break and cut her loose. Jesus, Max, this broad has got a pair of thighs on her. She's soft as kitten fur."

'Nasty said, "Carl, you sure got a weak spot for spades. This broad says she's broke. That black ass of hers ain't enough to buy a pass from me. If she ain't too shy to show what her Derby's like, maybe, I say just maybe, I might give her a break.

I'm driving into this alley. Carl, you test her lid and snatch. If you ain't raving how great it is upstairs and down when you finish, I'm gonna wheel outta this alley and toss her black ass in jail . . . I'm gonna book her on those eight counts of larceny. If she's lucky she'll get a deuce."

'Daddy, Blondie pushed my head down to his lap. Then I got on the back seat with him. That freak bastard, Max, turned around and kept his flashlight on us the whole time. I made Blondie holler.

'I finished with Blondie. Max got back there with me. For a half hour he called me filthy names. He punched and pinched me. I'm sure sore all over. Blondie begged him to stop. My ass feels like he split something back there. I had a rough time.

'Finally they let me out. Max told me to never let him see me again. I was scared so I came in. That's why the scratch is short. Max will bust me if he sees me again. You gonna have to find me another street to work.'

I said, 'You square-ass stupid bitch. You think you're a brain because you're hip that white men sneak through the stockade to lay black whores. Ain't a Nigger sealed in here that don't know that. It don't make you great because those white sick fools leave that fine pussy in Heaven to find your stinking black ass in Hell.

'You chicken-hearted bitch. You got a roust. They conned you to believe they could slap a bum rap on you. You're too dumb to know I'm gonna raise you. You rammed your funky finger in your sore ass. You took a powder from the track with a lousy double saw. You let those peckerwood coppers fuck you front, rear, sideways, and across. You simple bitch, I'm gonna find you another street to work? Now you got like a license to hustle this one?

'You ain't got to worry about Max and that other roller. Bitch, you can work it forever just so you don't get cancer of the cat or lockjaw. Bitch, if you don't get outta my face I'm going to the chair for slaughtering you. Get your clothes on. Get in the street and hump up some scratch. Bitch, don't come to that door unless you call me first. I ain't going nowhere.'

She had been taking sucks on the reefer while she was rapping. She was high when I gave her the rundown on how she had been conned by the rollers. She leaped off the bed and went to the closet. She dressed and jerked her head around the whole time.

She knew I was angry. She was maybe afraid after that slaughter crack that I might goose her in the butt with my knife. She got out fast. I had Silas bring me some food and take my shirts and things to the cleaners. I ate and snorted some Girl. Later I banged some. Except for the bump on my skull that still ached a little I felt all right.

I remembered Satan and the Demon wanting to see identification. I called Silas. He told me where to go. I could get a driver's license without a test for a saw buck under the counter. I dressed and made the trip. Sure enough I copped. I was back home in an hour.

I pulled a chair to the front window. I had my spy glass. It was still daylight. I didn't see the runt on the street. I spied into the greasy spoon across the street. The runt was sitting at the counter talking to a big black stud in overalls. He had trick engraved all over him. I saw them leave together and come across the street toward the Martin Hotel.

The scarfaced horn tooter who lived in four-twenty-two across the hall came out behind them alone. He got into a battered Ford and chugged away. It gave me an idea. After all I could blow the runt. I picked up the phone and asked for connection to apartment four-twenty-two. The pretty yellow ex-whore helloed. I was glad old Silas had given me a rundown on her. I could tailor my pitch.

I said, 'Now try to control yourself baby. I'm the tall stud with the dreamy bedroom eyes across the hall in four-twenty. I'm the guy with the pretty towel wrapped around his sexy hips. I got the same hips on now that you x-rayed. Remember that hump of sugar your peepers feasted on?'

She said, 'Maybe, but you shouldn't call me. I don't want an incident. What do you want? A lady doesn't accept phone calls from strangers.'

I said, 'A million dollars and a trip to the moon with a bored, trapped, beautiful bitch, you dig? I'm no stranger. I've been popping the elastic on your panties ever since you saw me in the hall.'

She giggled. I could hear the thrill in her voice. The horn blower had taken her off the track, but the whore was alive and thrashing inside her. She had class. She had done more than screw on the fire escape at high school.

She said, 'I don't drink and besides I don't know you.'

I said, 'You met me in your first hot dream, remember? You know that pretty joker in your little girl dreams that always faded when you woke up wet between the legs. You waited and wished.

'You lucky bitch, I've stepped out of your dreams. I'm alive and real across the hall from you. Get over here, I'm gonna turn you on. Don't worry about the watch dog. I saw him split out of the greasy spoon ten minutes ago. Baby, I'm gonna have to make one of my whores bake you a cake with a saw in it.'

She said, 'You're not married to one of them? I don't want my throat cut. I don't want to break an old habit, breathing.'

I said, 'Yeah, I'm married. I'm married to the whore game. You're still a member of the club yourself. You just ain't paid any dues lately. Maybe if you ain't full of shit I can put you back in good standing. Now get over here!'

She said, 'I'm raw. I'll have to slip on something. I'll come over for a minute. You're not a hype? I'm not hip to anything but grass.'

I said, 'No, sugar, I'm a lover and a beggar. I got black gunion, baby. You hip?'

I hung up. I went to the dresser mirror and powdered my

face. I brushed my hair with a damp brush. My mop was black, bright, and curly. I went to the closet and slipped on a wild yellow lounging robe. I had bought it the day before Dalanski busted me at the dance.

I had peeped at her hole card that day in the hall. I knew she was a freak. I remembered her eyes chained to my crotch. Now I didn't have on any towel. First chance I got I'd flash her into a boil, through the split in the front of the robe.

Maybe I could shoot some cocaine into that yellow virgin arm. That would open her up for sure. I might even steal her from scarface and put her back on the track tomorrow.

I thought, 'This fine bitch is my speed. She's not a hard-leg dog with a million miles on her. She's no more than nineteen and sexy as the rear end of a peacock. I'll play it cool and quiz her. Maybe some asskicker booted her off the track. Maybe that's how scarface copped.

'I'll stay in the pimp role, but I'll sweeten it with a little high-class bullshit. Maybe I'll rap some of that gigolo garbage I overheard the white pimps in the joint rapping.

'I better call Silas. I'm not ready for trouble with Scarface.' I went to the door and unlocked it. I picked up the phone and got Silas.

I said, 'Listen Jack, this is important. I'm gonna be rapping to the big-butt yellow broad who lives in four-twenty-two. I'm gonna give you and the broad on the desk a fin a piece. You gotta wire me here when Scarface shows. I'm not ready for him to wise up. Got me?'

Silas said, 'You lucky young sonuvabitch. A faggot in a Y.M.C.A. shower room ain't no luckier. You got salt and pepper, kid? We'll wire you. I'll stall the cage on the way up with him. Can I peep a little, kid, huh?'

I hung up. I felt a cool puff of draft on my ankles. I went into the living room. She had slipped into almost nothing. She was crossed legged in the chair at the window. She turned her head from the street and looked up at me.

She had on a thigh-long black negligee with pink butterflies sewn on. A pair of white silk panties gleamed through the black gauze. She curved inside it like a yellow Pretty Girl. Her ebony hair was steepled on top of her skull like a black satin crown. I saw a frantic tic jerk at a corner of her melon-red mouth. If she turned out to have entasis, I swore I would give up whores and get hip to the sissy game.

She said, 'Hi. I ask myself why I'm here?'

I said, 'Baby, don't drag the party. Don't ask yourself stupid questions. You can't escape that freak, desperate spark. You know baby, that awful sweet electricity that makes a farm boy kiss a ewe. The same power that yowls a hot tom cat in the alley. You hip to it? Now just relax. I'm gonna roll you up a bomber. Baby, your luck has changed. You've hit the jackpot. You found me. Oh yeah, my name is Blood.'

She said, 'Blood it's nice to meet you. I'm Christine. Chris I like better. I can't stay long. I have to be careful. My old man is very jealous.'

I said, 'Chris, you are gonna find out I'm a wild groove. You may stay a lifetime thinking it was only an hour. All we need is an understanding. All you need is a man.'

Over the top of Chris's head I saw the runt flash her eyes up at the window. She was just getting into a white trick's car. Twilight was sweeping away daylight with a deep purple broom. I went to the bedroom. I loaded an outfit and tilted it spike up in my pocket. I rolled two bombers. One with reefer, the other in cigarette tobacco. I snorted a thumb tip of cocaine. I got a towel and put it next to the gap under the front door. I lit some incense.

I gave Chris the bomber. I lit it and my dud. With a package like Chris, reefer might confuse me. I might wake up swindled. If she had been Garbo, I still wanted scratch before snatch.

I got another chair. We sat there facing each other in the twilight. I waited for the reefer to fill her skull. The bomber in her hand was now a roach. I cocktailed it for her. Her eyes were dreamy.

She said, 'God damnit, sweetheart, I'm high. You know Blood you're going to laugh when I tell you something. Guess what I was thinking when I saw you the first time in that towel?'

I said, 'You thought, "Oh my itching cat! That pretty brown

bastard looks like a pimp. I wish the hell I was still whoring. I sure would like to kiss Mr Thriller the Killer under that towel." Am I right, sweet freak?'

She giggled and scooted her chair flush against my knees. She slid her back down in the leather chair. She put the heels of her pink shoes on the seat of my chair.

I was sandwiched between her big yellow legs. The street lamp came on spotlighting her. She was still giggling. I fingered the ready jolt of cocaine in my robe pocket. I took it out and hid it against the side of my chair. I saw blue veins pulsing on her inner thighs.

The cocaine had me strung on an icy rack. I raised her right leg and rubbed my cheek against it. I crushed her knee-cap between my teeth. She moaned. I gazed deep into her eyes. She had laughed tiny pearls of tears that clung to her long, silky lashes. Under the street lamp her face was innocent and soft as a yellow fawn's. I felt old as Methuselah.

She said, 'Don't look at me like that. I know you can read minds. You give me the creeps with that look. It's like you're Svengali or that crazy Russian Monk I read about.'

I said, 'Chris, you're gonna be my whore. We gotta share things. That reefer was just an appetizer. Reeter is for low-class skunk broads. Heroin is for chumps bound for the grave yard. Cocaine is for brilliant, beautiful people.

'Chris, banging cocaine will spin a magic web of music and bells inside your skull. Every pore in your body will feel like Daddy's jugging his swipe in all over you. It will torch off a racy secret fire of life inside you. It's a miracle, Chris. You get all that thrill and no habit. I know you ain't chicken shit. Are you game to try?'

She said, 'If it won't scar me or hurt me. If it hurts, promise you'll stop. Don't give me a lot, Baby. Where you going to put it in?'

I took her left leg and put it on the arm of my chair. I saw a fat line high up on her thigh. I eased the spike into it. She flinched. The dropper flashed red. I pressed the bulb slowly. Her eyes widened. Her white teeth bit into her bottom lip.

I emptied the dropper. I pulled out the gun. She sat there

stiffly. She took her leg off the chair arm. She rubbed the inside knobs of her ankles against my sides. I saw her Adam's apple spasm.

I remembered how I puked the first time. I slid my chair back and raced to the bedroom to get the waste basket. I just made it back. She dumped a load into it. I flushed the mess down the toilet and rinsed the basket out. When I got back to her she was smiling and stroking her legs.

She said, 'I'm sorry I did that naughty thing, Daddy. Oh! Oh! But now I feel heavenly. Baby, I'm so glad I came over and got this feeling. Aren't those bells something? Baby, you got a lot of this? I want to do this every day. Stay like this every minute. Let's lie down. I want a formal introduction to Mr Thriller.'

I said, 'Bitch, when you come to me as my whore I'll keep your skull mellow. Now you gotta be joking about Mr Thriller. He won't have anything to do with a broke bitch that claims a square horn blower as her man. Let's go over there while he's away and get your clothes. You're not married to him are you?'

She said, 'How many girls do you have? Maybe your stable is too big for comfort. I get salty standing in a long line for my loving.'

I said, 'Whore, answer my question. What are you a roller or something? When you are my whore you don't worry about anything but your own ass and scratch. Now answer my question.'

She said, 'Blood, I didn't want to answer because I am married to him. Leroy, that's my husband, saved my life really. He's been wonderful to me. He used to be good looking. He didn't get so insanely jealous until after his accident.

'We've been waiting over two years for a settlement. Blood, honestly, you are my kind of stud. My life is so screwed up. I don't know what to do. I don't know what to tell you. Would you believe that you're the first fellow I've talked to in over two years? Blood, I don't love Leroy.'

That cocaine had her speed rapping. I couldn't cop her tonight unless I croaked Scarface. My plans had to change.

I had to unhook her from Leroy soon. She'd make bales of scratch. Maybe I could work an angle to get her and a slice of that settlement. Of course, I couldn't wait forever. If I had to, I'd cop without a slice of the settlement.

I knew Leroy was going to blow her. He didn't have a chance to hold much longer with that ugly face and that jealous bit. I had to find out if she would level with me all the way. Silas had told me she was an ex-whore.

I said, 'Chris, give me a fast rundown of your life story. I'll have all the answers for you when you finish.'

She said, 'If you let me sit in your lap.'

I nodded and she climbed onto my lap. She hooked an arm around my neck. Her cheek was against my ear. The cocaine thudded her ticker against my breast. Out of the side of my eye I saw the runt go into the greasy spoon. I was hoping she wouldn't use the phone just inside the door and interrupt the rundown.

I felt her balloon bottom blasting heat to the throbbing cup of my lap. Too bad I worked so hard at the pimp game. Mr Thriller was playing stiff con on me. He was just a fool at heart. The poor chump wanted to sucker out in that bed with this luscious doll. Good thing he had me to stand guard over him.

She said, 'I remember nothing but good until I was twelve. Then my mothe died. My father had been a kind, good man, until then. He always worked. He was a good carpenter. He changed quickly after Mama died.

'He took my bed down. He said he wanted me to sleep with him. He told me how lonely his bed was after all those years with Mama. Nothing happened at first. One night a month later I had a nightmare. A wild ferocious animal was sucking my breast. It was terrible. I woke up. It was Papa.

'I screamed. He slapped me hard. His face was all twisted and hateful. He looked like a crazy stranger. I blacked out. When I came to Papa was crying and begging me to forgive him.

'After a while I would just lie there, numb and let him use me. I hated his guts. In school I had the crazy feeling the students could see and feel my shame and filth. By the time I got fifteen I was a skeleton. By now he had me doing everything to him. I'm glad he's dead in Hell.

'Papa, the beast, was killing me. I was so nervous I couldn't wash dishes. I broke dozens. I wasn't eating enough to keep a bird alive. I collapsed one day coming from the grocery. I woke up in a hospital. My system was shot and I was pregnant. I stayed in the hospital a month. I stayed at Papa's a week after I got out. I took some money while he slept and left Wichita with the clothes on my back.

'I came here and got a waitress job. A young pimp named Dandy Louee started picking me up when I got off. I thought he was a millionaire. He dressed me up and turned me out. He was a cruel black bastard. He liked to beat me, and then screw me. He worked me in a house run by one of his whores. He kept his foot in my ass.

'Funny thing, I made money even when my belly was stuck way out. A lot of tricks who came there wanted a pregnant girl. I lost the baby while turning a trick. Dandy got five years on a white slave rap two months later.

'I got a bar-maid job and met Leroy. He was playing a gig in the spot. I was a sick girl. I fell out twice while serving the bar. The doctor said I needed rest. He said I couldn't expect to live long unless I rested. Leroy nursed me back to health.

'He was good to me. I needed some one who cared. I married him when I was just four months shy of seventeen. I went with Leroy on a string of one-nighters in the Midwest. The group broke up in Youngstown, Ohio. We were stranded. leroy got a job in an industrial cleaning plant. The second week a boiler exploded and you've seen his face.

'His lawyer says we can expect a ten-thousand dollar settlement any time now. Leroy is driving me crazy with his jealousy. I don't mind hustling. I'd be your girl, Blood. I go for you, Blood. Are things clearer now? What should I do?'

I said, 'You've had nothing but heartache. I feel so sorry for you, baby. Now I know you've got to be my woman. I gotta protect you. I gotta give you affection and understanding. Don't worry, angel, with me life will be smooth as the snow at Sun Valley.

'You'll be so happy you'll be out of your mind half the time. With our color combination we could make a sonuvabitching baby together after we get rich. Tell me does Leroy plan to work the Roost for a while?'

She said, 'Oh! I forgot to tell you. Last night was his last night. They want him for another six weeks, but he's going to drop the Combo. It's too much headache to get them to show for work sober and on time.

'He's out now with a booking agent. I think he might go with a big band on an East-Coast tour. I hope he gets it. Band leaders want band members' wives to stay at home. Daddy, please figure things out fast. I want to be your girl as soon as possible.'

I was sucking her scented cheek. I flogged my skull for a quick plot to tear the yellow gold mine from Scarface. The phone rang. She got out of her nest. I rushed to the phone. It was the excited broad on the desk.

She said, 'Forgive me for goofing. Four-twenty-two went up two minutes ago. I was having a hassle with a check out. I saw him come in. It didn't register until the second that I called you. You better clean house fast.'

I ran into the living room. I snatched her from the chair. I pulled her to the door. I cracked it. We peeped down the hall. Scarface was twenty yards away coming down the hall. He had a big stack of papers, maybe sheet music under his arm. He shifted the bundle to his other arm.

A paper fluttered to the carpet. He stooped to get it. I saw her door ajar. I stepped aside. I slapped her on the rump. She blurred across through her doorway. Scarface was standing with his mouth open staring toward his now locked door.

He was sure he'd seen her. His face was puzzled. I shut my door easy like. I stood with my ear against the door. A bomb of sound shocked my ear drum. Someone was punching his fist against my door. I ran into the bedroom and got my switch-blade. I came back to the door. I held the open blade behind me. I opened the door.

It was Scarface. He looked like Mr Hyde all right. His orange-brown eyes were spinning counter clockwise. I saw the bundle of papers in a careless heap in front of his door. His right mitt was deep in his coat pocket. I saw the faint outline of maybe a skinny lead pipe, or a gun barrel. I gauged the moves for a heart stab to beat his mitt out of his pocket.

I said, 'Yeah Jack, what is it. I'm on the phone with my bondsman. The court just raised my bond on a double-murder beef. I'm in a bad mood. I don't want to buy anything?'

He just stood there like a scarfaced zombie staring at me. He looked down at the carpet in front of my door. I looked down. A pink butterfly lay there like a silent indictment.

He heaved his chest and took a deep breath. It was like his last one. He stooped and picked it up. The eerie bastard took his other hand out of his pocket. Tears rolled down from his unblinking orange eyes as he stared at me. His scarred cheeks were quivering as he shredded the butterfly into pink lint on the carpet.

He turned and walked away. I shut my door and got a beak load of cocaine. I took the lounging robe off. It was dripping sweat. I showered. I sat in Chris's chair at the window. Her sweet odor was still rising from it. For an hour I heard a loud sobbing whine across the hall. It was Scarface chewing out Chris. Mickey said midnight. I hadn't eaten since morning, and I wasn't hungry. Cocaine was a strong con for the belly.

I thought, 'I hope that jealous chump doesn't croak her. It would be like making a big bonfire out of hundred dollar bills. If she wasn't his wife and I had a rod, I'd go over there and claim her.'

The phone rang. It was Silas.

He said, 'What happened, kid? Was she a whiz in the sack? Did the joker catch her? I been busy. I ain't had a chance to check with you until now. I was worried about you, kid. The broad told me she was late with the wire. I stalled him in the cage.'

I said, 'It was very close, Silas. I'm a pimp, I didn't stick her. I'll take care of you and the broad this weekend when I pay my rent. Silas, if you get any news on the broad or Scarface wire me fast.'

He said, 'Yeah, Kid, you know me. I stay hip to what goes

on around here. I'll keep you plugged in, Kid. Good night. I'm going home.'

I hung up and lay across the bed. I wondered if Max and Blondie had the runt hemmed up in an alley again. I smoked a reefer. I fell asleep. The phone woke me up. It was the runt.

She said, 'Daddy, it's your baby. It's after two, can I come home?'

I said, 'Bitch, what kinda lines you got?'

She said, 'I got thirty slats. I'm beat, Daddy. My tricks have been spades. You know how cheap and hard they are to turn. Can I come in?'

I said, 'Come on in. Take a bath. Watch your jib, bitch. Don't irritate me. I've got a lot on my mind.'

She'd been working more than twelve hours. She was beat all right. Within a half hour after her bath she was snoring beside me. I was dozing when the phone rang. I switched on the light. I picked up.

I said, 'Hello.'

Chris whispered, 'Daddy, I can't talk long. Leroy's asleep. He found a butterfly that fell off my negligee. He's been raving like a crazy man. He knows I was over there. I got bad news for us. The band spot is out. He called and turned it down. He's going to keep the combo and go through Ohio.

'His agent has a slew of one-nighters booked for him. He's taking me with him. Daddy, I won't forget us. I'll keep in touch. Maybe he'll go out before we leave tomorrow afternoon. I may get a chance to kiss you goodbye. I love you, Blood. I'm going to dream about Mr Thriller until I—'

I heard the drowsy whine of Leroy's voice calling her name the instant before she hung up. I turned and looked at the runt. Her big mouth was wide open. Frothy slobber ran down her chin. Her sour hair had started to kink at the edges. She needed to go to the beauty shop downstairs.

I thought, 'What kinda breaks am I getting? I'm sinfully good looking. I'm lying here with a lather-mouth dog. The ugliest joker in the world is across the hall. He's in the sack with a pretty bitch whose nose is wide open for me. Something's gotta be done. Maybe after I cop Chris, I'll have the brass ring in my mitt.'

I didn't sleep at all after Chris called. The runt woke up at noon. She went across the street and got our lunch. At two in the afternoon she was in the street.

Silas called. He told me Chris was checking out. I saw Chris and Scarface put their stuff in the car and drive away.

The runt came in at two A.M. with only twenty slats. She was shying away from white tricks. She was leery of Max and Blondie. I couldn't shake her out of it. She would rather turn spades for three or five dollars. She was afraid Max would catch her with a white trick.

10

The Unwritten Book

A week after Chris left I copped another bag of cocaine from Top. It was almost gone. The runt was only making expenses. I had one lonely C note and a double saw plus the porker silver. The weather was getting balmy. I needed fresh clothes. I was going to the bottom fast.

In the three weeks after Chris left I kicked the runt's ass a half-dozen times. I only left the hotel twice in almost a month. I was expecting Chris to call me and say she was on her way to me. Things were getting worse.

It had been two weeks since I saw Top. I decided to call him. Maybe he could hip me to a new spot to work for runt. My bankroll was thin. At ten A.M. I called Top. One of his broads said he was out of town. He wouldn't be back for a week.

I got a sudden thought. I asked her if she knew Sweet's phone number. She said she did, but she'd have to call and find out if Sweet wanted me to have it. She called back in ten minutes and gave it to me. I called him. He answered. He was in a good mood.

He said, 'Well, whatta you know, if it ain't grinning Slim. You still got that one whore or have your grinned yourself whoreless?'

I looked over at the runt. She was still asleep. She hadn't been in the street for three days. Her period had run five days. She claimed she was too weak and sick to go out. I had given her a terrible whipping the night before. I needed advice badly.

I said, 'Sweet, my bitch is falling apart. She's playing dead. If you don't pull my coat I'm gonna starve to death. You gotta help me Sweet.'

He said, 'Nigger, you ain't cracking to nick me for scratch are you? I don't loan my scratch to suckers who got whores and can't pimp on 'em. I ain't gonna support you and that lazy bitch.'

I said, 'No Sweet. I don't want scratch. I want you to run the game through my skull. I got a tiny bit of scratch. I gotta get my coat pulled before I tap out.'

He said, 'You got wheels? You know how to get out here? Now remember you get a roust out here, crack my name. Don't repeat your boner.'

I said, 'Yeah, I'm driving. I think I can find your pad. When should I come out there?'

He said, 'Quick as you can get here. You get here and grin in my face, I'm gonna throw you over the patio wall.

'Say kid, Peaches and me got a taste for some of that barbecued chicken down there in Hell. Bring one with you when you come.'

He hung up. My ticker was pounding like Chris had walked in the door naked with a million dollars. I shook the runt. She opened her eyes. I stood over her.

I said, 'Bitch, you better be in the street when I get back.'

She said, 'You can't do anything but kill me. I'm ready to die. I don't care what you do to me. I'm sick.'

I said, 'All right, bitch, just hip me where you want your black stinking ass shipped.'

I got in the Ford. I realized I hadn't put on a tie. I didn't have a lid. I looked into the rear-view mirror. I sure looked scroungy. Maybe he'd be alone. Then I remembered the lobby. What the hell did it matter.

I drove for about fifteen minutes before I saw a clean open barbeque joint. A black stud in a tall white cap was stabbing chickens onto a turning spit in the window. I went in. I came out with two birds. Peaches might be really hungry for barbequed chicken. It made solid sense to brown-nose Miss Peaches.

After making several wrong turns I found Sweet's building. I parked the Ford in almost the same spot at the curb where Satan had sapped me a month ago. A young white stud in a monkey suit was out in front. Crusader Sweet was doing his bit to reverse the social order.

I went to the desk in the lobby. I felt like a tramp as I waited for the pass. I got on the elevator. A different broad was at the controls. The spicy scent of the chicken wiggled her nose. She wasn't as pretty as the ripe-smelling broad. She sure kept her crotch from advertising. Maybe it was just that she didn't get heavy action.

I stepped from the cage. The friendly brown snake wasn't at his station to flop his mop for me. I figured it was his off day. The odds were a hundred to one he was in the sack somewhere with a six-foot blonde.

She was probably a little like the blonde coming up from the pit on her way to the cage. It was Mimi. She flicked her green eyes across my face. They were cold as a frozen French lake. She passed me. She looked like fancy French pastry in her sable stole. I wondered how I got the stupid courage to turn down her freak off.

I walked to the doorway of the pit. The stone broad was still in her squirting squat. Sweet was sitting on the couch. Miss Peaches beside him saw me first. She bounded across the carpet. I felt her choppers graze my hand. She snatched the bag of chicken. She flung it on the alabaster topped cocktail table in front of Sweet.

Sweet looked at me. I tightened my face into a solemn grim mask. I stepped down and walked toward him. He was wearing only a pair of polka-dot shorts. In daylight I noticed a mole on the broad in the picture over the couch.

I said, 'Hello Mr Jones. I hope those birds are still warm.'

He said, 'Kid, your map sure looks like that bullshit bitch you got is been shooting you through hot grease. I like that look you got today. Maybe you're getting hip the pimp game ain't for grinning jackasses.

'Get over here and sit on this couch. While baby and me eat our barbeque, rundown you and your whore. I wanta know where and how you copped her. Tell me everything you can remember about her and what's happened since you copped her. Rundown your whole life as far back as you remember. It don't matter which is first.'

I ran down my life for him. Then I ran down from the night I met the runt until the moment I left the Haven. It took maybe forty-five minutes. I even described the runt in detail.

Sweet and his greedy girl-friend had devoured both birds down to the bare bones. Sweet was wiping Miss Peaches' whiskers with a paper napkin. She put her head in his lap. She was jammed against my thigh. Sweet leaned back on the couch. He put his bare feet on the top of the cocktail table.

He said, 'Sweetheart, you're black like me. I love you. You got the hate to pimp. You a lucky Nigger to get your coat pulled by me. You flap your horns and remember what I'm gonna spiel to you.

'There are thousands of Niggers in this country who think they're pimps. The pussy-weak white pimps ain't worth mentioning. Don't none of them pimp by the book. They ain't even heard about it. If they was black, they'd starve stiff.

'There ain't more than six of 'em who are hip to and pimp by the book. You won't find it in the square-Nigger or white history books. The truth is that book was written in the skulls of proud slick Niggers freed from slavery. They wasn't lazy. They was puking sick of picking white man's cotton and kissing his nasty ass. The slave days stuck in their skulls. They went to the cities. They got hip fast.

'The conning bastard white man hadn't freed the Niggers. The cities was like the plantations down South. Jeffing Uncle Toms still did all the white man's hard and filthy work.

'Those slick Nigger heroes bawled like crumb crushers. They saw the white man just like on the plantations still ramming it into the finest black broads.

'The broads were stupid squares. They still freaked for free with the white man. They wasn't hip to the scratch in their hot black asses.

'Those first Nigger pimps started hipping the dumb bitches to the gold mines between their legs. They hipped them to stick their mitts out for the white man's scratch. The first Nigger pimps and sure-shot gamblers was the only Nigger big shots in the country.

'They wore fine threads and had blooded horses. Those pimps was black geniuses. They wrote that skull book on pimping. Even now if it wasn't for that frantic army of white tricks, Nigger pimps would starve to death.

'Greenie, the white man has been pig-greedy for Nigger broads ever since his first whiff of black pussy. Black whores con themselves the only reason he sniffs his way to 'em is white broads ain't got what it takes to please him.

'I'm hip he's got two other secret sick reasons. White women ain't hip to his secret reasons. The dumb white broads ain't even hip to why he locks all Niggers inside tight stockades. He'd love it if the Nigger broads wasn't locked in there. The white man is scared shitless. He don't want them humping bucks coming out there in the white world rubbing their bellies against those soft white bellies.

'That's the real reason for keeping all the Niggers locked up. To show you how sick in the head he is, he thinks black broads are dirt beneath his feet. His balls will bust if he don't sneak through that stockade, to those, to him, half-savage, less than human, black broads.

'You know, Greenie, why he's gotta come to 'em? The silly sick bastard is like a whore that needs and loves punishment. He's a joke with scratch in his mitt. As great as he thinks he is, he can't keep his beak and swipe outta the stink of a black ass.

'He wallows and stains himself. The poor freak's joy is in his suffering. The chump believes he's done something dirty to himself. He slips back into his white world. He goes on conning himself he's God and Niggers are wild filthy animals he has to keep in the stockades.

'The sad thing is he don't even know he's sick in the skull. Greenie, I'm pulling your coat from the bottom to the top. That rundown on the first Nigger pimps will make you proud to be a pimp.

'Square-ass Niggers will try to put shame inside you. Ain't one of 'em wouldn't suck a mule's ass to pimp. They can't because a square ain't nothing but a pussy. He lets a square bitch pimp on him. You gotta pimp by the rules of that pimp book those noble studs wrote a hundred years ago. When you look in a mirror you gotta know that cold-hearted bastard looking at you is real.

'Now that young bitch you got is gone lazy. She's stuffing

on you. That bitch ain't sick. I ain't never seen a bitch under twenty that could get sick. Your whore is bullshitting. A whore's scratch ain't never longer than a pimp's cold game. You gotta have strict rules for a whore. She's gotta respect you to hump her heart out in the street.

'One whore ain't got but one pussy and one jib. You got to get what there is in her fast as you can. You gotta get sixteen hours a day outta her. There ain't no guarantee you going to keep any bitch for long. The name of the pimp game is Cop and Blow.

'Now this young bitch you git is shitty all right. She knows you ain't got no other whore. I want you to go back to that hotel. Make that bitch get outta that bed and get in the street. Put your foot in her ass hard. If that don't work, take a wire coat hanger and twist it into a whip. Ain't no bitch, freak or not, can stand up to that hanger.

'Maybe your foot and fist can't move that young whore anymore. She's a freak to them. Believe me, Greenie, that coat hanger will blow her or straighten her out. It's better to have no whore than a piece of whore. Get some cotton and make her pack herself. The show can't stop when a whore bleeds.

'I'm gonna lay some pills on you. Give her a couple when you get her outta that bed. Don't give her any more reefer. It makes some whores lazy. Don't worry, kid, if you do like I say and blow her, I'll give you a whore. Kid, don't hold that whore to one block. Tell that whore all the streets go. Turn her loose. It's the only way to pimp. If she blows, whatta you lost. She stands up, you got a whore and some real scratch.

'You go back and put the coat-hanger pressure on her. If it don't blow her and she stands up for a week, you ought have half a grand in a week. Take that scratch and drive to one of the whore towns close around. Go to Western Union. Send that scratch back to yourself at your hotel. Use some broad's name as the sender.

'That lazy bitch you got will think she's got competition. Watch the sparks fly from her ass. She'll try to top that bitch that doesn't exist. Greenie, you listen to Sweet Jones. You'll be a helluva pimp.

'Never get friendly and confide in your whores. You got twenty whores, don't forget your thoughts are secret. A good pimp is always really alone. You gotta always be a puzzle, a mystery to them. That's how you hold a whore. Don't get sour. Tell them something new and confusing every day. You can hold 'em as long as you can do it.

Sweet is hipping you to pimp by the book. I'm the greatest Nigger pimp in the world. Now Greenie, is you skull going to hold everything I told you?'

I said, 'Thirty years from now I'll still remember every word. Sweet you won't be sorry you helped me. I'm gonna pimp my black ass off. I'll make you proud of me. I'll call you later and hip you to what the runt did under hanger pressure. Oh, yeah, don't forget to give me those pills.'

He got up. Miss Peaches stretched her legs. She jumped down and followed him. A sharp hooked nail in one of her rear claws snagged out an inch of cloth from my pants knee. I wouldn't have cared if she had clawed me naked. I was in a thrilled daze. With Sweet Jones on ready tap to pull my coat I was going to set a record on the fast track.

Sweet came back. He gave me a tiny bottle of small white pills. He put his hands on my shoulders. He looked down at me. His sub-zero eyes warmed to maybe zero.

He said, 'I love you, Sweetheart! You know, kid, I don't ever think I'm gonna grin in your face. I love you like a son. Any time I grin in a sucker's face I'm gonna cross him or croak him. Call me any time you need a rundown. Good luck, Greenie.'

I walked across the pit. I stepped up to the doorway. I glanced back. Sweet had Peaches in his arms. She was purring like a new bride. Sweet was squeezing her in a lover's embrace. He was covering her laughing face with kisses.

I checked Mickey when I got in the Ford. It was four P.M. I drove toward the runt. I tromped hard on the gas pedal.

I thought, 'No wonder Sweet is the greatest Nigger pimp in the world. He even knows the history of the black pimp.

'I ain't going to spare the runt's ass. I'm gonna go right

in with the pressure. I hope she's not in the street. Sweet promised me a whore if I blow the runt. Any whore of Sweet's is already trained to a fine edge. Maybe he'll give me Mimi.'

11

To Lose a Whore

I pulled the Ford into the curb across the street from the Haven. I didn't see the runt anywhere in the street. I peeped into the greasy spoon. She wasn't at the counter. I looked up at our window. I crossed the street and went through the lobby. I took the stairs to the fourth floor. I made three stabs at the lock with the key before I made it. I stepped inside. I was excited. I chain-bolted the door. I walked to the bedroom.

The runt was propped up in bed smoking a stick of gangster. Lady Day was tar brushing that mean, sweet man again. I stood by the side of the bed, next to the record player. I saw the edge of a paper plate sticking out of the waste basket. I took it out and put it on the bed.

Two navy beans were in a puddle of grease on the side of the plate. A pile of sucked, cleaned neck bones were heaped in the center of it. The runt had gone out to the greasy spoon and copped a hearty meal. She sure had a healthy appetite for a sick bitch. Her eyes were wild and big, looking up at me.

She fingered gently at the hole in my pants knee. I shut the box off. I ripped the record off the turn table. I broke it in half and hurled the pieces into the waste basket. She kept her eyes on the hole at my knee. She ignored the broken record. She played it cool.

She said, 'You'll have to get it rewoven, huh? Daddy, I'm feeling better. I felt good enough to go across the street for food. Maybe by tomorrow I'll feel good enough to go in the street. Baby, I would've went out after I ate, but my legs were too weak.'

I said, 'Bitch, I already passed the death sentence on you. It's good you had your last meal. I'm gonna send your dead ass to your daughter, Gay. Take off that gown and lie on your belly, bitch.'

I went to the closet. I took down a wire hanger. I straightened it into one long piece. I doubled and braided it. I wrapped a necktie around the handle end. I turned back to the bed. She was still propped in the bed. Her mouth was gaped open. She had both her hands clapped over her chest.

She was like a broad in a movie. She opens a door and there's Dr Jekyll just going into his frightful change. I saw her tongue tremble inside her jib. Her lips made a liquid plopping sound as they mutely pounded together. She rolled across the bed away from me. I raised my right arm up and back. I heard my shoulder socket creak.

Her gown was hiked up to her waist. Her naked rear end had scrambled to the far edge of the bed. I raced around the foot of the bed. She rolled to the middle. She was on her back. Her arms held her jack-knifed legs against her chest.

The whites of her eyes glowed like phosphorus. I brought the wire whip down. I heard it swish through the air. It struck her across the shin bones. She cried out like she was celebrating New Year's Eve.

She screamed, 'Ooh-whee! Ooh-whee!'

She jerked flat, rigid on the bed then smalled her fists against her temples. She sucked her bottom lip up into her jib. I slashed the air again. It sounded like maybe a dum-dum bullet striking across her gut button.

She moaned, 'Whee-Lordy! Whee-Lordy!'

She turned over on her belly. I tore the gown from her back. She was naked. She flailed her arms like a holy-roller. The whip whistled a deadly lyric as I brought it down again and again across her back and butt. I saw the awful welts puffing the black velvet skin.

I stopped and turned her over. The pillow stuck to her face. I snatched it away. There was a ripping sound. I saw feathers sticking to her tear wet face. She had chewed a hole in the pillow. She was thrashing her legs and mumbling.

Her chest heaved in great sobs. She was staring at me and shaking her skull. Her eyes had that pitiful look of Christ's on those paintings of the Crucifixion. Her lips were moving. I got on the bed. I stuck my ear near.

She whispered, 'I don't need any more whipping. I give,

Daddy. You're the boss. I was a dumb bitch. It looks like you got a whore now. Kiss me and help me up.'

I felt tears roll down my cheeks. Maybe I was crying in joy that I broke her spirit. I felt sorry for her. I wondered if I was falling in love like a sucker. I kissed her hard. I carried her into the bathroom. I placed her tenderly in the tub.

I turned the water on. A stream burst from the shower nozzle overhead. She squealed. I pushed in the shower bypass on the tub faucet. The warm water started filling the tub. I dumped a bottle of rubbing alcohol into the tub.

She looked up at me. I took the tiny bottle of pills out of my pocket. I shook out two into my palm. I took a glass off the face bowl. I handed her the pills. She put them in her mouth. She washed them down with the glass of water I gave her.

I said, 'Phyllis, why do you make your sweet daddy mean? Daddy's gonna kill his little bitch if she don't straighten up and whore like the star she is.

'Bitch, lie down in that water for a while. Then get in the street and get some real scratch for your man. You don't have to stay in this block. Just walk and work until you get respectable scratch to bring in. I can raise you if you take a fall. They gotta let you make a phone call. If I go out I'll check the desk here by phone every hour or so. Bitch, get down and star. You want your man, get him some real scratch.'

I went and sat on the bed. The sheet looked like a red zebra had lain down and his stripes had faded on it. I heard her sloshing the water in the tub. She was humming the record I'd smashed. Sweet's pills sure weren't hurting her.

Whores were strange people all right. She was silent while she combed her hair and fixed her face. She put on a red knit suit. She stood in front of me. She held her hand out. I saw dark stains on her stockings at the shins. Her eyes were bright.

She said, 'Daddy, I don't have a dime. Give me a coupla dollars, please. Don't worry, when I come in I'll have nice scratch.'

I stood up. I gave her a fin. I walked to the door with her. She turned her face up. I leaned down. I sucked her bottom lip, then bit it hard. She squeezed my arm and gouged her teeth into my cheek. She went down the hall.

I shut the door and went to the front window. I rubbed my cheek to see if the skin was broken. I saw her cross the street at the corner. She was walking fast. That whipping and those pills had made her well. She looked like a child. She was so tiny and sexy in her red suit. I wondered as she disappeared whether she'd come back. It was seven P.M.

I thought, 'I better stick here in the pad. Whipping a broad with a hanger is not a bit like a foot in the ass. Christ! I'd kill the bastard on the spot if he hit my bare ass with one. Sweet was right. She got outta that bed all right. I wonder if those slavery pimps invented the hanger whip.

'No, even hangers hadn't been invented then. I guess Sweet did. I'm gonna wait the runt out. If she tries to slip in here to steal her clothes, I'll croak her. I wonder why Chris hasn't gotten in touch? Maybe some fast pimp has already stolen that pretty bitch from Leroy. Maybe Leroy had one of his fits and croaked her.

'I wonder what the bitch will be like I get from Sweet if the runt blows? This is a hell of a feeling I got. I don't know if I got a whore or not. It would be a bitch if Sweet goes back on his word and leaves me whoreless on this fast track. I'm gonna get high. I'd better take the flight with gangster. Cocaine will only sharpen my grief.'

I took a shower. I stepped out of the tub. I got a towel from the wall rack. I saw splotches of red on the one beside it. I toweled off. I rolled a giant bomber. I put a fresh case on the pillow the runt had gnawed.

I propped myself against the head of the bed. I sucked the bomber down to a roach. The reefer and the sibilant mummering of tires against the street lulled me into deep sleep.

I woke up. I was still half-propped against the pillows. It was broad daylight. The runt hadn't come in. I had blown whoreless with that wire hanger. I lit a cigarette. It was seven A.M. I lay there staring at the entwined lovers on 'The Kiss' Statue.

I thought, 'The runt's got a pair of tits like that broad. Jeez, she was sure a freak. Some pimp is going to have a sweet bitch when he straightens her out. I wonder if that little bitch will miss me? She damn sure can't forget me.

'Hell, I can't worry about the mule going blind. I'll wait until noon or so. I'll rip open that whore grab-bag Sweet promised me. Maybe I was hasty to shut the door on Melody and his entasis. At this point I can get hip to anything except work. No one could know I was freaking with a stud.

'Christ, I wish beautiful Chris would call. What a thrill if she'd tell me she was rushing to me. To get her tight I'd maybe eat everything but the tacks in her shoes. I'm hungry. I'm not going to let my troubles abuse my skull and my belly.'

I got Silas on the phone. I ordered home fries and sausage. I got up and brushed my teeth. I skull-noted to call Top when he got back in town. Maybe he could find out who booked Leroy. Maybe I'd trace Chris that way. I'd get Preston's owl-head and take her from Leroy at gun-point.

I was listening to 'Mood Indigo' and thinking about the runt. I was remembering that day when I left Mama crying at the window.

I couldn't wait to get around the corner to the runt. Then I was sure I had a black gold mine sitting in the Ford waiting for me. In this tough pimp game you couldn't count your scratch until you had it in your mitt. Holding whores was like trying to cinch-grip quicksilver.

I thought, 'Poor Mama. I haven't called her or anything. I'm gonna call her when things get straight.'

12

To Gain a Stable

I heard Silas knock on the door. I went and opened it. Silas was a strange, beautiful sight. The slick sorcerer-bastard had my breakfast on a tray. He had turned himself into a cute black bitch in a red knit suit. It was the runt. I murdered the grin of relief in its jib womb. I twisted my face into a copy of Sweet's when he bounced my skull off his john wall.

I said, 'Bitch, I'm gonna' croak you. Since three o'clock I been calling all the hospitals and jails in town. I even called the morgue. Speak up bitch, what's your story?'

She looked up at me. She was smiling. She walked past me into the bedroom. I followed her. She sat the tray on the dresser. She ran her fingers deep into her bosom. She brought out a damp wad of bills. She gave it to me.

She said, 'Daddy, my last trick was a fifty slat, all night trick. I caught him at two this morning. Baby, I gave you a hundred and twenty eight slats.

'Silas had your breakfast on the elevator on my way up. With the two slats I gave him, I made a hundred and thirty.

'Oh, Daddy, I've found some good streets to work a coupla miles from here. It's in the neighborhood of a joint called the Roost. You were a sweet daddy to be worried about your baby. Oh! I almost forgot. Keep your fingers crossed. I may bring you a girl one of these mornings. She's wild about me. Her old man ain't nothing. He's a burglar.'

I said, 'Phyllis, there's more than one note in a song. You gotta string together a thousand nights like last night. Now take a bath. I'm gonna treat those scratches. Remember I don't want any junkie bitch. Make sure she's clean before you cop.'

I forgot about my breakfast. I went out and got into the Ford. I drove to the drugstore and got ointments and salves.

I called Sweet and told him the runt stood up. He reminded me to send that scratch to myself as soon as possible. I went back to the Haven. I sent Silas for hot food. I dressed her wounds. They sure looked bad.

Those go pills she had taken died. She fell asleep while I was doctoring her back. I ate and took a nap. By the end of the week, I felt like a pimp. I had an eight-bill bankroll not counting the porker silver.

One night about nine I got into the Ford. I drove less than a hundred miles to Terre Haute a small whore-town. I sent five bills to myself at the Haven. I used Christine as the broad's name.

Top was back in town so I stopped on the way home and copped cocaine, yellows, and bennies. The runt came in that morning around four. She had a hundred-and-five slats. She was on her way to stardom. We were in bed when I cracked on her.

I said, 'Baby, I think our luck is changing all around. I'm pretty sure Daddy's copped another whore. I met her in a bar about a week ago.

'It's a small world all right. She said she just moved out of this joint not long ago. She went wild over me. She's a fine young bitch. She begged me to go to Terre Haute with her. She's working a fast house up there. I told her I'd run up there after she sent her first week's scratch. She gave me her phone number up there. I gave her my address.

'Tonight I called up there. I asked her about my scratch. She told me five bills were on the way. Baby, if she's jiving we ain't hurt. If she sends it and it's respectable scratch your daddy's got a small stable.'

She said, 'Is she a white bitch? What does the bitch look like?'

I said, 'Bitch, don't get shitty now. What's wrong with a white broad helping two spades? She's a boot. She looks like what she is. A scratch-getting fine bitch in love with your man at first sight.'

It was a little after noon when the messenger brought the scratch notice. The runt went to the door and brought him into the bedroom.

I opened it. The office was a half mile away. I asked the runt if she'd like some air. She was eager to go.

It was a good thing I had gotten that driver's license. I had to go through a long routine. They even made me crack the amount I was expecting. I got the cash.

The runt was silent on the way home. Sweet sure knew the angles to put pressure on a whore's skull. In the next month I made two more trips to Terre Haute. Twice I went across town and stayed in a hotel over night until around noon. I was conning the runt I was visiting her stable mate.

The runt was really humping. She was averaging no less than a bill a night. Two months after the hanger whipping I took a furnished three-bedroom vacancy in Top's building. It was a gold-and-red dream after the Haven. The runt really freaked this pad off. I guess she felt at home at last. It was on the sixth floor.

I copped six two-hundred-dollar vines at sixty slats a piece. The booster lived on the second floor beneath me. The same week Top cut me into a stud who had a black La Salle car in mint condition.

He was out on an appeal bond and his lip wired him he was joint bound. I have the stud four bills in his mitt. I paid off the last two notes on the wheels.

I had two cars. I gave the runt her Ford back. She could cover and get down in a wider area.

I started hanging around out at Sweet's pad, sucking up the pimp game. I got home from Sweet's one morning around five. I heard the runt rapping to some one in one of the bedrooms. I pushed the door open. The runt was in bed with a tall, pretty brown-skin broad. She looked fifteen. They were naked. They stopped kissing and looked at me.

The runt said, 'Daddy this is Ophelia. I told you about her in the Haven. Her old man got one-to-three in the joint for burglary. She wants to join our family. Can she?'

I said, 'Ophelia, if you're not full of shit and you obey my rules you're welcome. Have you bitches been in the streets working tonight? I hope you just got in that bed to freak off. Phyllis, get outta that bed and get my double-action scratch.'

The runt went into the closet and brought me a roll of bills.

She said, 'A bill of this I made.'

I fast counted a yard and seventy-five slats. I took off my clothes and got between them. I spent an hour quizzing Ophelia and running down my rules. She was eighteen. The circus started. I was circus master. I had become too much pimp to freak off with a new package. They were the performers. She had put only six bits in my pocket. How cheaply did she get me if she blew tomorrow.

It was the night before my twentieth birthday in August. I had gone to the West Side to cop some dresses for Phyllis and Ophelia. I had left the booster's pad. I was loading the dozen or so pieces in the trunk of the La Salle. I slammed the trunk lid shut, and locked it.

I heard screaming and smashing sounds coming from a cabaret just down the street. I saw a hatless, gray-haired man come staggering to the sidewalk. He was holding his head. The side of his head looked shiny. I walked down the sidewalk toward him.

He was bleeding from a deep cut in his head. He was moaning and trying to stop the flow of blood with his hands. A dark thin joker ran out behind the old man. I saw something gleam in his hand as he raised his arm again and again.

I moved closer. The thin joker was savagely pistol whipping the old stud. He was beaten to his knees. He looked like some one had painted his face red.

The thin joker turned his face. The light coming from the open door of the cabaret shone on it. It was Chris's Leroy beating the old man. Twenty customers had come out. They formed a circle around the massacre. I moved to the outside of the circle.

Then I saw Chris standing on the other side of the circle. She was screaming and tugging at Leroy's pistol arm. Leroy had gone insane.

I moved around the circle closer to Chris. I stood behind her. I saw greasy stains on the back of her dress collar. Her hair looked frowzy and dull. Scarface was sure taking her to the dogs. I heard the screech of brakes. I saw two huge white rollers muscle through the crowd. Leroy was astraddle the unconscious figure, still pounding his pistol against it.

They shoved Chris backward. One of them put an armlock on Leroy's gun arm and took the pistol. The other vised his neck in a strangle-hold. They dragged him to the prowl car and threw him into the back seat.

A short middle-aged white broad stepped to the side of the fallen figure. She was wringing her hands. She was wearing a bar apron. She stooped and stroked the figure's brow.

One of them got on the front seat. He turned sideways guarding Leroy. He put a microphone to his lips. He was calling an ambulance, no doubt. The other roller came back and stopped beside the white woman.

He said, 'Anybody you know?'

She sobbed. 'Yes, he's my father-in-law.'

He said, 'What happened?'

She said, 'Everybody knows Papa Tony loves to kid around the girls. He's got a heart as big as New York. Everybody loves and understands him. Papa Tony came in the bar. He started kissing the cheek of all the girls at the bar.

'He kissed that one behind you. That maniac man of hers stopped singing. He leaped off the stage. He started to beat poor Papa Tony with his pistol. It's the first night the maniac has worked for my husband. If my husband, Vince, had been here that jerk's brains would splatter the sidewalk.'

The roller looked back at Chris. He started making notes in a small book. I knew he'd quiz her after he got the full picture. I touched Chris lightly on the shoulder. She turned and looked up at me. She got weak in the knees. She slumped against me. I took her arm and steered her down the sidewalk. I heard the distant whine of an ambulance siren.

I said, 'Chris, you had better split. That's a white man Leroy beat up. The white folks are going to cross you into it. After all you're the reason he flipped.'

We got into the La Salle. I moved it down the street toward the prowl car. I put on the brakes. A couple came from in front of the prowl car. They crossed the street in front of me. I had stopped beside the prowl car. Chris could have reached out and touched it.

I turned my head and looked into the rear seat of the prowl car. Leroy was staring at Chris. His eyes shifted to me. He leaped toward the front seat. The roller back-handed him. I saw Leroy's head dip out of sight as I pulled away.

I made book from that frantic leap of his that he remembered me. The La Salle moved quickly away from the West Side. Chris was crying. I stayed silent until I hit the fringe of the South Side.

Then I said, 'All right, Chris, I got you away from the heat. Tell me where you live and I'll take you home. Don't cry. You can bail him out when they book him.'

She sobbed, 'All right, you want to take me home? Turn around and take me to Leroy's jalopy. It's parked behind the bar where he blew his silly top.

'We got in town broke this afternoon. He didn't get the settlement. Maybe he'll never get it. I'm so disgusted. He was to get paid nightly for the gig. He does a blues singing bit now.'

I said, 'Bitch, you look like a bum. You conned me you'd keep in touch. You were gonna be my whore, remember? I shoulda left you back there to go to jail with your sucker-man.'

I realized I had a solid chance to cop her now. All I had to do was stay strong and bluff her.

Leroy was a cinch to get a bit. He couldn't make bail. Chris had no out but me. She sure looked like my third whore.

I coasted into the curb. I left the engine running. We were parked in front of a flea-bag hotel. I had maybe a twenty-five-hundred-slat roll in my pocket. I flashed for her. I peeled off a saw buck. I held it toward her. She ignored it.

She said, 'Blood, it wasn't that I didn't think about you. I wanted to call you. I wanted to keep my word. Leroy never let me out of his sight.

'He would even follow me to the toilet. You don't know how much I hate him. I hope he gets life. Don't cut me loose,

Blood. I'll keep my promises. I'm free now. I'm yours, baby. Tell me to jump in the river. I'll do it.'

I said, 'No, Chris, I'm afraid of you. I think Leroy has made a tramp jive-bitch outta you. I'm pimping too good to bring a headache into the stable. I'll always be your friend, Chris. My ticker is bleeding for you, baby. I gotta think of number one.

'My whores are humping sixteen hours a day in the street. They love it. I don't figure you got the guts and heart for the street track.

'Chris, for the rest of my life I'll be sad when I think of you. I'll have a lump in my throat when I think of what might have been. Take this saw buck, baby, and the best of luck always. Goodbye, Chris. Please split before I get weak and let you be my whore.'

I reached across her and opened the car door. My skull was hitting on all hundred-and-seventy-five cylinders. I was cinching her.

I remembered her name, Christine, on those Terre Haute money orders I'd been sending myself. She was the runt's ghost gadfly come to life.

She pulled the door shut. She hurled herself against me. She held on to me and wailed like maybe I was her dead mama on the way back to the grave after a brief visit.

She blubbered, 'Blood, please don't cut me loose. I'm not a lazy bitch. Give me a chance. I want to amount to something. Please take me with you. I won't let you down. I can hold my own against any bitch.'

I pulled out. I was headed home. I was a fox with a rare, pretty hen in my jib. I knew the runt and Ophelia were in the street. In the trunk I had six dresses I'd copped for Ophelia. I was sure they'd fit Chris.

I said, 'Bitch, I'm gonna gamble on you. I'm taking you to your new pad. You gotta understand one thing. You can't bring in scratch under a bill a night. You do, I may light my cigarettes with it or use it to wipe my ass.

'You're gonna meet and work in the street tonight with your sisters. I'm gonna give you a rundown. Flap your horns and remember it. It will bring you into the family with some stardust on your tail.

'Chris, you're lucky. A whore of mine croaked in Terre Haute just a week ago. Her heart stopped while she was turning a trick. She was a martyr. Her name was Christine. I went up there and blew a coupla grand on her funeral.

'I guess I felt guilty about blowing all that scratch on a broad I'd had for only a coupla months or so. I didn't tell the stable about her death. Maybe I went all out on her funeral because she had your name.

'I just don't know. Anyway, the stable never met her. They sure have a lot of respect for that long scratch she sent me every week from the whorehouse.

'Chris, you're that great humping bitch reborn. A week before she croaked she begged me to turn her loose here in the street. I turned her down because I knew she had a screwy ticker.

'So, Chris, I know you'll prove to the stable you are just as great in the street as you were in the house in Terre Haute. I'm taking you home to get pretty for the trick people, baby-bitch.'

13

The Iceberg

When she saw the pad she flipped. A pink silk dress from the trunk fitted her perfectly. After a bath and a shampoo she was again the gorgeous Chris I'd met at the Haven.

I gave her two go pills and took her to the street for the cut into Phyllis and Ophelia. It was midnight when I curbed in the block where they were working. They were walking together across the street. They looked over at the La Salle.

I blinked my headlights. They crossed the street and came toward me. The runt stuck her head through the window on Chris's side. Ophelia was stooping down, pinning Chris.

I said, 'Both of you get in.'

They got into the back seat. In the rear-view mirror I saw them look at each other, then at the back of Chris's head.

I said, 'Phyllis, Ophelia, meet Christine. She's gonna work the street with you. She's tired of giving up fifty percent of her scratch.

'She wants Daddy to have all she makes. I pulled her outta the whorehouse. What the hell, the whole family should be together anyway.

'Phyllis, I've told Christine a hundred times how great you are in the street. She's hip you know all the rollers and all the angles. I want you to take her under your wing out here for a week or so. I know there ain't a bitch out here that could pull her coat like you can. Now get outta the car and starve these other joker's whores to death.'

I watched them walk away chattering and laughing. It was like they were real sisters. I looked at my diamond-studded Longines. It was ten-after-twelve. How about it? I was twenty years old. I was living in a six-bill a month pad. I had three young fine mud kickers. I was a pimp at last.

I tilted down the rear-view mirror. I powdered my face. I sat there gazing at myself. Finally I pulled off. I was going to

Sweet's to report my progress. I didn't get much of a chance to rap to him.

Two rollers from Sweet's precinct were drinking and horsing around with two of Sweet's yellow whores. Sweet told them I was his son.

It tickled them witless when Sweet told them what Satan and his Demon had done to me. They told me not to worry. They would remember me and would wire the other precinct rollers not to roust me.

The rollers finally got crocked. The whores took them around the Chinese screen into bedrooms.

Then I said, 'Sweet, I copped a beautiful yellow bitch tonight. I got her humping on the track with my girls. Sweet, the bitch is crazy about me. I know I'll hold her for years.'

He said, 'Slim, a pretty Nigger bitch and a white whore are just alike. They both will get in a stable to wreck it. They'll leave the pimp on his ass with no whore. You gotta make 'em hump hard and fast. Stick 'em for long scratch quick. Slim, pimping ain't no game of love. Prat 'em and keep your swipe outta 'em. Any sucker who believes a whore loves him shouldn't a fell outta his mammy's ass.

'Slim, I hope you ain't sexed that pretty bitch yet. Believe me, Slim, a pimp is really a whore who's reversed the game on whores. Slim, be as sweet as the scratch. Don't be no sweeter. Always stick a whore for a bundle before you sex her. A whore ain't nothing but a trick to a pimp. Don't let 'em Georgia you. Always get your money in front just like a whore.

'Whores in a stable are like working chumps in the white man's factory. They know in their sucker tickers they're chumping. They both gotta have horns to blow their beefs into. They gotta have someone to listen while they bad mouth that Goddamn boss.

'A good pimp is like a slick white boss. He don't ever pair two of a kind for long. He don't ever pair two new bitches. He ain't stuck 'em for no long scratch. A pair of new bitches got too much in common. They'll beef to each other and pool their skull, plots, and split to the wind together.

'The real glue that holds any bitch to a pimp is the long

scratch she's hip she's stuck for. A good pimp could cut his swipe off and still pimp his ass off. Pimping ain't no sex game. It's a skull game.

'A pimp with a shaky-bottom woman is like a sucker with a lit firecracker stuck in his ass. When his boss bitch turns sour and blows, all the other bitches in the stable flee to the wind behind her.

'There ain't more than three or four good bottom women promised a pimp in his lifetime. I don't care if he cops three hundred whores before he croaks.

'A good pimp has gotta have like a farm system for bottom women. He's gotta know what bitch in the family could be the bottom bitch when mama bitch goes sour.

'He's gotta keep his game tighter on his bottom bitch than on any bitch in the stable. He's gotta peep around her ass while she's taking a crap. He's gottta know if it's got the same stink and color it had yesterday.

'Slim, you're in trouble until you cop the fourth whore. A stable is sets of teams playing against each other to stuff the pimp's pockets with scratch. You got a odd bitch. You ain't got but a team and a half.

'A young pimp like you is gotta learn not to cop blind. Your fourth bitch is gotta be right to pair with the third whore.

'She can't be no ugly bitch unless she likes pussy. She can't be smarter than the pretty bitch. She can be younger, even prettier, but she's gotta be dumber.

'Slim, all whores have one thing in common just like the chumps humping for the white boss. It thrills 'em when the pimp makes mistakes. They watch and wait for his downfall.

'A pimp is the loneliest bastard on Earth. He's gotta know his whores. He can't let them know him. He's gotta be God all the way.

'The poor sonuvabitch has joined a hate club he can't quit. He can't do a turn around and be a whore himself in the white boss's stable unless he was never a pimp in the first place.

'So, Kid, rest and dress and pimp till you croak. I ain't had no rest in a coupla days. I think I'll try to get some doss.

Kid, these skull aches are getting bad. Good luck, Kid. Call me tomorrow, late.

'Oh yeah, happy birthday, Kid. That rundown was a birthday present.'

My skull was reeling from his rundown on the way home. It was five A.M. when I got there. The runt and Ophelia were asleep. They were locked together like Siamese twins.

I picked up my scratch off the dresser. It was two and a quarter bills.

I went and looked in on Chris. She was in bed reading a book. She looked up and put the book across her belly. She reached under the pillow. She gave me a roll of bills.

I checked it. There was six bits. It wasn't bad for a new bitch who got to the track late. She held out her arms. She was naked. I had to cop her some sleep wear. To avoid her arms I lit a cigarette.

She said, 'Daddy, did I do all right?'

I said, 'Chris, you made a start. It's like the first buck of that million you're gonna make. I oughta frame it like a sucker who's opened a new hot-dog stand.

'I want you to put that book down. Get some doss. I want you to take a fin to Leroy tomorrow. Hip him I'm your man now.

'The family is gonna Cabaret tonight. It's my birthday today. I'll get a rundown of your first night when I wake up. I'm gonna cop you a partner for the street real soon, baby. Good night, Chris.'

When I woke up, it was one P.M. I turned on my side. Two big brown eyes were looking at me. It was Ophelia. She started kissing my eyelids.

She said, 'Daddy, you're so pretty. You got eyelashes just like a bitch's. Phyllis took Chris to visit that sucker in the shit-house. Daddy, can I kiss my candy?'

I said, 'Christ in Heaven, ain't I got a whore in this family without a hot jib. Go on bitch. Then get your kit and trim my toe nails and paint 'em. We're all going to get pretty for my birthday party tonight.'

She said, 'How old are you, Daddy? I bet you're nineteen.'

I said, 'Bitch, I'm a hundred-and-nineteen. I just got a pretty baby face.'

Chris and the runt got back from Leroy around three P.M. Chris had a serious look on her face.

I said, 'Well how did he take the news? Did he hang himself from the bars before your eyes?'

She said, 'Daddy, he fell apart. He would have killed me if he could have reached me. He cried like his heart was broken. He said he was going to kill you wherever he saw you. I feel bad, Daddy. He really upset me. I'm going to lie down.'

I thought, 'That square chump is sure a whingding. I'm gonna put the hurt to him fast if I run into him.'

We partied at a swank white joint near the Gold Coast. We got home at four A.M. I was sober. The whores were stoned. I went and got into my bed. I dozed.

An hour later I woke up. The three whores were crowded into bed with me. They were stroking and kissing me all over.

Mr Thriller sure ached to be a circus performer. I was having trouble convincing Mr Thriller he had to take only one at a time. He was a pimp not a freak.

The ring-master put the show on and stayed cool. It was eight o'clock before I got to sleep.

It was a month before I copped the fourth whore. She was a cute tiny seventeen-year-old broad, about Chris's color. The stable had brought her home from a coffee joint at closing time. They took their breaks there.

The little broad was a waitress in the joint. She was curious about the whore game. She was wild to wear flashy clothes. She thought I was rich when she dug the pad. The excitement in her eyes hipped me I could make a fast cop.

I took her into the living room. I cracked her into saying she'd be my woman and stop slaving for thirty a week.

Then I gave her the pitch to tie the knot. She was sitting in a chair. I stood looking down at her. Her eyes never left my face. It was maybe like a rattle-snake charming a robin.

I said, 'Jo Ann, I gotta congratulate you. You're not only lucky, you're smart. You knew when you saw me that I was going to be your man. I'm hip that you were just waiting to meet me.

'You have wanted since you were a little girl to live an exciting, glamorous life. Well, Sugar, you're on Blood's magic carpet. I'm gonna make your life with me out-shine your flashiest day dreams.

'I'm a pimp. You gotta be a whore. I don't have squares. I'm gonna be your mother, your father, your brother, your friend, and your lover. The most important thing I'm gonna be to you is your man. The manager of the scratch you make in the street. Now, sweet bitch, have you followed me so far?'

She whispered, 'Yes, Blood, I understand.'

I reached down and took her hand. I took her to the window overlooking the city. I held her against me.

I said, 'Look out there, baby angel. Out there is where you work. Those streets are yours because you're my woman. I've got five Gs in fall money. If you get busted for anything, even murder, I can free you. Baby Bitch, this family is like a small army. We got rules and regulations we never break.

'I am really two studs. One of them is sweet and kind to his whores when they don't break the rules. The other one comes out insane and dangerous when the rules are broken. Little baby, I'm sure you'll never meet him.

'Never forget this family is as one against the cold, cruel world. We are strong because we love each other. There's no problem I can't solve. There's no question I can't answer about this game.

'Tomorrow I'm going to start filling your skull with everything about this game and street. I'm going to make a star outta you angel. Don't ask any outsider anything. Come to Chris or me.

'My little baby, I'll protect you with my last drop of blood. If any mother-fucker in those streets out there, stud or bitch, hurts you, or threatens you, come to me. He will have to cut my throat first, shoot me first. I take an oath to protect you for as long as you are my woman. Baby, I know that's for always. Now repeat after Daddy, baby.'

She squeezed tightly against me. She was in a trance looking up at me.

She chanted along with me. 'From this moment I belong to Blood. I am his whore. I will do everything he tells me. I won't ever fuck with his scratch. I will hump my heart out every night. I've gotta make a bill a night.'

She slept with Chris that night. After the first week I knew she was the perfect partner for Chris.

Sweet was right. Chris and Jo Ann ran Phyllis and Ophelia into a panting lather in the street. I started wanting that fifth whore.

Leroy got a year for the beating he gave Papa Tony.

About six months later Top and I were at the Roost bar. A loud-mouth joker beside me was arguing with a stud on his other side. I had my back to him, facing Top.

Top and I had been shooting stuff for several hours in his pad. I was so frosted with cocaine I felt embalmed. It was maybe like I was at the Roost and I really wasn't. I had raised my glass of Coke to my jib. I was being fascinated by the tiny bubbles popping inside the glass.

I was trying to count them before they all popped away.

I heard an explosion behind me. My skull was numb. It was maybe like the noise behind me happened a year ago on an ice floe in the Arctic somewhere.

I saw a light gray lid that stirred a faint memory. It wobbled across the log and stopped in front of where Top had been.

I thought, 'That's a Knox forty. I had one once that color.'

That crazy joker Top was on the floor between the log and his stool. His eyes were wide in fear. He was looking up at me like he thought I had gone bats and was going to croak him. I laughed at him.

I heard running feet behind me. I looked over my shoulder. The joker who had been arguing with Loud Mouth was running through the door with a rod in his hand.

I looked behind me. Loud Mouth was on his back, out cold. He had a long, red gouge across his temple. Some of the frost melted away in my skull.

The bullet that grazed Loud Mouth had torn my lid off.

The joint was still. Top was standing and dusting himself off. The joint had emptied. I reached over and picked my lid off the bar.

I took a casual look at the entrance, exit holes in the top of the crown. I stuck it on my head. Top was staring at me. I tilted my glass and drained it. I turned to Top. Loud Mouth was groaning and coming to on the floor.

I said, 'Jack, let's get outta here before the rollers come. I ain't got time for a quiz. You know Top, if my skull had been pointed, I'da had a bad break.'

Top followed me out the door. We got into his Hog in front of the Roost. Top was still staring at me. His jib was gaping.

He said, 'Kid, I saw it but I don't believe it. I've seen some cool studs in my time, but I ain't never seen nothing to equal that.

'Kid, you were cold in there, icy; icy, like an iceberg. Kid, I got it. You're getting to be a good young pimp. All good pimps got monickers. I'm gonna hang one on you.

'Kid, you've outgrown Young Blood as a monicker. How about Iceberg Slim? Kid, it's a beautiful fit. Iceberg Slim, how about it, and I thought it up. Cocaine sure chills you. I guess you picked the right high for you.'

14

The Mistake

By the end of the year I had copped a new thirty-nine Hog. I had blown Jo Ann ninety days after I got her. She was too possessive and she didn't really have the guts for a long stretch in the street.

I didn't cry when she left. While I had her, Chris kept her humping. I was thousands ahead of her when she slipped away from Chris in the street.

A week later, I copped a young whore that was a whiz in the street and was hip to boosting. She went ape over Chris. She'd go downtown and come home with shopping bags loaded with fine dresses and underclothes for herself and her sisters.

Later she hipped Chris to boosting. I let them go down together with a stud who drove for them. They filled my closet with beautiful vines.

Top got five years on a narcotics rap. The federal heat tricked him into a four-piece sale to an undercover agent. I sure missed him. I hung out at Sweet's more than ever.

My name was ringing. The monicker Top hung on me stuck. Everybody was calling me Iceberg, even Sweet. Only I and the several peddlers I copped from knew that my icy front was really backed by the freezing cocaine I snorted and banged every day.

I pimped strictly by the book for the next three years. I traded in a Hog each year. I never had less than five girls in the family.

I moved out of Top's building and let the family stay there. I took a suite in a swank midtown hotel. I had the privacy, the jewelry, and all the flash and glamour of a successful pimp.

I had managed to solve the fast track. I was fast becoming one of its legends.

Top had gotten out. He was in Seattle with relatives serving out his short parole paper. Only one of his women stuck with him. The rest got in the wind when he fell.

The runt was still bottom woman. Ophelia was still hung up on her. Chris was proving every day she had the qualities for a bottom woman.

I noticed the runt was acting like she might be wearing thin fast. The other two whores I had, had been stable mates. I copped them when their pimp shot an overdose of H.

I was at Sweet's when Pearl Harbor was bombed. I had stayed all night. I was still in bed.

The friendly brown snake had brought my breakfast. I was just finishing when Sweet walked into the bedroom. He sat down on the side of the bed.

He said, 'Berg, Uncle Sam just got his throat cut. The Slant Eyes, just put the torch to Pearl Harbor. Whores gonna make more scratch now than ever before. Berg I got a feeling this Second World War is gonna hurt the pimp game in the long run.'

I said, 'Sweet, how do you figure that?'

He said, 'You know a whore ain't nothing but an ex-square. A good pimp wears out a lot of whores in his lifetime. If there ain't no big pool of squares for the pimps to turn out, then stables gotta get smaller.

'The defense plants are gonna claim thousands of young potential whores. Those square bitches are gonna get those pay checks. They'll get shitty independent. A pimp can't turn them out.

'The older square broads are going into the plants too. Thousands of them got teenage daughters. They'll have the scratch to fill the bellies of those young bitches. They'll put nice clothes on their backs. Why the hell should they whore for a pimp. They can pimp on Mama.

'The worse thing is those plants are inviting whores with strict pimps to split and square up. If the war lasts a long time, pimps will have to turn pussy to hold a whore.

'Berg ain't but one real Heaven for a pimp. He's in it when there's a big pool of raggedy, hungry young bitches.'

The war was raging. The defense plants were grinding out

war goods around the clock. Thousands of young and old broads were slaving in them.

As far as I was concerned, the pool was still full of fine fish. I had three original girls and three new cops.

It was December, nineteen forty-four. Sweet was still pimping good for an old man. He was down to seven women, but this was great pimping for a stud his age. Top had settled out West.

I had held Chris, Ophelia, and the runt a long time. Since 'thirty-eight, I had copped and blown sixty to seventy whores and turnouts.

The turn-over in turnouts was big. Some of them would hump for a month and split. Some a week. Others a couple hours before they cut out. Sweet had been so right years ago. The pimp game was sure cop and blow.

I spent Christmas day with Mama. She was really happy to see me. She hadn't seen me since 'thirty-eight. She cried as always when I left her.

The runt was getting tired and evil. Several of those turn-outs she had run away from me. All new turn-outs I was giving to Chris to polish in the street.

I started sending the runt to small towns near army camps. Some of them were out of state. Sometimes Ophelia went with her. A week before I met Carmen, the runt and Ophelia had come back from a weekend in Wisconsin.

The runt and the other five girls were with me when I copped the seventh girl.

She was almost a perfect copy of the runt at eighteen. She had a prettier face than the runt had at eighteen. Her features were more regular. Time and street had bulldogged the once cute Peke face of the runt.

We were at a cabaret. Carmen was behind a twenty-six game table in the barroom. I left my table and went to the john. I passed Carmen on the way. She gave me a strong lick.

On the way back I stopped and tossed a quarter on her table and rolled the dice trying for a score of twenty-six. I hit twenty-six, so I bought us a drink with the score. I stood beside the table and quizzed her. She was from Peoria. She'd been in town a week.

We had old Party Time in common. She had met him up in Peoria where he was still living. He had a whore in a house up there. She had worked in the same house. She had run off from her pimp and she was wide open for a fast cop.

We rapped for fifteen or twenty minutes. I could tell she went for me. She looked at the clock. It was almost closing time. I invited her to have breakfast at the family's pad.

We'd had breakfast. I was leaving with Carmen. I was going to my place to put her under contract. The runt followed me outside to the hallway. She called me.

I gave Carmen the key to the Hog. She went toward the elevator. I didn't move toward the runt.

I said, 'Bitch, you wanna' rap to me, come to me.'

She had a tight evil look on her face. She walked slowly up to me. Top was right. These bottom broads, when they started to rot really funked up a stud's skull.

She said, 'You ain't thinking about bringing that bull-shit bitch into this family are you? That phony bitch ain't shit.'

I said, 'What the hell. You mean you're gonna turn down a chance to Larceny a new bitch away. You stinking bitch, nobody tells me what bitch to have. You got the nerve to crack some bitch is phony. I had to almost croak you to make you real.'

I noticed two of the latest cops were in the open door. They were eyeballing down the hall at our show.

She shouted, 'Nigger, you were a raggity nowhere scarecrow until you got me. You didn't have no wheels. You muscled me for mine. Nigger, I'm the bitch that made you great. Without me right now, you'd go to the bottom fast as shit through a greasy funnel.'

I made a bad mistake. I shoulda maybe used Top's jellied skull technique to get rid of her. Instead I left-hooked her hard as I could against the jaw. There was a pop like a firecracker going off. She fell to the carpet in a quiet heap. I kicked her big rear end a dozen times. I walked to the elevator. I looked down the hall. I saw Ophelia and Chris dragging her toward the apartment.

The runt got her broken jaw wired up. She split with Ophelia. Chris said she tried to take two of the newer girls with her too. I had made a pimp's classic blunder. I had blown a tired bottom bitch in the rough.

Carmen was an easy cop. A pimp wants everybody who can hump his pockets fat. He's in real clover when he cops a fine young whore who wants him. Carmen really wanted me. She was starting with Chris.

Six months later Sweet called me early in the morning. His voice was laced with excitement. I jerked erect in bed.

He said, 'Berg, I got a wire the FBI is nosing around some of the broad lock-ups. They're quizzing whores. Your name has been cracked more than once. It looks like they already got a solid beef to go on. It's my guess they're trying to build a five or six count rap against you.'

I said, 'Sweet, I bet it's that stinking runt. Christ! Sweet, I've sent her and Ophelia across state lines a dozen times since the war started. They're trying to ram a white-slave rap into me, Sweet. What would you do?'

He said, 'I would give one of those nice sweet jokers on the West Side expense scratch and a ball-peen hammer. I'd tell him as soon as I read they was found in an alley with their skulls caved in he could get a cinch two grand.

'It would be easy to trap 'em. They're whores. He'd be just another freakish trick wanting to party with two whores.

'Tell you what, Berg, get them whores outta that crib over there fast. Move outta your pad today. Go groundhog. Switch your whores to new stomping grounds. Stay outta the street after you move. Call me when you get outta there.'

He hung up. I thought, 'I'm a sucker. I shoulda destroyed the runt Top's way.'

I had moved the stable and myself to new pads by seven that night. Chris, my new bottom woman was the only one in the family who knew the reason for the move.

I took the Hog and put it in a garage I rented from an old

widower. The garage was behind his house in a respectable neighborhood.

I got a cab to one of my stuff connections. I was going underground. I had to have at least a piece of stuff. I had copped and was walking down the street looking for a cab.

I passed a barber shop. I got a glimpse of the white-spatted dogs of a joker in the barber's chair, next to the window.

I thought, 'Geez. that square joker is pitiful. He ain't hip. Spats went out with high-button shoes.'

I was walking fast. I had the sizzle on me. I needed a cab in the worse way. I was almost a half block from the barber shop. I thought I heard some joker yelling, 'Run! Run!'

I looked back over my shoulder. A tall skinny stud in a barber's apron was on the sidewalk. His white spats flashed on his feet. He was screaming and flailing his arms like a minstrel clown singing 'Mammy.'

He was loping down the sidewalk. The out-of-fashion bastard was yelping, Son! Son!' He galloped by the neon lights toward me. His wrinkled brown-skin face changed colors like a chameleon.

He ran into me and clutched me like I was a winning sweepstakes ticket. He was panting and sweating like a whore on soldier's payday. I could smell witch hazel and the stink of emotion sweat. I saw white specks of barber's talc on the bald crown of his head. I couldn't see his face. He had it buried in my chest.

He was blubbering, 'Oh son, precious son. Sweet Jesus answered an old man's prayer. He's let me see and hold my one and only son before I got to my heavenly rest.'

I had the damnedest thought while he made love to me. I wondered if my skull had chipped any paint off that wall he threw me against when I was six-months old.

I stiff-armed him away. I stared coldly into his face. I saw a weak blaze of anger light his dull brown eyes.

He said, 'God, don't like ugly, son. You saw your father back there. You ignored me, didn't you?'

I said, 'Shit no I didn't see you. I thought you had croaked.

Look Jack, I'm happy to see you, but I'm in an awful hurry. See you around.'

He said, 'I did my part to bring you into this world. You ain't gonna treat me like a dog. Where do you live? You look prosperous. What's your line? Are you with some big company? Are you married to some nice girl? Do I have any grandchildren, son?'

I said, 'You haven't heard about Iceberg Slim? He's famous.'

He said, 'You don't associate with black filth like that I hope.'

I said, 'Look Jack, I *am* Iceberg. Ain't you proud of me? I'm the greatest Nigger that ever came outta our family. I got five whores humping sparks outta their asses.'

I thought he was going to have a heart attack. The apron was quivering over his ticker. He was supporting himself against a lamp post. His face was gray in shock under the street light. I jerked my shirt and coat sleeves up past spike hollow. I stuck the needle-scarred arm under his nose. He drew back from it.

I said, 'God damnit Jack, what's the matter. Shit I shoot more scratch into that arm a day than you make in a week. I've come a long way since you bounced my skull off that wall. Stick your chest out in pride, Jack. I been in two prisons already. Shit, Jack, I'm on my way to the third any day now. You ain't hip I'm important? Maybe one of these days I'll really make you a proud father. I'll croak a whore and make the Chair.'

I walked away from him. I caught a cab at the corner. The cabbie u-turned. I looked at my old man. He was sitting on the curb beside the lamp post. His white spats gleamed starkly in the gutter. He had his head on his knees. I saw his back jerking up and down. The poor joker was bawling his ass off.

I got home. I called Sweet. I banged a load of cocaine. It was the best I'd copped since Glass Top went to the joint.

15

In a Sewer

After I had called Sweet and banged the cocaine, I had chilling thoughts.

'I've got five whores just like poor Preston had when Sweet crossed and destroyed him. I wonder if Sweet will dream up a cross to steal my whores from me? He knows where I'm padding. It would be as easy as lifting a telephone receiver. Sweet swears he loves me like I'm his son.

'These seven years on this fast track have hipped me to one solid truth. To a pimp there's nothing more important than copping whores. While I'm holed up, I'll keep my stable headaches a secret. I won't give him a cue to volunteer his help. It would be a bitch to have him handling my stable. I'm sure glad Chris is a boss bottom bitch.

'Oh! this pressure is really screwing my skull around. Sweet wouldn't cross me. I gotta stop mistrusting the only friend I got. I mean more to Sweet as his friend than any whore.

'Maybe I should make a run for it and set up shop in some other city. Christ! Why do I have to be red hot with Federal heat? Why couldn't it be city or state heat? On this fast track I've only been busted and mugged once. A dozen other times I paid off on the street.

'That FBI is a sonuvabitching genius. No, I'd better keep my hot ass in town right here in this cruddy pig sty.

'The runt's a whore. Maybe her new pimp or a trick will croak her. Then I could walk into the FBI office and stick my black ass out to be kissed. They'd have no case without the runt as a witness.'

'The runt took Ophelia on all those out-of-state trips. I gave the runt instructions and expense money. I ain't never told Ophelia to cross a state line. The runt was screwing Ophelia. That was really the runt's bitch.'

'It's a good thing I holed up in this rat's nest. The FBI would never look for a good pimp in a sewer.'

It was December, nineteen forty-five. The war was over. The world was licking its bloody wounds. Drugs and the pimp game had hardened away my baby face. My hair was thinning. I was turning twenty-eight but I looked forty.

For seven years I had devoted myself to getting hip to that pimp's book. I had labored with the zeal of a Catholic Brother agonizing for the Priesthood. I had thought and acted like a black God.

I was now trapped in my dingy one-room kitchenette. It was in a very old two-story building. I was on the first floor in the rear in number ten. Down the hall at night, rats would come scampering and squealing from the alley. They came under the back door which hung crookedly on its hinges.

I had a vague disturbing doubt in my skull. Was it possible I wasn't even a poor imitation of a God? Maybe I was just a sucker black pimp on his way to a third bit in the joint.

Chris was the only one of the stable that visited me. We'd bang cocaine together. I wouldn't let her know how worried I was. God couldn't have skull aches.

I couldn't let the others see me in a crummy setting. After all how could a God live like a square chump? Chris knew all the reasons why. To her God's farts still had the fragrant odor of roses. I worked out with Chris a smooth system. Even the best pimp has to keep some personal contact with his whores.

The system was simple and for a while effective. Chris and I would go out into the hall to the phone on the wall. She could call the stable at their pad. It would always be three or four o'clock in the morning.

One of the girls would pick up. Chris would pretend to be a long-distance operator. It was rare luck that Chris had a talent for mimicry. They didn't get hip to it. It would always be a person-to-person call from me to one of them. Chris and I conned them the calls came from New York, Boston, and Philadelphia.

I would get on the line and talk to all four of them. There

were extensions in all four bedrooms. I could con and tighten my game on all of them at the same time.

The first call we made was supposed to be from New York. It took maybe a minute for me to have all their horns to receivers.

I said, 'Well girls, I know you've missed Daddy. You've all probably wondered, when in the hell is Daddy coming back to town? Jesus Christ! Has he forgotten a whore needs to see her man some time? Sure we're in his corner. We prove that when we hump our asses off in the street. We check our scratch into Chris to send to him.

'Goddamnit, what could be so important that he neglects his whores? Well girls, I'm gonna show the kinda confidence Daddy's got in you. I'm gonna hip you to a million-dollar secret. I know all of you will keep your jibs buttoned.'

Chris cut in crisply and said, 'Three minutes are up, Sir. Please signal when through.'

I continued, 'You are the luckiest whores alive. Your man's got a genius white engraver for his pal. He used to be an engraver for the government. We've got some plates he's just finished. We've turned out three-hundred of the prettiest hundred-slat bills the human eye has ever seen. They're perfect. Even the government couldn't get hip to a difference from real scratch. There ain't any.

'We got one problem we're gonna solve if it takes a year. We've run outta the special paper the government prints it's scratch on. My white genius pal even knows how to make the paper. We are playing it cool and traveling and copping inks and other stuff we need. It's tough to cop some of it, but for millions who's going to give up? As soon as we get the paper made up we're gonna run off a coupla-million or so slats.

'I'm gonna breeze back into town the only millionaire pimp in the world. I'm gonna buy a beach and a mansion in Hawaii for my stable. If we run outta scratch, we'll just run off another bale.

'So stay cool and keep humping. Oh yeah, Chris got a cab to the airport an hour ago. She should be getting home in a coupla hours or so. She's bringing each of you a piece of that beautiful lettuce. Spend it on anything you want. Take it anywhere, even a bank. Believe me, it's perfect.'

I hung up. I had electrified them with the story. I could hear the excited thrill in their voices when they chorused goodbye. I told Chris to crack the genius had a way to make all the serial numbers on the bills different. I already knew what my story would be whenever I got the heat off me.

I could stall them a lifetime. I could say the genius got busted on another beef. I had to wait until he got out. He wouldn't tell me where the plates were hidden. He could even croak while doing his bit.

Chris called the next day. The whores were walking on air. They rapped all night about that perfect queer. I was sure I had found the way to hold my stable. I felt like a genius myself.

Each time I talked to the stable after that, the genius and I had just copped another vital item we needed. It wouldn't be long now I assured them. Sweet had dropped the word in the street that I was on the West Coast taking off long scratch from a rich square broad.

It was getting almost impossible to sleep. I would almost jump from my skin when a tenant would knock. I would think it was the heat. The tenant would be calling me to the phone in the hall. When I did fall off into fitful sleep I'd have nightmares. Those dreams about Mama would hog-tie me on a sweaty rack of misery. I had an awful fear of another jolt in the joint. The guilty daydreams on the heels of the nightmares were torturing my skull.

I stopped banging cocaine. It only magnified my terror and worry. I remembered how serene Top used to look after a bang of H. He'd sit and coast like he was in a beautiful peaceful dream. Maybe he'd been right. Maybe sable H came after mink cocaine.

Chris came on Christmas Eve. She stayed until Christmas Day afternoon. She brought me pajamas, cologne and robes from herself and the girls. She had given them scratch from me.

My one-room kitchenette hideout was crammed wall to wall

with trunks and suitcases. I had all those fine threads and no place to go. I was a lonely pimp bastard!

Sweet came to see me at midnight in January, the tenth I think. He took off his velvet-collared Melton benny. He hung it in the tiny closet. It had been ten below zero or colder for a week.

It was a brand new year, nineteen forty-six. The new Hogs were out for the first time in several years. The garage rent was paid for a year for my old Hog. Chris had gone out several times to run its engine for a while.

I thought, 'Christ, it would be a kick to trade off and flash through the fresh air in a new Hog.'

It was the first time Sweet had visited me. He was getting white around his temples. There was less fiery voltage in his gray eyes. That H and the fast track had him looking terrible. He was getting old all right. He sat down on a suitcase at the head of the bed. I was lying down. Miss Peaches was an old lady, but still gorgeous in her mink coat and fur bootees. He slipped off her coat and shoes. He put them on the dresser. She sat on the floor looking up at me.

He said, 'Berg, I got bad news for you. The street wire says city rollers are carrying a mug shot of you around. You're really hot now. I gotta wire that pimping Poison is nosing around your girls in the street. If you ain't got Chris tight, he'll steal her. She's gonna hip him where you're hiding.

'Maybe you oughta get outta this joint tonight. Take another hide out. Don't let Chris or any whore you got know where you are. I'm your bosom buddy, sweetheart, and I love you. I'll keep the stable in line for you.

'In the meantime I could figure an angle to get your balls outta the hot sand. All you gotta do is call your girls. Tell 'em you want Uncle Sweet to look out for 'em for a coupla weeks. It's easy, Pal.'

I just lay there for a long moment feeling myself tremble. If he had been lovable Henry, my stepfather, saying he hated me, I couldn't have felt worse. True, I had conquered the fast track, but that sucker inside me I couldn't kill was hurting the hell out of me. I looked at him. Somehow I kept my voice steady and the pain outta my eyes.

I said, 'Jeez Sweet, I'd have a bitch of a time trying to cop another friend like you. I feel like bawling just to think about it. I ran down my life story to you. You know I love you like I loved Henry. Maybe I love you, Sweet, more than I love Mama.

'Don't think I'm a chump square when I say it. Sweet, you taught me to be cold-hearted. You're the only person on Earth who could hurt me. The jokers in the street call me Iceberg.'

'They'd laugh their asses off if they knew I was weak for a stud I love like a father. Sweet please don't hip them I got a sucker weakness. Don't ever do anything to croak my love for you. Sweet, if you ever do, they'll all get hip.

'I'll maybe fall apart and run through the streets wailing like a crazy bitch. Sweet, I'll wait and think for a day or so. Poison can't steal Chris. I'll kick things around in my skull. Maybe you should be looking out for the stable.'

The whole time I was talking, he had run his index fingers along the sword edges of his pant's creases. His gray eyes had found the suitcases and cluttered room fascinating works of art. He swallowed air and tented his bejeweled fingers under his first chin.

He said, 'Berg, this joint is wrecking your skull. Sweet would chop his right arm off before he'd cross you. You're the only friend I got, sweetheart. Shit, Honey, you could have a hundred whores and I could be whoreless. I'd ask you to give me a bitch. I wouldn't try to steal no whore from you, Darling. You need anything? I gotta split. I got two whores I gotta pick up downtown.'

I said, 'No Sweet, I don't need anything. I'll rap to you tomorrow. If you hear anything, wire me fast. I'm sure glad you dropped by.'

I heard his heavy feet pounding down the linoleum in the hall. They stopped. I heard them getting louder. He was coming back. I looked around the suitcase where he had been sitting. I didn't see anything he had left. He thumped the door. I opened it. He had Miss Peaches in his arms. He was flashing the first gold toothed grin I'd ever seen on his face.

He said, 'Berg, I forgot to tell you. They found old Pretty Preston frozen stiff in the alley back of the Roost. The poor bastard had wrapped himself in newspapers. The Greek fired him a week ago for staying near the fire and not pulling marks on the sidewalk. The drunk half-white bastard thought the newspapers could stand off ten below zero.'

He turned and walked down the hall. I shut the door and fell across the bed. At three Chris called. I told her to stay away until my next phony long-distance call to the girls. I told her Poison might try to tail her, and maybe the FBI.

She told me they didn't have a chance. She went in front doors of a half-dozen buildings then out the back doors before she came to me. When she got to my place she'd come in the back door and walk through the front door. She'd go through the alley then through the back door again before she came to my door.

Maybe they couldn't keep a tail on her. I told her to stay away to play safe. I told her not to call from the pad. It would be a bitch if one of the girls picked up an extension.

Sweet called the next morning at one A.M. The broad next door answered the phone. She knocked on my door. I slipped on an overcoat and walked into the hall. It felt like zero out there.

He said, 'Berg, I just got the wire. Poison stole your young bitch, Fay. I hope she ain't hip to anything that can cross you. Berg, you gotta make some moves. I'll keep my horns to the wire.'

He hung up. I was in trouble. I went and got back in bed.

I thought, Poison's gonna quiz that stinking bitch. She's gonna spill that queer scratch con I've been playing. To tighten his game on her he's gonna wake her to the con. He's gonna tell her I'm hiding out in the city.

'It's a good thing Chris is in on the con. I could blow whoreless in an hour if she wasn't. I need her to take the rest of the stable underground. Maybe I shoulda split outta town when I first got hot. I gotta move the rest of the stable fast.

'Poison is a cinch to pull their coats to the con I played. It's the ace to play for a fast cop of maybe the other three. They'll be salty as hell with me if he gets a chance to wake 'em up. Hurry Chris and call!'

At three Chris called. I ran to the phone in my pajamas. I almost froze to death talking to her.

She said, 'Daddy, I had to call you from home. Poison just left with Fay and her clothes. The black bastard has wised up the whole family to that game we played. Dot, Rose, and Penny are larcenied to the gills. They're crying and packing their clothes. I can't hold them. They hate me. Poison came into my bedroom before he split. He acted and rapped like I was already his whore. If I'd had a pistol I'd have croaked the strong bastard.

'He said, "Well Miss Bitch, your Nigger is finished. You're the only whore he's got left. I know a fast pretty bitch like you don't want no pimp you gotta solo for. With my Fay cop, I got eight whores. I'm on the inside of this game. None of my whores take falls. I'm top pimp in town.

"You're the best whore in town. There ain't nobody but me you can take for your man. Bitch, come to me and you can be queen boss bitch of the eight-whore stable. Get your clothes and get outta here with me and Fay. Iceberg is going to the Federal joint."

She said, 'Daddy, what happens now. Maybe Poison will come back and gorilla me. I'm so upset, I know any minute I'll scream myself into a padded cell.'

The zero drafts blasting through the gap under the back door kept me from passing out. I felt cold sweat dripping down my shaking legs. My throat was having dry convulsions. My voice sounded like it came from an echo chamber.

I stammered, 'Chris, don't lose your cool. This is Iceberg remember? Like always I'll put an angle together. Now listen carefully. Pack your things. Go down and get the building flunky. Pay him to take you to a hotel near the garage where the Hog is stashed.

'Check in and leave your things. Go to the Hog. Drive back and pick up your stuff. Go downtown and check into a hotel. Drive the Hog back and stash it back in the garage. Take an El train back to your hotel. Call me then.'

I went back and washed my face in cold water. I looked in the mirror. I looked like I had on a Halloween fright mask. I sure didn't look a bit like a fresh-faced kid any more. The whites of my once-bright eyes were blood-shot and faded. The deep black circles looked like some tricky practical joker had conned me to ram inked spyglasses against the sockets.

I started looking for a yellow. I had to put a damper on my nerves. I had a little cocaine. I didn't need racing. I needed some skull pacifying. I was out of yellows.

Somewhere in one of the suitcases I had a notebook. The phone number of a connection no farther than fifteen blocks away was in it. Maybe he had yellows. If not, what the hell, I'd cop a cap of H. One cap couldn't hook me. Horse was a cinch to kick the jitters outta my skull.

It would be two hours at least before Chris would call back. I found his number. I called him. I told him, in code, I'd pick up six caps within the hour.

I had a fat roll of scratch in a sock pinned inside the sleeve of a trench coat. I started to take it with me. I stuck it in my benny pocket. It bulged like a grapefruit. I'd be back before long. I pinned it back inside the sleeve.

I had close to sixty-eight hundred slats stashed there. I fished out three saw bucks. I slipped pants and a shirt over my pajamas. I put on shoes and a heavy benny.

I was in a helluva hurry. I pulled the door shut. I heard the spring-latch lock. Less than five minutes after I had talked to the peddler, I was on the way. It was four A.M. when I left. The wintry winds almost snatched my lid off my skull. It felt good though. It was the first time I'd walked in the fresh air for months.

A bleak overcast blotting out the sky. Slipping and sliding on the icy sidewalks, I finally got to the connection. He lived on the second floor over an all-night chili joint. The joint was crowded. There was no one on the sidewalk. I went up the rickety stairs and copped five caps of H. He put the caps into the cellophane shell from a cigarette pack. He twisted the end and balled the package.

I took it and went down the stairs to the street. I had the

sizzle in my hand. I started to walk by the chili spot on my way home. Two neatly dressed brown skin studs were standing on the sidewalk in front of the joint. Its bright lights floodlighted the sidewalk. It was like walking a show-up stage at a police station.

From the side vent in my eye I saw them pinning me. They stiffened. One of them reached toward his chest. I looked back. He was showing his buddy a small square of paper. I started walking fast away from them.

I remembered the sizzle. I downed it and walked faster. I knew they couldn't see in the darkness that I had dropped it. I glanced over my shoulder. I saw a rod in the hand of the taller one as they ran toward me. I ran.

They were bellowing, 'Halt! Police! Halt! Stop or we'll shoot!'

I had reached the corner and was halfway around it. I saw a four-man squad of white detectives. They were cruising toward me in a police car. They threw a blinding spotlight on me. I froze. They all looked at me. I saw a shotgun muzzle ease out of a fast-lowering rear side window.

The two rollers chasing me skidded around the corner. In a way I was glad to see them. Those rollers in the cruiser probably hadn't croaked anybody in a week. I really didn't want them to break their luck on me.

The two held on to me like I was Sutton. The white rollers shut off the spotlight and moved slowly down the street past us. The shorter one had handcuffed my hands behind me. He showed his buddy the picture. They looked up at me.

The taller one said, 'Yeah, it's the bastard all right. Look at the eyes.'

They searched me head to toe. They saw the lone saw buck I had. They hustled me back around the corner. We passed a skinny black joker standing on the corner. He nodded at me. I recognized him. He was in my building. I had sent him for groceries and change for the phone a dozen times.

I got a fast glimpse of the picture as the roller slipped it back inside his coat pocket. It was me. I remembered the pearl-gray sharkskin suit and black shirt. Top and I had been together four years ago. The two white rollers who had hit on us hated Top because he had white whores. They wouldn't take a pay off. They booked us on suspicion of homicide and mugged us. Top and I were out in less than two hours. It was the one and only time I had been taken in on the fast track.

They put me into the rear seat of an unmarked Chevy. They were in the front seat as the tall one drove away.

I said, 'Gentlemen, it's not gonna put any scratch in your mitts to take me in. Let me give you the price of a couple fine vines to cut me loose.'

Slim said, 'Shit, you couldn't cop one bullshit vine in a hock shop with the scratch you're carrying.'

I said, 'I got more scratch at my pad. Knowing I'm Iceberg you can believe that can't you? Just run me by there, I'll get it, lay a coupla Cs apiece on you and fade away. How about it?'

Slim and Shorty looked at each other.

Shorty said, 'You think we're suckers? You got a Federal Warrant for white slavery outstanding. We didn't hear a word you said about that chicken shit four Cs.'

I said, 'All right, so we're all like black brothers. The bad difference is the FBI wants to lynch your brother in court. You gonna throw me to the white folks for hanging? I'll give you two grand apiece to beat the FBI outta their pound of black meat.'

Slim said. 'Where's your pad?'

I thought fast. It had been a mistake to crack about my pad. If I told them they could take my whole stash and still bust me or croak me. I was a fugitive. They might even come back to the stash after they took me in. I had the key to the kitchenette in my pocket. I tested them.

I said, 'You know Sweet Jones. He's a friend of mine. I can get four Gs from him five minutes after we get to his place. I can't take you to my pad. I got a close friend there. Suppose after we got there you'd change your minds about the deal. You'd have to book him for harboring me.'

Slim said, 'We can't cut you loose. We couldn't do it if you gave us forty Gs. I just remembered you were in that spotlight back there. One of those downtown men could have made you. Sorry brother, but what the hell? Federal joints ain't bad to pull a bit in. Thanks for popping up like you did. You make a great pinch for us.'

16

Away from the Track

They locked me up in central jail. At dawn a jail trusty brought a basket of bologna sandwiches down the line of cells. A moment later another trusty brought a gigantic kettle of black stinking chicory. I passed up the delicacies.

The tiny cell was too small for two men. Eight of us were in it. I was lying on the concrete floor. I was using my rolled up benny as a pillow. My lid shielded my eyes from the bright bare bulb in the corridor.

My cellmates were bums and junkies. Two of them were getting sick. They were puking all over. The bums were stinking almost as bad as the junkies. A drunk lying beside me dug his fingernails into his scalp and crotch over and over. He scratched his back against the floor. He had to be lousy. It was rough going for a pimp all right.

I thought, 'If someone had told me a year ago I'd be back in a shit-house I'd have thought he was nuts. Christ! I hope nothing happens to Chris. She's the only link to the outside I can trust to get my clothes and scratch.

'I know after she calls and can't get me at the pad she'll check out all the shit-houses. It's a good thing I'm not in the Federal lockup at County Jail. Here she can grease a mitt and see me. I hope she makes it before the U. S. Marshal shows to move me.'

At nine the turnkey came and called out my name. I went to the cell door. He looked hard at me through the bars. He twisted the cell-lock open. I stepped out into the corridor and followed him.

He took me to a break-proof glass window with a speaking hole in it. I saw Chris on the other side of it. She was crying. I couldn't blame her. I felt like crying with her. I bent down and put my mouth to the hole. She stuck an ear against it on her side.

I said, 'Baby, there's nothing to cry about. You're Daddy's brave bitch, remember? Now listen. I want you to give the copper at the property desk a double saw or so for the key to my pad.

'I want you to get my scratch outta the sleeve of my green trench coat. Rent a safe-deposit box. Then move my stuff to your hotel. The Feds are gonna take me back to Wisconsin. They call it the point of origin for the runt's beef.

'They'll set a bond for me there. I'll get a slick lip in Wisconsin. Baby, you keep checking. Get to Wisconsin a day before I do with the scratch. I'll need it for the lip and bail, understand Sugar? Once I get bail, I'll get our stable back and beat this rap.'

I took my jib from the hole and put my horn there.

She said, 'Daddy, I'll do everything the way you say. I understand. Daddy, I'll go and get the key to your latest hideout. Where did you move? I thought you were going to wait for my call?'

It didn't register. Maybe I was cracking up under all the strain and grief. Maybe I had moved before I got busted. I raised my head and looked at her. Her eyes were questioning. I pointed my index finger at the hole. I decided to risk my theory that I hadn't moved.

I said, 'Chris, Goddamnit! I haven't moved! All my stuff is still on West Ave. Now come on, girl, this is not the time for jokes from Daddy's witty bitch. You knocked on the door, I wasn't there. Naturally, I couldn't be, I was down here.'

She said, 'Daddy, I didn't have to knock. The door was wide open. Both trunks and all the suitcases were gone. In fact the only thing left was your hair brush. I put it in my purse. Daddy, all this is too much for me. I must be losing my mind.'

I stood there glaring hate at her. Her eyes were wide, staring at me.

I thought, 'Poison or Sweet has stolen this Judas-bitch from me. I'm in a cross. One of them has rehearsed this bitch. She's a sonuvabitching actress. A sucker looking at that innocent look she's got would have to buy the con. I hate this bitch worse than I do the runt. If I could just get my hands around her throat. I'd love to see her tongue turned black, flopping across her chin.

'Well, I can't croak her through that glass wall. No matter what. I've gotta stay Iceberg, I can't let her take back a chump emotional scene to report. She and her new man are not gonna get their kicks at my expense.'

I turned and walked away from her. I saw the turnkey at the far end of the corridor with his back to me. Good thing for me he hadn't been close enough to lock me back in the cell right away. I was twenty feet from her when it exploded in my skull.

I thought, 'It's the skinny flunky! It's the skinny flunky! It's the bastard that saw me get busted! He rushed back and sprang that spring latch. I gotta go back to Chris and really play some game. If she gets hip I don't trust her she'll blow for sure. She's the only stick I got to fight with.'

I turned back toward her. She was still standing there. She was crying harder than before. I walked to the glass and spoke into the hole.

I said, 'Chris, a joker in the building saw me get busted. He cleaned me out. Baby, we've been so close. I had a crazy thought that if you'd been there I wouldn't have been robbed. What the hell, Sugar, I'm the bastard that kept you away. It wasn't your fault at all.

'Christ! I'll be glad when this is over. Give a lip here in town a half a yard or so. Have him come to County Jail and bring me whatever papers are needed to sell the Hog. Get the slip on the Hog from the property desk. It's in my wallet. We should get twenty-five hundred or so for it. Bring that scratch and all you can hump up on to Wisconsin.'

They moved me to Wisconsin. Chris came to County Jail there and put three-thousand dollars in my jail account.

Mama came to see me. She was in pieces. She thought the Government was going to give me fifty years.

At my hearing bail was set at twenty thousand. A bondsman put up the face amount. His fee was two Gs. I got the state's best criminal lip. I gave him a G retainer.

Chris and I went back to the track. I stayed out on bail four months. I had two turn-outs and three seasoned whores during that time. None stayed longer than a month.

Everybody in the street knew about that rap over my head. I guess the whores didn't want to fatten a frog for snakes. Sweet and I didn't see much of each other. I didn't feel close to him any more. I was a pimp on the skids. Poison was top pimp.

Every slat I got my hands on I wired to the lip. I had to. I was getting one continuance after another. Finally I went to trial. The runt and Ophelia were there. They were afraid to look at me. They gave the Government a penitentiary case all right.

They grinned at each other when I got eighteen months. Mama fainted. Chris boo-hooed. I had a good lip though. With the counts against me I could have gotten ten years. Chris went back to the track. She swore she'd stick until I got out.

Leavenworth was what the government called a class-A joint. It was big and escape-proof. It was run by master psychologists. There was no screw brutality. It wasn't necessary. The invisible mental shackles were subtle but harder than the steel bars. Alcatraz was the grim trump the officials held over our heads.

It was a joint of con cliques. The most dangerous clique was the Southern cons. They hated Negroes!

I had references as a cell-house orderly from other joints. I got a spot in a cell house with mostly pimps, dope dealers and stick-up men.

I was out at night until ten exchanging newspapers and magazines for the cons. I'd been in the joint about six months. I stopped in front of a cell to rap to a pimp pal. He was excited and standing gripping the bars of his cell door. He was a yellow version of Top. They called him Doll Baby.

He said, 'Berg, you told me I couldn't steal the beautiful bitch. Well, the bitch sent me a kite this morning. She's transferring to the shoe shop. I already got the spot picked out where I can sock it into her.

'I told you that square-ass peckerwood she's got couldn't out-play me. The bitch is got four bills on the books. She's getting me a big order on commissary this week. Shit, on the street or in the joint it's all the same to pimping Doll Baby.'

I had seen the beautiful bitch. He was a lanky white boy with watery blue eyes and bleached corn-silk hair. A fat red-faced Southern con was madly in love with him. The beautiful bitch would lie in the fat con's arms in the yard and pick at the pimples on his face. The con was feared by everyone. He was the leader of a treacherous band of Southern cons.

I said, 'Doll, you better cut that bitch loose. Her old man is from Mississippi. He's a cinch to cut your heart out in that yard. He can't let a Nigger steal his broad. Take my advice, pal. I like you. You've only a year to go.'

The next time on the yard I saw Doll and his bitch billing and cooing on the grass. They didn't see any of the ball game. The game was over. The fat con and his band of Southern shiv men had been evil eyeing Doll's show. I was fifty yards back of Doll when it happened.

Hundreds of cons were pressed together filing from the bleachers and playing field. I saw Doll throw up his hands and scream. He disappeared. The gray tide moved on. Three screws were standing over him. He was on his back. Blood was gushing from his open mouth. Blood seeped from holes in his jacket.

He lived, but he had a bitch of a time making it. He stayed bitchless for the rest of his bit.

Chris stopped sending me scratch or anything. I got a wire she'd squared up and married a pullman porter. She even had a baby. I wondered if the sucker knew what a boss bitch he had.

I was filing out to sick call one morning. A group of cons on the other side of the road was filing to work. I saw a con marching behind a dark-complexioned con raise something that glinted in the sun. It was a shiv. He was chopping away at the con. Finally the con folded dead. Screws rushed up and took the hatchet man away.

I was two months from release. I had stopped to rap to an old con forger who knew Sweet. We were shooting the breeze about stick-up men and how they stacked up in the skull department with pimps and con men. We were rapping loud. I knew the night screw was at his desk four tiers down on the ground floor.

I said, 'Pops, a stick-up man is gotta be nuts. The stupid bastard maybe passes a grocery store. He sees the owner checking his till. Right away a stupid idea flashes inside his crazy skull. "That's my scratch."

'The screwy heist man walks in. Maybe the grocer is a magician or an ex-acrobat with a degree in Karate, worse an ex-marine. The silly sonuvabitch doesn't realize the awful odds. He ain't got enough in his dim skull to think about the trillion human elements. Any one of them can put him in his grave. The suicidal sonuvabitch maybe has his back to the street with his rod in his mitt. Pops, the stick-up man is champ lunatic in the underworld.'

Pops agreed and I walked away down the tier. I heard a hiss from the cell next to Pops. A new transfer was standing at his cell door. He was skinny with a rat face. I stopped. He was sneering at me. His hands were trying to crush the rolled-steel bars.

He stuttered, 'You you lousy pim-pim-pimp mother-fucker. You you pu-pu-pussy-eating sonuvabitch. You you ain't going to live your bit out.'

I went fast to get a rundown on the nut from a stud on the tier below.

He said, 'Ah, Berg, I hope you haven't crossed that dizzy bastard. He croaked a stud in Lewisburg. They hung fifty on him. He's a heist man. You better watch him close. He's a cinch to make the Rock or loony bin.'

It was a week later just after the cell house filed out to the shops. The cell-house screw had signalled sick call. I was standing in the back of the cell house on the flag. I was lighting a cigarette to smoke before I started mopping and waxing the flag.

Somewhere above me an excited voice shouted, 'Look out, Berg.'

I looked up and chilled. A plummeting shadow flashed like black lightning in my eyes. I heard a whooshing whistle as it scraped gently against the cloth of my shirt at the tip of my shoulder. A dozen cymbals clashed as it grenaded against the flagstone at my side. I looked down. A steel mop wringer lay in three pieces. There was a Rorschach crater in the flagstone. It's outline was like a head-shrinker's blot.

I stared at it and idly wondered what the prison head-shrinker could make of it. He was a slick joker. Months ago he had told me, 'Pimps have deep mother hatred and severe guilt feelings.'

I looked up. It wouldn't take a head-shrinker to figure this one. The rat-faced heist man was grinning down at me. He was on his gallery on the fourth tier near the ceiling. He had stayed for sick call to bomb my skull off. The crater symbol was easy. Rat-face hated pimps without guilt feelings tied in. That night I took a pack of butts to the con who had screamed out the warning to me.

The nutty bomber went to solitary. Two weeks later he tried to gut a con with a shiv made from a file. They shipped him to the Rock. I was ecstatic to see him go.

During my bit I had read the second cell-house full of books. I had read mountains of books on psychiatry, psychology, and the psychoneuroses. I couldn't have done a smarter thing. I'd have to be my own head-shrinker when the white folks entombed me for a year in that steel casket in the future.

I got all my good time. I was released in the early spring of nineteen forty-seven. I stopped off at Mama's for a week. Then I went back to the fast track.

I had sixty slats and the joint vine on my back. The clothes I'd bought while on bail were with Chris. Maybe her pullman porter was my size. Anyway, I wasn't going to do a Dick Tracy for a few used vines.

Sweet was still in the penthouse. He had blown down to only three whores. Poison had made a bad pimping blunder. He had turned out a white square and put his foot in her ass. It was the last straw for the downtown brass. They bounced him off the force. He had one whore. He bird-dogged her. He took his scratch off after every trick like a Chili Pimp.

I rented a pad by the week. It was in the same slum district where the flunky had beat me for my roll and clothes. I had no flash and glamour, no pimp front. I was just another pimp down on his luck. I was starving for a whore.

In a pimp's life, yesterday means nothing. It's how you are doing today. A pimp's fame is as fleeting as an icicle under a blow-torch. The young fine whores are wild to hump for a pimp in the chips. A pimp in bad shape can't get the time of day from them. A pimp's wardrobe has to be spectacular. His wheels must be expensive and sparkling new. I had to get the gaudy tools to start pimping again.

17

Trying a New Game

I had three choices. I could cop a piece of stuff on consignment from a contact I had made in the joint. I could peddle it retail and get nine or ten grand in weeks. I could take a dog, a broken-down whore with trillions of mileage on her. Maybe I could keep my foot in her ass and grind up a bankroll.

I decided to take the third out. Do a slick fast hustle. I met a pimp named Red Eye in a junkie joint. He had just finished a state bit the week before. He was whoreless like me and itching to pimp again. We were crying on each other's shoulder at the bar.

He said, 'Ice, ain't it a bitch? No matter how much pimp a stud is, these dizzy bitches demand he's got a front. Now we ain't hustlers, but I got an idea. Ice, you're a helluva actor and you can rap good as a con man. I know a stud who's hip to every smack peddler and fence on the West Side. I got a rod and a real copper's shield.

'All we need is a Short and a third stud to drive. Neither one of us is well known over there. Besides there's a flock of youngsters dealing now who were squares when we left the track. I'm a roller-type stud. With the weight you put on in the joint you'd make a perfect copper.

'Ice, if we only knock over three of 'em, we split maybe ten to fifteen Gs between us. Our finger man is a junkie punk. We give him and the driver peanuts. Ice, those forty-seven Hogs are a pimp's dream. I gotta have one. Whatta you say? Are you in?'

I said, 'Red Eye, I'll go for it. I sure as hell ain't going to put a mop in my hand out here. I don't have wheels, but I've got a little scratch. I'll spring to rent a short. You know someone with one? How about a driver?'

He said, 'Ice, lay a double saw on me to cop a short. I know a stud for the driver. Meet me right here in this joint tomorrow night at nine. We can take off our first mark.'

I said, 'Don't crack my name to that driver. Call me Tom, Frank, anything.'

I didn't get two hours sleep that night. It worried me to be part of a hustle that required a rod.

I thought, 'Maybe I'd better back out. I could maybe find a young hash-slinger in a greasy spoon. I could turn her out in a hurry. She'd be a long shot for stardom. At least she'd make enough scratch for chump expenses.

'You can't start pimping with a turnout. It never works out. A pimp with no whore and no bankroll is a sucker to try the turnout on a mulish square broad. No, I guess the Red Eye deal is all I got.'

Red Eye got to the joint at ten-thirty. The driver was a huge stud with a rapper like a girl's. I noticed his big meat-hooks shaking on the steering wheel on our way to the West Side. Red Eye ran down our first mark. His light-maroon eyes were whirling. He had a skull full of H.

He said, 'Paul, our first mark is a bird's nest on the ground. It's a broad. The finger showed her to me last night. She and her old man got the best smack on the West Side. It's so good studs from all over town are rushing to cop every night.

'He and the broad deal out of a bar three blocks from their pad. They deal mostly in eights and sixteenths. On a weekend night like this one they take off maybe five Gs. The stud is got a rep as a fast-rod joker. He ain't got no direct syndicate connections as far as I know.

'We ain't got to worry about him tonight. He's in New York copping a supply. The broad will leave the bar around midnight loaded with scratch. She'll have a few packs of smack on her too for the evidence to shake her. Her real name is Mavis Sims.

'She's gonna go to her short parked behind the bar. She ain't afraid of being heisted. Everybody is scared shitless of her old man. She's got a small rod strapped to her thigh. She ain't going to pull it on the police though. That's us, strange rollers from downtown. We gotta move fast on her when she hits that lot behind the bar. She's a slick bitch. We gotta be real rollers. We can't wake her up we're fakes. She's a strong bitch. I'd have to blow a hole in her if she reached for her rod.

'There will be a pack of hard studs in the bar. They would love to croak us on that lot to please her old man. We gotta move her fast outta the neighborhood to play her outta the scratch. We gotta be careful the rollers don't join our party. Her old man is doing a lot of greasing in the district.

'Perry is gonna park our short in the street beside the lot. We arrest the broad and you play on her while Perry drives. I ain't going to rap and maybe queer things. Ice, after we cop her it's up to you for the shake. You got to convince her.'

Perry was really nervous. He pulled into the curb next to the bar lot. His skull was jiggling on his bull neck like he had Parkinson shakes. I was silent.

Red Eye's rundown had me wondering how it shaped up as a bird's nest to him. It looked like maybe a bird's nest for Dillinger. If the mark hadn't been a broad I'd have split and got on an El train.

I wondered if she'd seen me before I went to the joint. What if she made me right away as Iceberg and plugged me in the skull. Her old man might have outfit friends. If he did we'd be found in an alley with our balls rammed down our throats. We were standing in the shadows ten feet from the broad's short.

I said, 'Red, I better take the rod. When we step out on her, shine the flashlight right in her eyes.'

She was walking fast when she came into the lot. Her light blue chiffon dress was billowing in the April breeze. She was walking wide legged like a whore after a long night in a two-dollar house.

My legs were trembling like a stud dog's hung up in a bitch. I looked down at the badge pinned to the wallet in my palm. It glittered like molten silver in the moonlight. The thirty-two pistol in my right hand weighed a sweaty ton.

She was twirling a key ring. In the utter silence the clinking sounded like the U. S. Marshal's handcuffs. She had her hands on the door handle. I stepped out of the shadows. Red Eye was behind me. I wondered if she could hear my ticker hammering. Red Eye put the light in her face. Her yellow forehead wrinkled in surprise. Her sexy jib flapped open. I grabbed her wrist and tried to crush it.

I roared, 'Police, what's your name and why are you sneaking around back here?'

She stammered, 'Gloria Jones, and I was coming to my car. I always park it here. Now get out of the way. I'm going home. The captain of this district is a personal friend of my husband's.'

Red Eye had turned off the flashlight and moved behind her. She was looking down at the badge. She was trying to yank her wrist free.

I said in a low heavy voice. 'You lying dope-peddling bitch. Your real monicker is Mavis Sims. We're from downtown. Your old man's no pal of ours. We're gonna bust you, bitch. I'll lay odds we've caught you dirty. Come on, bitch, before we get rough. Anything I hate it's a stinking smack dealer.'

We hurled her into the back seat of our short. Red got in beside her. I was up front with Perry. I turned facing the rear seat. There was silence as Perry drove out of the district toward central headquarters. Miss Sims was squirming in the seat. Her right hand was out of sight behind her. She was getting very jerky. I remembered that rod she was carrying. I started the shake.

I said, 'Al, this suspect is acting peculiarly. Perhaps you'd better pull over. She might have concealed some evidence behind the seat.'

He pulled over. Red moved toward her. She slid to the window on the other side.

She said, 'Officers, I'm clean. It's worth fifty apiece to cut me loose. If you bust me, I'll be out in an hour. Take me back to the bar. I can get the hundred and fifty from the bar owner.'

I said, 'No dice, sister. We got specific orders to bring you in. Now don't make him slap a broad around. He's gonna frisk you. He don't have to wait for a matron to do it downtown. It's proper if he thinks you're armed and we're in danger.'

He patted the inside of her thighs. It was there, a twenty-two automatic jammed under the top of her stocking. He took it out and shoved it in his pocket, searched her bosom, purse, shoes, and hair. She was sure clean except for the rod.

I felt like a real chump. All this trouble for nothing. He was scratching his chin. The junkie punk had put a bum finger on the broad.

I was at the point of shoving her out. Then it struck me. Where did my street whores hide their scratch? In the cat! In the cat, where else? The clincher was this broad's wide-legged walk. I had noticed it on the lot. She was leaning forward staring at Perry's face.

I said, 'Joe, it's gotta be up her cat. Bitch, stretch out and put your legs across his lap.'

She said, 'The hell I will. You phony Niggers ain't rollers. That big one at the wheel used to bounce at Mario's.'

She was wise. The double saw I gave Red Eye had tapped me out. We had to know if she had treasure up her cat.

I wondered how he'd handle it. I didn't wonder long. He turned brute. He punched her hard in the nose. It was like he had cut her throat. Blood splattered over the front of her dress. I felt a light spray on my face.

She opened her mouth to scream. He smothered it with a terrible slam to the gut. She went limp. He pulled her across him. He darted his paw between her legs.

When he brought his mitt out it made a kissing sound. He had a long shiny plastic tube between his index and middle fingers. It stank like rotten fish.

The broad was moaning and holding both hands to her nose. He unwrapped the package. The pouch was bursting with scratch. In the center of the roll I saw the cellophane edges of packaged dope.

He got out and opened the door on the broad's side. He dragged her out to the sidewalk. He got in the front seat. Perry gunned away. I kept a sharp eye on Red Eye as he counted the scratch in his lap.

Red Eye and I netted two grand apiece. Red Eye took the packages of H. The broad dealer had forty-four hundred in the pouch. Perry and the junkie finger man got two bills apiece.

It was a week before we tried for the second mark. We shouldn't have. He was a reefer peddler and fence. We thought he had big scratch on him. We didn't have a driver. We had the mark in the short. Red Eye was driving.

We were playing the peel off. The mark was in the back seat. I was in the front seat. I asked for his identification. He handed me his hide. I saw it had only a few slats in it.

We were pulling to the curb to search him. A two-man squad car passed. The mark saw them and started screaming. They stopped and dragged Red Eye and me out to the street. They kicked and beat hell out of us. They took us down.

The mark was slick. Right there on the street he cracked we took a C note from him. If he'd known about our roll, he could have beefed for four Gs.

The rollers saw our rolls and tried to pin every stick-up on the books against us. We went on every show-up for a week. We didn't get a finger. They booked us for armed robbery of the mark.

18

Jailbreak

An agent for a fixer came to the lockup. He assured us we could avoid five to ten for armed robbery. We could get the charge reduced to a workhouse bit for a price.

We tapped out and got a year apiece in the work house. it was like a prison only tougher. A joint is always rough when there's graft and corruption. Only cons with scratch are treated and fed like human beings. The walls were just as high. Most of the inmates were serving short thirty- and ninety-day bits.

The joint was filthy. The food was unbelievable. The officials had an unfunny habit of putting pimps on the coal pile. I did a week on it. I was ready to make a blind rush at the wall. Maybe I could claw up the thirty feet before I got shot. I was really desperate.

After the first week I came out of shock. I started thinking about a sensible way to escape. I just couldn't get my skull in shape for another bit. It was too soon after the last one. By the middle of the second week I'd had a dozen ideas. None of them stood up under second thoughts.

I shared a tiny cell with a young con. He was only eighteen. He idolized me. He'd heard about me in the streets. I slept on the top of a double bunk. There were three counts. One in the morning, one after night lockup. The third at midnight.

One night I missed standing up for count at the cell door. I was so beat from heaving coal I'd collapsed on my bunk. I woke up an hour after the count. It gave me an idea. I kicked it around in my skull. Like all good ideas it kept growing, crying out for my attention.

I thought, 'I wonder how much and what of me that screw saw when he counted me?' I tested him three nights in a row. I'd lie on the bunk when he came through to count. Each time I'd lie so he saw less of me. The last time he counted me there was only my back, rear end, and legs visible to him.

I got excited. I knew it would be easy to get extra pants and a shirt. I could stuff them into a passable dummy. I knew my first problem was to find a way to get out of line when filing from the coal pile.

My second problem was I couldn't leave a dummy in position in the cell during the day. Cell-house cons and screws would pass on the gallery and discover it. I decided to solve my outside problem first.

At the end of the day a screw would line us up at the coal pile to be counted. We would then file two-hundred yards into the mess hall for supper. After supper we would file through hallways to the cell house for count.

There were several cell houses. All of the cell houses phoned in their tallies to the office. If all the tallies equaled that number of cons in the entire joint then the count was right. A loud whistle blew and the day screws could go home.

There was no cover between the coal pile and the mess hall. A screw with a scoped, high-powered rifle manned a wall that ran parallel to our line of march. It looked impossible. I lost hope. On my twenty-eighth day in the joint I noticed something.

I had been on an official pass-out of some kind. It was very near supper time. I passed the dress-in station and shower room. The front door was open. I glanced in. In the rear of it a screw was hook-locking a wooden door.

I stopped and pretended to tie my shoe. He then walked up two or three stairs and swung a steel door shut inside the shower room. He started lining up his cons for the march to the dining room.

I had noticed the shed before on the marches to the dining room. It was maybe thirty feet from the line of march. The door had always been shut. I had thought it stayed locked all the time. I couldn't have checked it with that rifleman on the wall and a screw marching with me.

In the cell that night I was as excited as a crumb crusher at Christmas time.

I thought, 'Maybe that shower screw sometimes forgets to lock that shed door. Maybe he's even later locking it than today. I couldn't see what the hell was in the shed. I know there's gotta be old clothing or something I can hide under when he comes to hook that slammer. I gotta get outta this joint. I can't pull my bit here.

'If the kid will handle the dummy end, I'll take a chance. I'm gonna talk to my cellmate about that dummy. If he'll help me, I can escape like a shadow.'

I looked down over the rim of my bunk at him. I had written several bullshit letters for him to his girlfriend. So far they had kept her writing and sending him candy and cigarette money. He was a good kid. I didn't think he'd rat.

I said, 'Shorty, what if I told you I could beat this joint?'

He said, 'Iceberg, you're jiving. You can't make it out of here. There are five steel gates between this cell and the streets. How're you planning to do it?'

I said, 'Kid, as beautiful as it is I can't do it without your help. Now here it is.'

I ran it down to him. At first he was leery. I told him to take the dummy from the floor under his bunk. Put it on mine. As soon as the whistle blew, unstuff the shirt and pants. Put the blanket stuffing back on my bunk. Sometime during the night before the midnight count, throw the pants and shirt over the gallery to the flagstone.

When the midnight hell broke loose he'd be clean. No one could prove or even suspect he had dismantled the dummy. I asked him to give me the name of a relative of record. I told him I would send him a C note from the first whore scratch I got.

I got his promise to handle the cell end of the plan. An hour later I gave a cell-house orderly two packs of butts for an extra blanket. I had the stuffing. I took off my shirt and pants and stuffed them for rehearsal. He sat at the cell door with a mirror watching the gallery both ways. In twenty minutes he had the position and the rest of it down pat.

I didn't close my eyes all night. At midnight I saw the screw counting heads. He was due for a shock soon. I knew that if something went wrong they'd probably beat me to death out there on the yard. I had to go through with it. No con misses his freedom more than a pimp. His senses are addicted to silky living.

I took packs of butts to the coal pile the next day. A yard runner got me a shirt and pants. I put them on over the ones I wore. That night in the cell I made up the dummy. I put it under the kid's bunk and gave him a pep talk until midnight. I even promised him I'd keep in touch and when he got out I'd teach him to pimp.

I thought the last day on the coal pile would never end. I would be sunk if there was a routine cell-house shakedown. Finally we lined up. My throat was dry and my knees were wobbly. We were approaching that shed. The screw on the wall walked twenty paces away. Then about faced and walked back facing the coal pile gang.

I'd have to break for the shed when he walked away. I'd have to be in there when he turned if it wasn't locked. If he didn't shoot me the yard screws would beat me to a pulp. The coal-pile screw was ahead of me. He could turn and look back at any moment. No other moment in my life has been so tense, so wildly adventuresome. I didn't even know if there wasn't a fink in the line. I tell you it was something. If my ticker had been faulty I'd have passed out.

The screw on the wall was walking away. The shed seemed miles away. I slipped out of line and raced for it. I could hear an excited whispering from the cons behind me. I touched the shed door-handle. For an instant I hesitated. I was afraid I'd find it locked. My sweat-hot hands pulled it toward me. It was open!

Just before I stepped inside I looked up at the wall. The screw was standing looking in the direction of the shed. I shut the door. Had he seen me. I looked around the shed. There was nothing to hide under or behind. I could hear the cons in the shower room. They were getting ready for supper.

The steel door was half open. That screw would be out at any second to hook the shed door. There was no place to hide. It had been all for nothing. I heard a voice and the scrape of feet at the steel door. The screw was coming out into the shed! I looked up at the shed ceiling. I looked over the steel door.

There was a line of rusty bars a foot long over the door flush against a grimy window. I leaped up and grabbed two of them. I swung my feet and legs up just as the screw walked in to lock the door. I was jack-knifing my legs just six inches from the top of his blue uniform cap. I hung there like a bat. I held my breath. He passed beneath me. I saw flakes of rust fall from the bars onto the top of his cap. It seemed forever to my agonized aching arms and legs.

I heard the steel door crash shut. I started breathing again. I hung up there for another long moment. He might come back for some reason. I swung my paralyzed legs down and released my grip on the bars. I sat on the stone steps fighting for breath. The shed was quiet as a tomb. I could hear my ticker staccato.

The worst wasn't over. That 'all is well' whistle had to blow. If it didn't blow they'd come looking for me with fists, clubs, and guns. I peeped through a crack in the door. I put my ear to it. The yard was bare. I could hear the clatter of steel plates in the mess hall. Finally all was quiet. The count was going on.

I thought, 'Even if the kid goes through with his end, this one night the count screw will poke that dummy to stand up to the cell door. That whistle ain't gonna blow. It's been too long already. Those cold hearted bastards are on the way already. They'll beat and stomp me crippled.'

The whistle blew! The beautiful sound of it was like a faucet. It flooded my eyes with tears. I did a dusty jig on the shed floor. It was dusk. It wasn't over. The only way to get over the wall was to scale and climb to the top of a cell house in the far corner of the yard.

Lucky for me the cell house sat in a deep recess, otherwise its roof would have towered above the wall. It was the only building close to a section of wall. Other buildings stairs stepped almost to the roof of the cell house. Maybe I'd been too eager to escape. I'd not put together a rope or hook. I'd have to use hands and feet. It sat six feet away and twenty feet above the wall.

There was only one screw on the wall after the count cleared. He'd be in his cubicle reading the newspaper or a magazine. If he looked up he couldn't miss seeing me in the glare of the yard lights.

My uniform was dark green, stained black with coal dust. Maybe on the street I'd look like any sooty steel mill or coal worker. I hadn't done too badly so far with short-term planning.

I had until midnight to get over the wall and out of the city. I had no scratch. I'd passed out a small fortune in tips to hotel maids, bellhops, and bartenders. Now all of them were rich compared to me. I knew several I could go to and get a few dollars. They could be found at their places of work.

There had been all the show-ups the month before and my conviction. My face would be remembered by the rollers in those neighborhoods. I thought about Sweet? I remembered his crack at the hideout to set me up for the cop of my stable. I threw him out of my skull.

I couldn't trust any of the pimps I knew. I'd always been a threat to them. Iceberg was really on his own. I'd have to make it to one of Mama's sisters, thirty miles away in Indiana.

It was now pitch black inside the shed. I raised the hook and pushed the door open. I looked out into the yard. I stepped through the door into the yard. All was quiet. I pushed the door shut. I heard a dull metallic noise. I pulled it toward me. The hook had fallen into its loop. The shed door had hooked from the inside.

I thought, 'That freak accident would confound the investigators for sure.'

I raced to the side of the mess hall. I'd have to get on its flat roof. I took hold of some window bars and pulled up to a standing position on the sill. I reached over and grabbed the drain pipe. I swung over and shinnied up to the roof.

I looked to my left. I could see the silhouetted figure of the wall screw in his cubicle. I looked across and up at the cell-house roof abutting the wall. It was a long way. I walked across the roof toward the next building. I was near the far edge of the roof. I looked back at the wall cubicle. The screw was out walking the wall. He had that deadly rifle cradled in his arms.

I flung myself flat on my back on the black roof. I hoped I was invisible to him. I lay there panting. I wondered what a screw's manual said about an escaping con target. If he saw me would he scope for a skull, heart, or gut shot?

Finally he went back into the cubicle. Lucky for me the mess-hall roof was connected to the chapel building. The connection was a concrete ledge. It was less than a foot wide and about twelve feet long. My heavy prison brogans seemed as wide as the ledge. They slipped on the glazed ledge. The wild late April winds made the walk as secure as a stroll across a teeter-totter two stories above the ground.

I stood at the end of the ledge and looked up. I stretched my right arm up and stood on tip-toes. The chapel roof was two feet above my fingertips. I'd have to go back a few feet on that glassy ledge. I'd have to get up enough speed coming back to make a two-feet leap. I'd have to grab the outside rim of the roof's drain gutter. I wondered if it could stand my weight.

I carefully backed up six feet. I stood there trembling looking up at the rim. I looked back. The screw wasn't on the wall. I had to forget how narrow the ledge was. I threw a leg out. I whipped the other toward it. I pumped them over the gritty glaze. I heard the whispering hiss of the leather soles tromping the ledge. My arms were outstretched to the black sky. My eyes were riveted upward to the gutter rim.

I leaped upward. I felt my feet soar off the ledge. I taloned the rim. I hung from it dangling in space. My fingernails sent red-hot needles of pain through the tortured flesh at their roots. I chinned up and hurled a leg across the roof top. I rolled onto it. I lay there gasping as I watched the rifleman walk his beat. He went in.

I struggled up the steep sloping roof to the top. The edge of the cell-house roof was three feet away. I leaped straight ahead. I flopped on my belly. The tips of my brogans were in the drain gutter. The cell house roof was even steeper. It was coated with squares of slippery shale. I looked up toward the top. It seemed a city block away. I started bellying up it. I dug my brogan tips into the small cracks between the shale squares.

I finally inched to the top. My chest was flaming. I lay astraddle the six-inch top of a double precipice. The two sides of the roof formed a steep pyramid. I was on top of it. The six-inch top seemed as thin as a wire. Through a dizzy haze I saw the lights of the city winking in an ocean of blackness.

I got to my feet. I started walking the tight wire like a circus performer. The winds were savage up here. They kicked and punched me. I teetered and swayed on the wire. I looked down over the right precipice to the street far below. Through a fuzzy blur I saw auto headlights darting through the night like tiny fireflies. My skull almost blacked out. I jerked my skull away and glued my eyes to the wire.

It was like an age before I reached the end of the cell-house. If the screw came out now I'd be in full view. Even from the inside, he could spot me. I stood shivering. I looked down twenty feet to the top of the three-foot wide wall. I couldn't turn back. I couldn't just stand there. It was a cinch I couldn't expect to keep balance if I hit the wall feet first.

I dropped, legs opened wide. I heard my trousers rip. The inside concrete edge of the wall top gouged into my inner thigh. My rear end crashed against the concrete. My skull reeled in pain as I sat in the cold saddle. I swung my gouged left leg from the inner side of the wall. I scooted back on my belly to my fingertips.

I hung there for a moment. I felt blood running down my left leg into my shoe. I let go. I struck feet first. My butt and back took the rest of the shock. I lay there on my back in a drunken fog of exhaustion, pain and breathless joy.

It was at least ten minutes before I could stand. I limped away for a hundred yards. I turned and looked back at the joint.

I thought, 'Those dirty white folks are gonna pace the floor. Their ass holes are gonna twitch. They're gonna call me a million black-Nigger bastards and sonuvabitches. One thing they can't deny in their cruel secret hearts. I outsmarted them. It's gonna hurt 'em to the rotten quick that a Nigger did a black Houdini outta here. No screws' skulls busted and no bars sawed.

'They're gonna foul their chances to catch me after the midnight count. They'll search the yard and joint for a week. Their asses will turn blue. Their skulls won't let 'em believe a Nigger was clever enough to ghost outta here.'

I turned and hobbled toward the State of Indiana.

19

The Ice Pick

I was lucky. I caught five rides to get to my Aunt. It was five minutes to midnight when she opened the door. At first she didn't recognize me. She made me welcome.

In a week my leg had healed and I felt strong. Her husband was my size. He gave me an outfit and fifty dollars. I went to the whore section of town. A bunch of New Orleans pimps were in town. They had their thieving whores with them. Three days later I stole one.

Her name was No Thumbs Helen. She was at that time one of the slickest from the person thieves in the country. We got about in a 'forty-seven Hog. She was a magician. For almost a year she left a trail of empty wallets across five states.

We were in Iowa when Helen stung a rich sod-buster for seventy-two hundred. I was in bed when she threw it on the bed. Excited! Sure I was. My heart boomed like bombs going off. She didn't know it. I was icy cool. I casually scooped it up and counted it. I had a poker face.

I said, 'Now listen, bitch. Run this sting down. I gotta know how hot this scratch is. Did you get all the sucker had? I'll be a salty sonuvabitch to read in the papers that you missed a bundle.'

Her rundown told me it was best to split. We got in the Hog and went to Minneapolis. The second day I copped a young whore. She wanted to be a thief. I took her to Helen at our hotel. Helen chilled when she saw the pretty bitch.

She blew her top. She drew her knife. The young whore fled. I disarmed Helen and punched her around. Helen went to work. I fell asleep. I woke up fast. Helen was jabbing her knife into me. I rolled away. She had stabbed me in the forearm and the side of an elbow. I took a golf club and knocked her out.

I never tried to stable her after that. I didn't feel like a real pimp with one whore. I decided to steal the technique of stealing from Helen. I could use it to train other whores when I cut her loose. Finally I picked her skull. The technique went as follows.

She would lurk in some shadowy doorway or alley entrance. When a trick came by she'd go into a con act. She'd stand wide-legged and bend her knees to an almost squatting stance. She'd whip up the front bottom of her dress. She'd expose the gaping, hairy magnet to the bugging eyes of the sucker. The pull was magnified by her stroking her cat.

She'd say to the sucker, 'Please pretty sweetie, I am so hot this pussy is burning up. I ain't had no dick in six months. Come here and do something to it.'

He'd step into the doorway already blind hot to sock it in for free. His instinctive wariness blackjacked to sleep by the raw event. She'd bombard the sucker with a flow of sweetly passionate sexy bullshit as she tightly embraced him.

She had located his wallet, usually in a rear trouser pocket, with the sensitive tips of her fingers. She'd dry grind her belly against his scrotum. She'd complain that his belt buckle was hurting her. She would be panting in phony passion as she unbuckled it. It would release the tension on his pants pockets. She'd caress the head of his swipe with her fingers.

She'd stroke the tip of his ear with her tongue. The very tips of the airy light index finger and thumb of the free hand flicked the buttoned pocket open. The index and middle fingers scissored on the wallet and slid it from the pocket. The trick would be excited and hot. He wouldn't have felt the glowing end of a cigarette on his ass.

With both hands behind his neck, she'd remove the scratch from the hide. She'd up the sexy chatter and the strong grind against his scrotum. She'd roll the bills into a tight suppository shape. She'd slip the wallet back into the pocket. She wouldn't forget to rebutton the pocket. She was ready to blow the sucker off, get rid of him. She'd crack that she had to pee. Stooping quickly, she'd ram the rolled bills up her cat. She'd sight a passing car. She'd fake alarm.

She would say, 'Oh, my God. There's Riley, the vice cop. Listen Honey, go to the Park Hotel up the street and register as Mr and Mrs Jones. I will be there in ten minutes, Pretty Dandy. I sure want some of your good dick.'

The sucker would pat the reassuring bump of his wallet. It was still there in the buttoned pocket. He'd amble off to the hotel. The thief would make it home. She'd completely change her appearance. She'd go back into the street to sting another sucker.

There was an accident. She got pregnant. I found a croaker who made her one again. The game went down as usual. The bubble burst in a small town in Ohio.

The sky-rocket came crashing down then I ran into an old pal. He was now called New York Joe. I hadn't seen him since I was fourteen. My mother had taken him in for a few weeks when his widowed mother died. He got sick and had to go to a hospital. I'd take a bus to see him and bring him tid-bits. I'd sit with him and console him. I liked him. Our friendship was brief. He got out of the hospital and left town.

He was wholesaling cocaine and the sample he gave me was almost pure. I made an appointment to cop a piece. I didn't know he had learned in New York to cross everybody, even old friends. I found out the stuff he gave me was phony. I rushed back to him figuring he had made a mistake and would square things with me.

I said, 'Joe, you've made a mistake, man.'

He took me inside. He said, 'What's the trouble, Jim?'

I said, 'Man, this is bullshit. This ain't the same stuff that I sampled.'

He said, 'Well listen, Ronald went out to the stash. That mother-fucker is crossing me.'

He drew his gun from a shoulder holster. At the time I didn't know it was all con.

He said, 'Should I go out there and kill that sonuvabitch? What do you want me to do?'

He started working his eyes. His eyes were bugging and going through all that crazy act.

I said, 'No, man, just give me my scratch back.'

He said, 'I'm so mad I should croak you both.'

I was relatively young. I had never run into this New York stuff before. I was spooked.

I said, 'Forget about it.'

He was going through contortions. I was in his town. I had a thief with at least seven beefs on her. I was out the three grand. I might have gotten croaked. Later I knew it was stuff: New York stuff. In later years, I figured it out. He maybe had always hated me because I had more education than he had.

A week later Helen got busted on seven counts. I signed the Hog over to a lip. She got five to ten. I should have wired a bomb to the starter before I turned it over to the lip.

A stud told me Joe had fingered Helen. He almost ruined me. He tapped me out, got my thief busted. He literally ran me out of town broke, and with no whore.

I heard whore-catching was good in Detroit. I took my last ten-dollar bill and caught a Greyhound. Detroit was the promised land for pimps all right. The town was teeming with young fast whores. The local pimps were soft competition.

I was walking, but I was sharp as a Harlem sissy. Anyway, these whores were a different breed than the ones back in the city. They were gullible, and a fellow didn't have to play his heart out to cop them.

The first package I copped was a beautiful seventeen-year-old green-eyed version of Pepper. Her name was Rachel. I was to keep her thirteen years.

My next package was a huge, black dangerous jasper named Serena. In addition to being a whore, she ran a fast sheet setup for a dozen whores. They tricked out of her joint. Within eight weeks after I hit Detroit I was cruising the streets in a sparkling new 'forty-eight Fleetwood. I had a fat bankroll.

Within ninety days after the Serena cop, I had copped two more young broads. A week later a small-time pimp came to town from Rhode Island. He had a beautiful young whore with him. He was jealous. He followed her in the street. I stalked her. He forgot to follow her. I stole her. I'd had her several months when the town got shaky. The rollers forced Serena out of her joint. I put her in the street.

Then I heard about a small town in Ohio – Lima – that was

jumping with good tricks and wide open. I could possibly open up a couple of houses there.

My luck was soaring. With my pad rent and a pad a piece for the girls I needed a tighter setup to cut down my nut. My skull was whirling as I drove the Hog to pick up my stable in the street. They got in. I tossed their scratch in the glove compartment.

Dawn was breaking as the big Hog scooted through the streets. My five whores were chattering like drunk magpies. I smelled that stink that only a street whore has after a long, busy night. The inside of my nose was raw. It happens when you're a pig for snorting cocaine.

My nose was on fire. The stink of those whores and the gangster they were smoking seemed like invisible knives scraping to the root of my brain. I was in an evil, dangerous mood despite that pile of scratch crammed into the glove compartment.

'Goddamnit, has one of you bitches shit on herself or something?' I bellowed. I flipped the wing window toward me.

For a long moment there was silence. Then Rachel, my bottom whore, cracked in a pleasing-ass kissing voice, 'Daddy, Baby, that ain't no shit you smell. We been turning all night. Ain't no bathrooms in those tricks' cars we been flipping out of. Daddy, we sure been humping for you. What you smell is our nasty whore asses.'

I grinned widely, inside of course. The best pimps keep a steel lid on their emotions. I was one of the iciest. The whores went into fits of giggles at Rachel's shaky witticism. A pimp is happy when his whores giggle. He knows they are still asleep.

I coasted the Hog into the curb outside the hotel where Kim, my newest, prettiest girl, was cribbing. Jesus! I would be glad to drop the last whore off. I could get to my own hotel to nurse my nose with cocaine and be alone. Any good pimp is his own best company. His inner life is so rich with cunning and scheming to out-think his whores.

As Kim got out I said, 'Goodnight Baby, today is Saturday. I want everybody in the street at noon instead of seven tonight.

I said noon, not five minutes after or two minutes after. At twelve sharp I want you down, got it, Baby?'

She didn't answer. She did a strange thing. She walked into the street around the Hog to the window on my side. She stood looking at me for a long moment. Her beautiful face tense in the dim dawn.

Then in her crisp New England accent she said, 'Are you coming back to my pad this morning? You haven't spent a night with me in a month. So come back, okay?'

A good pimp doesn't get paid for screwing. He gets his pay-off for always having the right thing to say to a whore right on lightning tap. I knew my four whores were flapping their ears to get my reaction to this beautiful bitch. A pimp with an overly-fine bitch in his stable has to keep his game tight. Whores constantly probe for weakness in a pimp.

I fitted a scary mask on my face and said, in a low, deadly voice, 'Bitch, are you insane? No bitch in this family calls any shots or muscles me to do anything. Now take your stinking yellow ass upstairs to a bath and some shut-eye. Get in the street at noon like I told you.'

The bitch just stood there. Her eyes slitted in anger. I could sense she was game to play the string out right there in the street before my whores. If I had been ten years dumber I would have leaped out of the Hog and broken her jaw, and put my foot in her ass. The joint was too fresh in my mind.

I knew the bitch was trying to booby-trap me when she spat out her invitation. 'Come on, kick my ass. What the hell do I need with a man I only see when he comes to get his money? I am sick of it all. I don't dig stables and never will. I know I'm the new bitch who has to prove herself. Well Goddamnit, I am sick of this shit. I'm cutting out.'

She stopped for air and lit a cigarette. I was going to blast her ass off when she finished. I just sat there staring at her.

Then she went on, 'I have turned more tricks in the three months I have been with you than in the whole two years with Paul. My pussy stays sore and swollen. Do I get my ass kicked before I split? If so, kick it now because I'm going back to Providence on the next thing smoking.'

The Ice Pick | 237

She was young, fast with trick appeal galore. She was a pimp's dream and she knew it. She had tested me with her beef. She was laying back for a sucker response.

I disappointed her with my cold overlay. I could see her wilt as I said in an icy voice. 'Listen square-ass bitch, I have never had a whore I couldn't do without. I celebrate, Bitch, when a whore leaves me. It gives some worthy bitch a chance to take her place and be a star. You scurvy Bitch, if I shit in your face, you gotta love it and open your mouth wide.'

The rollers cruised by in a squad car. I flashed a sucker smile on my face. I cooled it until they passed. Kim was rooted there wincing under the blizzard.

I went on ruthlessly, 'Bitch, you are nothing but a funky zero. Before me you had one chili chump with no rep. Nobody except his mother ever heard of the bastard. Yes, Bitch, I'll be back this morning to put your phony ass on the train.'

I rocketed away from the curb. In the rear-view mirror, I saw Kim walk slowly into the hotel. Her shoulders were slumped. Until I dropped the last whore off you could have heard a mosquito crapping on the moon. I had tested out for them, solid ice.

I went back for Kim. She was packed and silent. On the way to the station, I riffled the pages in that pimp's book in my head. I searched for an angle to hold her without kissing her ass.

I couldn't find a line in it for an out like that. As it turned out the bitch was testing and bluffing right down the line.

We had pulled into the station parking lot when the bitch fell to pieces. Her eyes were misty when she yelped, 'Daddy, are you really going to let me split? Daddy, I love you.'

I started the prat action to cinch her when I said, 'Bitch, I don't want a whore with rabbit in her. I want a bitch who wants me for life. You have got to go. After that bullshit earlier this morning, you are not that bitch.'

That prat butchered her. She collapsed into my lap crying and begging to stay. I had a theory about splitting whores. They seldom split without a bankroll.

So, I cracked on her, 'Give me that scratch you held out and maybe I'll give you another chance.'

Sure enough she reached into her bosom. She drew out close to five bills and handed it to me. No pimp with a brain in his head cuts loose a young beautiful whore with lots of mileage left in her. I let her come back.

At long last I was driving toward my hotel. I remembered what Sweet Jones, the master pimp who turned me out, had said about whores like Kim.

'Slim,' he had said, 'A pretty Nigger bitch and a white whore are just alike. They both will get in a stable to wreck it and leave the pimp on his ass with no whore. You gotta make 'em hump hard and fast to stick 'em for long scratch quick. Slim, pimping ain't no game of love, so prat 'em and keep your swipe outta 'em. Any sucker who believes a whore loves him shouldn't a fell outta his mammy's ass.'

My mind went back to Pepper. Then back even further and I remembered what he had said about the Georgia.

'Slim, a pimp is really a whore who has reversed the game on whores. So Slim, be as sweet as the scratch, no sweeter, and always stick a whore for a bundle before you sex her. A whore ain't nothing but a trick to a pimp. Don't let 'em Georgia you. Always get your money in front just like a whore.'

I was on the elevator riding to my pad. I thought about the first bitch who had Georgied me, when I was three. She had flim-flammed me out of my head. She would be old and gray now. If I could find her, I would sure get the bitch's unpaid account off my conscience.

I snorted a couple of caps of cocaine. Two hours later I took a yellow. I fell asleep.

When I woke up at noon, I knew I had to make a move. Rachel's parents were trying to cross me. Kim might split back to the sucker. My whole stable, except Kim, were local girls. A pimp is asking for trouble when he doesn't move his action away.

Control is easier and tighter away from the familiar setting. A girl in strange surroundings depends more on her man. She needs his advice and guidance more. Girls copped in smaller towns have to be moved fast.

That night I went to Ohio. I put down the foundation for the move. I rented two houses and furnished them beautifully. I made contact with a fellow who collected the oil for the heat. I got the okay to go at a C a week for each house. I moved my whole family there. I was just in time. A month later Detroit folded and the lid slammed down.

There was a good dope connection in the new town. I started capping H with my C. I'd mix them and shoot speedballs. When I went to bed I got sound sleep. I seldom had those bad dreams. I got hooked on H. It didn't worry me. I was getting long scratch.

I was thirty years old. For the second time in my pimping career I could see solid success and lots of long green in my future. How could I know that elephant bitch, Serena would get jealous? She brought the whole green-back house of cards crashing down around me. I missed a murder rap by a fraction of an inch. The fraction was in Serena's chest.

Within the year that I had set up my houses, tricks from all over the county were beating a path to them. They were wild to sample those luscious young freaks. Pimping had never been better.

I was in a wonderful mood as I walked in the sunshine. I noticed Serena was coming up the street with a sack of groceries in her arm. She had croaked two people in New Orleans. She walked toward me smiling. When she got close to me, she got the ice pick out of the sack. She jabbed it toward my chest. At the time I was quite quick, so I leaped back. The point of it slashed the edge of my pocket right over my ticker. She was trying to drive the point right through my ticker.

I was without a pistol at the time. I could buy a pistol from any hardware store. I bought a '32 and a box of fifty bullets. I took it up to her pad and loaded it at the kitchen table.

She said, 'Daddy, what's that for?'

I said, 'That's to croak any bitch that tries to hurt me.'

She said, 'Oh, Daddy, you know I was just upset. Forget about it.'

I said, 'No, I'm not going to forget about it. I'd kill my own mother if I thought she was going to hurt me.'

Later that evening about midnight, the other girls and I were returning from a cabaret. I put the key in the door. I opened it and smelled the heavy odor of Tabu. The heavy scent that only Serena used. I hesitated. My eyes became accustomed to the gloom. I saw Serena standing over in the corner of the living room with an ice pick in her hand. She had slipped into Rachel's house through an open basement window. I drew my gun.

I said, 'Serena!'

She said, 'Yes, mother-fucker, I'm killing you and them whores this morning.'

She started crying.

I said, 'Serena, don't come by that end table. If you do I'm going to kill you. You know I always keep my word.'

She said, 'I wouldn't give a mother-fuck.'

She lunged past the end table. I shot her. When I shot her the only thing that saved her life was the fact that she had a forty-six inch bust. The fatty tissue absorbed the bullet at almost point-blank range.

When I shot her, blood splattered. I struck her in an artery. It blew all over my face, all over her. Her dress had a ringlet of sparks. I set her on fire. She had elephant toughness. It didn't even knock her down. The bitch grabbed at me. She had dropped the ice pick.

She grabbed her chest and said, 'Daddy, don't kill me!'

I was tempted. I really intended to kill her. I started to shoot her through the head. I didn't. I don't really know why except there were witnessess, those four whores. She staggered past us through the door and down the street. We all got into the Fleetwood and raced out of town leaving everything.

I sped toward Mama. I hadn't seen her since that Christmas visit. Her hair was snow white. Jesus! Was she excited and happy to see me. I told her what had happened. She got a friend to drive her back there. She loaded all the clothing on a trailer. She visited Serena in the hospital.

Serena begged my mother to tell me to come back. She wouldn't file charges. It was all her fault and she loved me. I knew that if I had gone back Serena would have driven a butcher knife through my heart in my sleep.

20

Stable Moves

It had been a sucker move to come to Mama. Fortunately she had moved from over the beauty shop. She now lived in an almost all-white neighborhood. Here I was with four idle whores in a closed town where I had fallen three times. It was the point of origin for the white slave rap that the copper-hearted runt had crossed me with. There were a couple of sneak ten-dollar houses in town.

I stayed inside the house at Mama's. Every joker in town knew me. They all had diarrhea of the mouth. I couldn't put my action in the street in this hot town. They'd had an easy go in Ohio. They were soft. I could put them down only in a town where I had a fix. I knew none of them, if busted, could stand up under the clever grilling of the FBI.

I had a ten-G bankroll. I was housing and feeding four whores in an expensive hotel. I was a pig for banging speedballs. No fresh scratch was coming in. With only a ten-G stick I knew I would soon be in trouble. I had to make a move fast. It was bad for morale of the stable to keep them on their asses.

After a week of confinement at Mama's house, I slipped out of town to cop H and C for myself, and gangster for the girls. While in the city I looked up Sweet. I was careful because all the heat in the neighborhood knew me.

Sweet insisted I give him all the details of my escape. He shook his skull in awe when he heard them. Miss Peaches had died of old age. His eyes were sad when he told me about it. Glass Top was still out West in Seattle. Patch Eye did a little bookie business for him. Sweet had lost his glory. He looked a hundred years old. His backbone was the old white broad who owned the building.

Sweet had just beat a murder rap. He had killed some pretty jerk from St Louis who had insulted him in the Roost. The poor chump had called Sweet an ugly, gray-ass bastard. Sweet had drawn his pistol on him. He prodded him into an alley. He made him kneel and then he pissed on him. This was too much to take, so the kid lost his temper. Sweet shot him through the top of the head.

Sweet was laughing, in a good mood as he told me about it. It had cost him five grand to beat it. He told me he got a wire that Red Eye got life for croaking a whore in Pittsburgh.

Sweet had a complete answer to my problem. He said that since Serena hadn't beefed I should go back into Ohio. No state was better at the time for house or street. Before I left I went to his john. The door had a padlock on the outside.

He looked at me grinned, and said, 'Pal, my crapper is out of order.'

I went downstairs to the john in the bookie joint. On the way out I asked Patch Eye why Sweet didn't get his toilet fixed.

The old ex-pimp, without looking up answered, 'Shit, ain't nothing wrong with the crapper. That cold bastard has his two whores locked in there for fucking with his scratch. They been in there three days.'

I walked toward my car. I wondered how long Sweet would keep them there and how long the whores could live with just water.

I got back from the city. I stopped downtown at Rachel's suite. I stayed for the night. I outlined the move. The next morning I was looking out the window down on the street. There was a stooped white-haired joker dumping barrels of hotel garbage into a huge truck. It was Steve. I'd know him in hell!

A hot-flash shot through me. I don't know what happened after that. Rachel told me I snatched my thirty-two from my coat pocket in the closet. I ran to the service elevator in my pajamas. She followed me all the way to the street. I didn't say a word. The truck had pulled away when we reached the sidewalk.

She got me back upstairs. It had been a sucker play for a fugitive. Lucky for me no rollers showed on the scene. I dressed and told Rachel I'd be back later and I wanted the rest of the stable in her joint.

I stopped at a leather-goods shop and bought a small valise. It was about the size that a doctor carries. I stopped at several banks and cracked some of my big bills into enough singles to fill the bag. I went to Mama's to prepare the flash. I filled it almost to the brim with singles. I put the remaining big bills on top. I was getting ready to ship my stable. With my plan I could ship them without a strong fix. Even new whores think twice before leaving a rich pimp.

That afternoon they were all in Rachel's plush suite. She was the boss bitch. They had twenty-five dollar a day, neat rooms on the same floor. I walked in. They were smoking gangster and eager for my speech.

They were anxious to get back on the track. I had loosened the catch on the bag. I casually hurled it onto the table before them. A bale of hundred-dollar bills jumped from the bag. Reefer enhances what you see. I saw on those whores' faces that they were seeing every dollar of the mountain of greenbacks they had given me for the years I had been their man.

Confidence flooded their eyes. I finished my briefing and my instructions. I had built my shining castles in the air. Brother, I could have sent those whores to Siberia, in bikinis, in the wintertime. Keeping her wife-in-laws and my scratch straight up there in Toledo was the first acid test for Rachel as a bottom woman.

I stayed around Mama's for a week. She was bugging me to embrace the Holy Ghost and the Fire. She begged me to square up and repent my sins. No, it was a little late for that. I moved on to Ohio again.

Cleveland was only a short hop to Toledo. I set up a mad apartment in the larger city. Cleveland was jumping. I was ready for the best pimping of my career. Kim ran off with a wealthy white trick. I didn't miss her. Both towns were crawling with young fine whores. The name of the game was still cop and blow.

Within four months I had the three girls in Toledo and five in Cleveland. I was pimping good. I had a connection for stuff.

All was perfect except for one thing. Rachel's name was ringing. Every pimp, con man and rich dope-peddler was shooting for her. They offered soft, irresistible propositions.

Her head was getting as big as a pumpkin. I didn't want to lose her. I had another more serious reason for wanting to hold her. If I blew her, she might pull a runt on me and go to the FBI. I got it through the wire that a slick con-man out of New York was using his beautiful jasper white girl as bait to cop Rachel. The same wire said that Rachel was getting weak for the broad.

I went to Toledo one early morning to Rachel's. Sure enough there they were, the three of them in Rachel's bed. Believe me they hadn't gotten in there to recite bedtime stories. I was cool, icy as always. I let her con me that it was a party, all business of course. That wire had described that bastard con player and his freak woman.

I was in trouble. If it had been any other bitch in the stable except Rachel it wouldn't have been worth a fleeting thought. I couldn't lose Rachel, my bottom woman, in this shitty fashion to some ass-hole con player.

It could kill my career as a pimp. The news would flash in a dozen states. No, I couldn't afford to lose her. I still had that expensive friend riding with me, that monkey on my back. Sweet would have had the solution to this tough problem right off the top of his head. Sweet, the week before, had shot himself in the temple.

He left a bitter note, 'Good-bye squares! Kiss my pimping ass!'

I felt nothing when I got the wire. I left her apartment and drove out into the country. I spun the wheels in my skull. I got the key to the riddle. It was cruel but perfect. If it worked I'd never have to worry that she'd blow or cross me with the FBI.

Rachel called me the next day. She told me she had just sent me three bills. She got them for the party I had crashed. When she cracked, I knew I had to go through with the cross. The three bills she was sending had to be scratch she had been holding out. That con bastard was too pretty and slick to spend three fat-ones with a whore. I had to make an honest whore of her from now on.

I faked excitement when I told her about a sucker who was visiting Akron. It's a small town, thirty miles from Cleveland. I told her I got a wire that the sucker had hit the numbers for twenty Gs. He had it all with him in his hotel room.

I sold her that she could take it off smooth and easy. She said she would be down the next day to get briefed in detail.

I had already driven to Akron and set the stage for her. I had rented a hotel room in a fair hotel. I contacted a dignified looking old ex-slum hustler down on his luck. He spruced up a wino friend of his for the play.

The whole arrangement – clothes, room, and a bill apiece for the actors – came to a half-grand. The slum hustler was to wait in a pool room nearby for my call.

Rachel got to my apartment at three P.M. We got to Akron around six. I told her one of the bellhops had told the sucker she would be there before seven. He was waiting for her.

I slipped a small vial of mineral oil into her palm. I told her it was Chloral Hydrate. Only two drops would knock the sucker out. I told her I would be waiting in the hotel bar for her.

She stopped at the desk. Sure enough he was expecting her. She went up. She came down within an hour nervous and jumpy. The sucker was out cold. She had searched the room. She couldn't find the scratch. I went back to the room with her. I went through another search. The wino was lying there motionless. We gave up searching. We moved toward the door. I looked back at the wino.

I said, 'Say Baby, he looks bad to me.'

I knelt beside him blocking her view with my back. I wiped my brow and turned my face toward her. My eyes were wide in alarm.

I said, 'Baby, he's dead I think.'

Most women, even whores, are terrified of dead bodies. She stood there paralyzed.

I said, 'Don't get panicky. Shut that door. I've got it! I know an underworld croaker here in town. Maybe he can bring him to. I know he will keep his mouth shut for a price, even if.'

She knew we couldn't leave a murdered man here. She had stopped at the desk first before coming up. She was painfully aware of the big gap between theft and murder. I picked up the phone and got the pool room. I gave the fake doctor the hotel and room number. He came within five minutes carrying his empty bag.

She couldn't see into it. I had told her to hide in the closet. Too many people had seen her already. He stooped down beside the wino. He fumbled with his pulse, his eyelids.

Finally he stood up and said, 'He's dead. I can't help him. I'll have to call the police.'

I could almost hear Rachel's heart booming in the closet. We haggled for her benefit for ten minutes. Finally we had a deal. For five bills, he would keep his mouth shut. He would also contact a hoodlum who would get the body out of there and dispose of it. He left. Rachel and I got out of there fast.

Driving back to Cleveland, Rachel was in a trance. She squeezed tightly against me. I kept telling her she had nothing to worry about. After all we were together for life and her secret would always be safe with me. She found out about the hoax years later.

Rachel straightened up with that murder pressure on her. Toledo was on fire and in one month my three girls got nine cases between them. I pulled them out into Cleveland. Cleveland was lousy with pimps and whores and boosters from all over the country.

The mob of hustlers set the torch to Cleveland. By nineteen fifty-three the streets were so hot a whore was lucky to stand up a week between falls. I was a fugitive. For almost a year I never left my apartment. I couldn't risk arrest and a fingerprint check. I was down to four girls. That year in the apartment was cramping my style.

Mama had hit a romantic and financial jack-pot. She had moved to Los Angeles. She called me every week pleading with me to visit her. She wanted me to meet my new stepfather, and stay for a while. I kept stalling her. I had heard that the smack in California was only six percent. The pimps out there were only half serious. This makes for bad pimping conditions.

Several Eastern pimps had gone to the coast in good shape. They had returned torn down. They said the Western whores were lazy and were satisfied with making chump change. The Western pimps had spoiled them.

I gave myself logical arguments against the move to California. Why should I expose my well-trained whores to that dangerous half-ass scene out West? What if I blew my family out there in the hinterlands?

I was thirty-four now. In any square profession I would have been in my prime. As a pimp I was getting elderly. I was stern and strict on my women.

Rachel wired me that a stud with a stable of boosters was in town with a load of wild Lilli Anne suits and Petrocelli vines at twenty percent of retail. She got me his number the next day.

I called him and got an appointment to look his stock over. I only left the apartment for important reasons. I decided I would cop a piece of stuff and a fresh outfit before seeing him.

He was staying at a crummy hotel on the East Side. He let me into a cracker-box three-room apartment. He sounded me down to make sure of my pedigree.

'So, you're Iceberg, huh? I was in your town not long ago. Philly sure is hot.'

He knew me by reputation and that I was from Chicago.

I said, 'Yes, I'm Iceberg from the Windy.'

He said, 'Say Jim, how 'bout old Red Eye? I saw him in New York last month. He's pimping a zillion. Surely you know him.'

I gave him that look, like I had caught him frenching a sissy.

I said, 'Listen carefully, Jack. I don't have time for bull-shit. I knew Red Eye. You saw him last month, Jack? You better see a head-shrinker. You're flipping your top. Red Eye caught the big one in Pittsburgh five years ago. He's doing it all.'

He gave me a grin like he had swallowed a bottle of snot. He got the sizes from me. He said to cool it in his pad. He had to go to his stash across the street to get the merchandise.

I glanced into the tiny bedroom. There was a naked broad lying on the bed.

I said to myself, 'I wonder what kind of dog that is.'

I went to the bed and looked down at her. She was drunk, stoned. It looked like the runt. This broad was buxom, almost fat. I knew one way to be sure. I had lashed the blood out of her with that hanger whipping years ago. She would still have the scars. I flipped her over on her belly. They were there.

I stood there looking down at her. I remembered that tough bit in Leavenworth. Here at my mercy was that stinking bitch, Phyllis. Just the sight of her made me crazy.

I grabbed a cologne bottle off the dresser. I jerked the big top off. I got my bag out. I dumped enough of the twenty percent stuff into the top to croak a sick junkie. She was clean.

I spotted a bottle of mixer water on the floor. I filled the top and struck a match. I held it beneath the top. I rammed my gun into it. I drew up her reckoning.

I stabbed the outfit into a vein just back of her knees. Her red blood streaked up into the joint. I was just about to press the pacifier bulb. I looked out the window. I caught a glimpse of the joker darting across the street. He had a steamer trunk headed toward the front door of the hotel.

I froze, jerked the spike out of her. I thrust the loaded outfit inside my shoe underneath my instep. I pinned the bag to my shorts between my legs. I collapsed into the living-room chair just as he came through the door. I was sweating like hell. He was suspicious. He kept looking from the corner of his eye at his broad.

He thought I had been riding her in his absence. I wondered how long he'd had her. He was a wrongdoer. He'd cut her loose when he got hip to what he had. Sooner or later someone would pull his coat. He'd find out the runt had sent me to the joint. I was getting what I wanted from the merchandise. He slipped into the bedroom and checked her cat out.

I left with the dozen items I had bought. I knew I had bought going-to-California clothes. I had quizzed him about his plans. He was going to stay in Cleveland for weeks. I had to leave town. Now.

Phyllis was sure to get the wire from him that I was in town. I knew she wouldn't hesitate to drop a dime in the phone to the heat. She had to know about the escape. I drove away. I tried to picture the expression on her face when her man cracked to her that Iceberg had been up there alone with her while she was stoned.

I got a flight that night for L.A. It's fabulous when a pimp's bottom girl can be trusted to handle his scratch and his whores. She was welded to me by that murder cross. The stable would drive out later in the Hog.

Mama was radiantly happy out there and my stepfather was a wonderful square. They lived in a big house. L.A. was worse than the reports I had gotten. I got around in Mama's Coupe de Ville. After the second night I went into the whore and pimp stomping grounds.

I stayed around Mama for another week then went up to Seattle. Glass Top's name wasn't ringing. In fact he was almost unknown. One stud told me Glass Top had croaked.

I copped a gorgeous hash-slinger up there. I turned her out that week. Lucky I did. I lost a girl back in Cleveland. Her appendix burst. I pulled the three left into Seattle.

After I had been in town six months, fate dealt me one off the top for a change. My bag was empty and the stuff in town was around six percent. I had to shoot three spoons to stay well. The girls were humping up a storm, I was getting no inside grief.

I was sitting in the Hog one day. An old withered stud walked past me. He came back and stooped down looking at me.

He shouted, 'Ice, my old pimping buddy.'

I took a close look. It was Glass Top. He got in. He patted the scraggly processed hair on his nearly-bald head. He'd done a long bit in the state joint. He wasn't pimping. An old square broad was feeding him. He was a drunk. Until I left town I bought him bottles and rapped with him. He croaked two days after I left town.

I ran into the croaker who aborted Helen. He had lost his license and done a short bit back East for an abortion. We started rapping a lot to each other. He knew most of the hustlers I knew so we had much in common. He kept telling me how bad I looked. He told me how handsome I'd been when I brought Helen to him.

He needled me. He expressed doubt that I had the guts to kick. He was game to help me kick if I was game to kick. I decided to let him help me. He warned me I would have to follow his every instruction. He had a house in town. He still took a fast buck from his old hustle.

Rachel was the only girl in the family who knew I was hooked. None of the rest knew. I was going to stay at the Doc's to kick. They thought I was out of town.

He used the system of reduction. We reached the tearing, puking, none-at-all stage. Let me tell you that beautiful croaker bastard was immune and rock-hard. I tried the raving, crying con on him. He would jab a needle into me to tranquilize me, so he couldn't hear my bleating. I tell you, if you have ever had the flu real bad, just multiply the misery, the aching torture by a thousand. That's what it's like to kick a habit.

It took two weeks. I was weak, but with an appetite like a horse. In another two weeks I was stronger than I'd been in years. The Doc will always be my man. If he hadn't come to my rescue, and I had kept that habit until nineteen sixty, I would have been a corpse within a week in that steel casket waiting for me.

21

The Steel Casket

Seattle had played out. It was nineteen fifty-eight. My step-father died leaving Mama all alone back in California. Her letters were full of her grief and loneliness. I had blown down to Rachel and the young hash-slinger I'd turned out.

I had put on fifty pounds since I kicked the habit. I weighed more than two-hundred pounds. Time had scissored away my hair in front. I didn't look much like the mug shot of that sleek escapee.

I smoked a little gangster and snorted cocaine now and then. I actually copped a cap of H once with my C. I wanted to mix it in a speedball. It was hard to flush the H down the drain.

At almost forty I was ancient as a pimp. I looked like a black, fat seal in my expensive threads. For the first time in many years I had rediscovered my appetite for good food. I was slowing down. I spent most of my time reading in bed. The end of my pimping career wasn't far in the future.

I made the decision to go back to the fast track. I stayed away from old haunts. I had put my two girls to work in the street near downtown. Most of their tricks were white. I stayed in a nice hotel near by. They lived together in the same hotel. Three months after I got back, a fire changed my pimping setup. The change set up the chain of events that busted me for the escape.

I was taking a walk. I stopped to watch flames gut an apartment building. An old brown-skin stud was watching beside me. He was a sure-shot craps hustler. He also sold working togs to whores in houses in ten states. After the fire we went and had a drink together. We liked each other right away. For the next month we saw each other every day. I started going with him to the whorehouses to peddle his merchandise.

I'd always had contempt for whores who worked houses.

They gave up fifty percent of the scratch to a madam. I'd always believed a good whore went to the street to meet the trick. Even when I had the houses in Ohio my whores got their tricks in the street.

Lazy, half-ass whores worked houses and let the trick come to them. My friend, Bet 'Em Big, convinced me whorehouses were the thing for me. His points were that the wear and tear on a pimp was less. The houses were protected and the madams were responsible for falls. Also a girl didn't need the complicated turn out for houses.

A pimp's blows would be at least fifty percent less in the houses. He told me at my age I could grind up a bankroll in the houses. Then I could open a couple of my own and live to get a hundred years old. I wouldn't live that long under the stress and strain of the street.

Two months later I had both my girls in houses. I got my scratch every Monday in money orders by registered mail. Just like he said, it was an easy way to pimp. The fifty percent off the top, I couldn't miss. I never had it.

The girls would work maybe a month or two before coming in to visit me. I spent the time between with Bet 'Em Big. He was a real pal. He blew his top when I ignored his advice and tapped almost out for a new fifty-nine Hog.

I loved him like a father. He knew all the percentages on craps and people. His friendship and wisdom maybe helped me to stay away from H. Maybe if I hadn't gone to jail, I would have gone back to it. I was tempted a dozen times.

I moved Stacy, the younger whore to a house in Montana. It was March. She was up there for the season. This meant every six weeks or so I'd have to go up there to service her and tighten my game. She was lonesome. She'd call and write to tell me how much she missed me.

She fell out with the madam and started working in a house run by a stud in the same town. I told Bet I was going up to visit her.

He said, 'Ice, you can't take good advice. You were a sucker to go broke on that new Hog. Now here is more good advice. Ice, not only should you not go up there, you better pull that fine bitch out of there. I know that stud. He's a snake. Pull her out! I know a spot in Pennsylvania just as good. Inside of two days you can pull her and place her.'

I didn't take his advice. I took a train up to visit her. I rented a room in a motel. I registered as Johnny Cato. It was on the outskirts of town. The only Negroes ever in town were whores in houses and pimps come to visit them.

She'd come to the motel in early morning after work. She confessed to me that she woke up one day and found her boss in bed with her. In her alarm she struck him on the head with a heavy brass clock. It didn't chill him. He wiped the blood away and gave her fifty slats to get his rocks. He begged her to quit me and be his woman. It was a bitch of a time to tell me.

It was the third and last day of my visit. It was Sunday night around nine. She didn't work Sundays. We were playing around. I had my pajamas on. I had a cap of C in a pocket. I was just lighting a cigarette when a roller-type knock shook the door and me. I went to the door.

I said, 'Yes, who is it?'

He said, 'Police, open the door.'

I opened it. It was two red-faced Swede rollers. One was porcine, the other lanky. I put my shaking hands into the pajama pockets. My finger tips touched the scorching hot cap of cocaine. I hoped I was keeping the fear out of my face. I gave them a wide toothy smile. They came in and stood in the middle of the room. Their eyes were racing about the room. Stacy was open mouthed in the bed.

I said, 'Yes gentlemen, what can I do for you?'

Lanky said, 'We wanta see your ID.'

I went to the closet and got the phony John Cato Fredrickson ID. I put it in his palm. I felt cold sweat running down my back. They looked at it, then looked at each other.

Lanky said, 'You are in violation of the law. You signed the motel register improperly. Why didn't you sign your full name? What are you trying to hide? What are you doing here in town? It says here you're a dancer. We don't have a club in town that books entertainers.'

I said, 'Officers, my professional name is Johnny Cato. I've got nothing to hide. My full name had always been too long for the marquees. I've fallen into the habit of using the shorter version.

'My legs went out last year. I don't dance anymore. My wife and I decided to go into business. We are making a tour of this part of the country. We think that in your town we've found the ideal site for a Southern fried chicken shack. My wife has a secret recipe that should make us rich up here.'

Porky said, 'You're a Goddamn black lying sonuvabitch. Every one of you Niggers come up here to open another cat house or suck your whore's pussy. You and that bitch aren't married. You're a low life pimp and she's your whore. I've seen her around. I'm telling you boy, get your Nigger ass out of town. We don't want you here.'

I said, 'Yes Sir, I'll forget about the restaurant like you say.'

They turned and walked out. I knew Stacy's boss had put his finger on me. It was too late to catch the train back to the city. There was one a day at eight P.M. I knew they'd be back. I was trapped. I'd heard radio bulletins warning that the highways were snowed under. I couldn't even walk out of town. I snorted the sizzle and sat trying to figure a way out.

The chief of police came back at three the next afternoon. I let him in.

He said, 'Boy, I'm not satisfied. I'm going to forget about the phony registration. Now there's a more serious matter. If you and this young woman aren't legally married you've broken a law I can't overlook. When and where were you married?'

I thought fast. I tried to remember a court house fire from the newspapers. I couldn't.

I said, 'Sir, we were married three years ago in Waco, Texas. I just can't understand why you doubt we're married.'

He said, 'I'm going to take you in. I'm going to check your story. If you're telling the truth, I'll let you go. If not you'll get a jail sentence.'

He took us down. We were mugged and fingerprinted. Afterwards we were taken to his office.

He said, 'Boy, you lied to me. I called Waco. There's no record of your marriage.'

They locked us up. An hour later we walked out on two-hundred dollar bonds each. We got a cab to the motel. I understood the bond delay. The joint had been searched. We got her stuff from the whorehouse and sat in the train station until eight P.M.

We got back to the city early that morning. I knew when my fingerprints got to Washington the FBI would rush back the news I was a fugitive. I had to get out of town.

The police chief knew my destination when I left his town. Bet 'Em Big called Pennsylvania. Stacy was parked, ready to leave for the new spot the next day. The chief must have flown my fingerprints to Washington.

The city rollers, with a captain of guards from the joint busted Stacy and me. I was held for the escape. Stacy for harboring me. There was one angle I couldn't figure. All the way to the lock-up it bothered me. How did the city police and that screw know just where in that big city to put their hands on me?

I had been transferred to County Jail when I figured it out. I have made many stupid mistakes in my life. None was more stupid than the one that put me back in the shit house. I had a letter in my bag from Stacy. The rollers that searched our room while we were in jail made a notation of my city address. I had played the hick coppers cheap and here I was with my balls in the fire.

Rachel rushed to me from the whorehouse. I fought the charge of escape. After all, they couldn't prove it to the extent they could tell in court how I had escaped. At my first hearing, I told the judge I hadn't escaped. I told him one night before midnight a screw unlocked the cell and took me to the front gate and released me. I had a friend who had supplied the scratch for the underground release.

It was a very thin story, but it was strong enough to forestall my return to the joint. I was sure bad things would happen to me back there. Bet visited me. He offered to do anything for me. I was lost. No one could help me.

Mama came from California to visit me. She was sick and old. In fact she was dying. She had heart trouble and diabetes. I don't see how she made the trip. It was an old scene. I was in a barred cage. She was crying on the outside of it.

She sobbed, 'Son, this is the last time we are going to see each other. Your Mama's so tired. God gave me the strength to make the long trip to see my poor baby before I got to sleep in Jesus' arms. Son, it's too bad you don't love me as much as I love you.'

I was crying. I was squeezing her thin, pale hands in mine between the bars.

I said, 'Now look Mama, you know we all got Indian blood in us. Mama you ain't gonna die. Mama, you'll live to get a hundred like Papa Joe, your father. Come on now, Mama, stop it. Ain't I got enough worry? Mama, I love you. Honest Mama. Forgive me for not writing regular and stuff like that. I love you, Mama, I love you. Please don't die. I couldn't take it while I'm locked up. I'll take care of you when I get out. I swear it, Mama. Just don't die. Please!'

The screw came up. The visit was over. His hard face softened in pity as he looked at her. He knew she was critically sick. I watched her move slowly away from me down the jail corridor. She got to the elevator. She turned and looked at me. She had a sad, pitiful look on her face. It reminded me of that stormy morning long ago she had stood in the rain and watched the van taking me to my first prison bit. I get a terrible lump in my throat even now when I relive that moment.

A week passed after Mama visited me and went back to California.

I went into court for the third and last time. The judge ordered me into the custody of the joint's captain of screws. Stacy was released.

The captain and his aide were grimly silent. Their prison sedan sliced through the sparkling April day. I was on the rear seat. I gazed at the scurrying, lucky citizens on the street. I wondered what they'd use on me at the joint, rubber hoses or blackjacks? I felt so low. I wouldn't have cared if I'd dropped dead right on the car seat.

We went through the big gate into the joint. The warm April sun shone down on the ancient grimy buildings.

The yard cons leaned on their brooms. They stared through the car window at me. The sedan came to a stop. We got out. They took off my handcuffs. I was taken into the same cell-house from which I'd made the escape thirteen years before. I was locked in a cell on the flag.

In the early afternoon a screw marched me to the office of the chief of the joint's security. He looked like a pure Aryan storm trooper sitting behind his desk. He didn't have a blackjack or a rubber hose in his hand. He was grinning like maybe Herr Schickelgruber at that railroad coach in France. His voice was a lethal whisper.

He said, 'Well, well, so you're that slick blackbird who flew the coop. Cheer up, you only owe us eleven months. You're lucky you escaped before the new law. There's one on the books now. It penalizes escapees with up to an extra year.

'Ah, what a shame it isn't retroactive. I am going to put you into a punishment cell for a few days. Nothing personal mind you. Hell, you didn't hurt me with your escape. Tell me confidentially, how did you do it?'

I said, 'Sir, I wish I knew. I am subject to states of fugue. I came to that night and I was walking down the highway a free man. Sir, I certainly wish I could tell you how I did it.'

His pale cold eyes hardened into blue agates.

His grin widened.

He said, 'Oh, it's all right my boy. Tell you what, you're a cinch to get a clear memory of just how you did it before long. Put in a request to the cell-house officer to see me when you regain the memory. Well good luck, my boy, 'til we meet again.'

A screw took me to the bath house. I took a shower and changed into a tattered con uniform. A croaker examined me, then back to the cell house. The screw took me to a row of tiny filthy cells on the flag. My first detention cell was on the other side of the cell house. The screw stopped in front of a cell. He unlocked it. He prodded me into it. It was near the front of the cell house. I looked around my new home.

It was a tight box designed to crush and torture the human spirit. I raised my arms above me. My fingertips touched the cold steel ceiling. I stretched them out to the side. I touched the steel walls. I walked seven feet or so from the barred door to the rear of the cell. I passed a steel cot.

The mattress cover was stained and stinking from old puke and crap. The toilet and wash bowls were encrusted with greenish-brown crud. It could be a steel casket for a weak skull after a week or two. I wondered how long they'd punish me in the box.

I turned and walked to the cell door. I stood grasping the bars, looking out at the blank cell-house wall in front of me.

I thought, 'The Nazi figures after a week or so in this dungeon, I'll be crying and begging to tell him how I escaped. I'm not going to pussy-out. Hell, I got a strong skull. I could do a month in here.'

I heard a slapping noise against the steel space between the cells. I saw a thin white hand holding a square of paper. I stuck my arm through the bars of my cell door. I took the paper. It was a kite with two cigarettes and three matches folded inside.

It read, 'Welcome to Happiness Lane. My name is Coppola. The vine said you're Lancaster the guy who took a powder thirteen years ago. I was clerking in an office up front. I took my powder a year and a half ago.

'They brought me back six months ago. I've started to cash in my chips a dozen times. You'll find out what I mean. I've been right in this cell ever since. I got another year to go with the new time stacked on top for the escape. I got a detainer warrant from Maine for forgery up front.

'We're in big trouble, buddy. The prick up front has cracked up four or five cons in these cells since I came back . . . There's six of us on the row now. Only three are escapees. The rest are doing short punishment time like two days to a week. I'll give you background on other things later, I know what screws will get anything you want for a price.'

I lit a cigarette and sat on the cot. I thought, Coppola is a helluva stud to keep his skull straight for six months on Happiness Lane. He doesn't know I'm just here for a few days.'

That night we had a supper of sour Spanish rice. I heard the shuffling feet of cons filing into the cell house. They were going into their cells on the tiers overhead. The blaring radio loudspeakers and the lights went off at nine. Over the flushing of toilets and epidemic farting, I heard my name mentioned. The speaker was on the tier just above my cell.

He said, 'Jim, how about old Iceberg, the mack man? Jim, a deuce will get you a saw buck the white folks will croak him down there. A pimp ain't got the heart to do a slat down there.'

Jim said, 'Jack, I hope the pimp bastard croaks tonight. One of them pimps put my baby sister on stuff.'

I dozed off. After midnight I woke up. Somebody was screaming. He was pleading with someone not to kill him. I heard thudding sounds. I got up and went to the cell door. I heard Coppola flush his john.

I stage whispered, 'Coppola, what's happening, man?'

He whispered, 'Don't let it bug you, Lancaster. It's just the night screws having their nightly fun and exercise. They pull their punching bags from the cells on the other side. It's where drunks and old men are held for court in the morning.

'Buddy, you ain't seen nothing yet. Don't give them any lip if they ever come by and needle you. They'll beat hell out of you. Then take all your clothes off and put you in a stripped cell. That's one with nothing in it, just the cold concrete floor. Buddy, there are at least a dozen ways to die in here.'

All the rest of the night I lay staring at the blank dirty wall in front of me. I wondered what Rachel and Stacy were doing. I had to make contact with a screw to mail some letters on the outside for me. The joint censors would never let whore instructions pass through. Every few minutes a screw would pass and flash his light on me.

That morning I watched the cell-house cons file past my cell on the way to breakfast and then to their work. All new arrivals the day before were also in this line.

That afternoon, I got letters from Stacy and Rachel. They

had also sent money orders. They missed their strong right arm. They were working bars downtown. Bet was handling any falls they might take.

Coppola within the first week hipped me to the angles of survival. I had a screw who would take letters directly to the girls. He would get his pay-off from them. He would bring me cash from them.

I got a letter from Mama. I could hardly read the shaky writing. She sent me religious tracts inside it. I was really worried about her. The tight cell and the fear of a year in it was getting to me. The little sleep I got was crowded with nightmares. I was eating good at high prices. I still lost weight.

The first month I lost thirty pounds. Then I got bad news twice within the fifth week. I got a letter from Stacy. Bet had been found dead on his toilet stool at home. It really shook me. He had been a real friend. I got a very short note from Rachel. She was in Cleveland.

It said, 'I ran into an old doctor friend of yours the other night. He was looped. He bought me a drink. Lucky for me the bartender asked how you were doing. The doctor spilled his guts. He told me about a dead patient of his who came back to life. My worst wishes. P.S. Please drop dead. I'll keep the Hog.'

The joint waived the balance of Coppola's time to face the rap in Maine. The skull pressure was getting larger. The cell was getting tighter. With Coppola gone I was in real trouble the third month. It was like a deadly hex was at work to crack me up.

None of the screws would cop heavy drugs for me. I settled for whiskey. I stopped using the safety razor. I didn't want to see the gaunt ugly stranger in my sliver of mirror. It wasn't just the cell. It was the sights and sounds of the misery and torment on the row and in the nightmares.

Mama was bed-ridden. She was too sick to write. I got telegrams and letters from her friends. They were all praying that I'd get out before Mama passed. I got a pass to the visitors' cage. A screw took me and stood behind me the whole time.

It was Stacy. She was pregnant and living with an old hustler. Her eyes told me how bad I looked. Her letters dropped off to one a month with no scratch.

At the end of the fourth month my skull was shaking on my shoulders like I had palsy. A con on the row blew his top one night around midnight. He woke up the whole cell house. At first he was cursing God and his mother. The screws brought him past my cell.

In my state the sight of him almost took me into madness. He was buck naked and jabbering a weird madman's language through a foamy jib. It was like the talking in tongues Holy Rollers do. He was jacking-off his stiff swipe with both hands. I gnawed in my pillow like the runt to keep from screaming.

The next day I put in a request to see the Nazi. Nothing happened. A week later I was sitting on the john with my head between my knees. I heard the morning line moving to breakfast. The line had stalled for a moment right outside my cell door.

I looked up into a pair of strange almost orange eyes sunk into an old horribly scarred face. It was Leroy. I had stolen Chris from him many years ago. He still remembered me. He stared at me and smiled crookedly as the line moved out.

I got my screw to check his rap sheet. The screw gave me the whole rundown. Since nineteen forty Leroy had been arrested more than a hundred times for common drunk. He had also been committed to mental hospitals twice. I was forty-two. I was twenty when I stole Chris from him. I asked the screw to pull strings to send him to another cell-house. I gave him a rundown on the Chris steal and how weak Leroy had been for her. The screw told me he couldn't cut it.

Leroy was doing only five days for drunk. Leroy had to stay in the cell-house. I wondered how Leroy would try for revenge. I had to be careful in the morning for the next five days. I had to keep my feet and legs away from the cell door. Leroy might score for a shiv and try to hack something off when he passed my cell. I worried all day about what he would do. Could he somehow get gasoline and torch me?

That night I heard the voice for the first time. The lights

were out. The cell-house was quiet. The voice seemed to be coming through a tiny grille at the head of the cot.

A light always burned in the breezeway behind the grille. The pipes for all the plumbing for the cells were there. I got down on my hands and knees and looked through the grille's tiny holes. I couldn't see anybody.

I got back on the cot. The voice was louder and clearer. It sounded friendly and sweet like a woman consoling a friend. I wondered if cons on one of the tiers above me were clowning with each other.

I heard my name in the flow of chatter. I got back down and listened at the grille. A light flooded the corner. It was the screw. I spun around on my knees facing him. The light was in my eyes.

He said, 'What the hell are you doing?'

I said, 'Officer, I heard a voice. I thought someone was working back there.'

He said, 'Oh, Oh, you poor bastard. You won't pull this bit. You're going nuts Slim. Now stop that nonsense and get in that cot and stay there.'

The cell-house lights woke me up. My first thought was Leroy. I got up and sat on the cot. Then I thought about the voice. I wasn't sure now. Maybe it had been a dream.

I wondered whether I should ask the screw about it. One thing for sure, dream or not, I didn't want to go nuts. My mind hooked on to what I'd heard the old con philosopher say about that screen in the skull. I remembered what the books at Federal Prison said about voices and even people that only existed inside a joker's skull.

I thought, 'After this when I get the first sign of a sneaky worry thought, or idea, I'll fight it out of my skull.

'Maybe I wasn't dreaming when I heard that voice. If I hear it again I'll have some protection. I'll keep a strong sane voice inside to fight off anything screwy from going on.

'Every moment I'll stand guard over my thoughts until I get out of here. I can do it. I just have to train that guard. He's got to be slick enough not to let trouble by him. I'll make him shout down the phony voices. He'll know they're not real right away.'

I got up and went to the face bowl. I heard the rumbling feet of the cons coming off the tiers. I was washing my face. I heard a series of sliding bumps on the floor behind me. It was like maybe several news-boys all throwing your paper on the porch in rotation. Then I smelled it. I turned toward the door. I squinted through the soap on my eyelids. I had been bombed with crap.

It was oozing off the wall. The solid stuff had rolled to my feet. Pieces of loosely rolled newspaper were the casings. Cons were passing my door snickering. I felt dizzy. A big lead balloon started inflating inside my chest. I remembered the inside guard. He was new and late on the job. I puked.

I shouted over and over, 'Watch out now, it's only crap, it's only crap. It's just crap. Watch out, it can't hurt you. It's only stinking crap.'

A screw stood at the cell door twitching his nose. He was screaming, 'Shut Up!'

He opened the cell. I got a bucket of hot water and a scrub brush. I cleaned the cell. The screw asked me who fouled my nest. I told him I didn't know.

My screw came to see me at noon. He told me how Leroy had enlisted the crap-bombers. Leroy told them I had put the finger on him years ago when he got the bit for the Papa Tony beating. My screw dropped the truth around the cell-house. All the bombers were down on Leroy. They dared him to bother me again. I was safe from Leroy.

I didn't mourn when Leroy finished his five-day bit.

It was the end of my sixth month. I beat down worry, voices, and countless thoughts of suicide with the skull-guard plan.

A friend of Mama's sent me a telegram. Mama had been stricken. The hospital doctors had given her up. Then she bounced back. She was very sick now, but still alive. The telegram gave my skull gimmick a tough test.

I had a very sad day around the middle of the seventh month. A booster from New York busted on his second day in town was on the tier above me. A con on my row several cells down called me one night to borrow a book. A moment later I heard my name called from up above. He came down next morning and rapped to me. His job was in the cell-house.

The booster asked me if I were the Iceberg who was a friend of Party Time. I told him yes. He didn't say anything for awhile. Finally he told me Party had often spoken of me as the kid he once hustled with who grew up to be Iceberg the pimp.

He told me Party had copped the beautiful girlfriend of a dope dealer when he got a bit. Party turned her out. The dope dealer did his bit. The broad tried to cut Party loose to go back to a life of ease.

Party went gorilla on her. He broke her arm. Two months later Party copped some H. He didn't know his connection was a pal of the dealer who got the bit. It was H all right mixed with flakes of battery acid. I didn't sleep that night.

I had come to a decision in that awful cell. I was through with pimping and drugs. I got insight that perhaps I could never have hoped to get outside. I couldn't have awakened if I had been serving a normal bit. After I got the mental game down pat I could see the terrible pattern of my life.

Mama's condition and my guilty conscience had a lot to do with my decision. Perhaps my age and loss of youth played their parts. I had found out that pimping is for young men, the stupid kind.

I had spent more than half a lifetime in a worthless, dangerous profession. If I had stayed in school in eight years of study I could have been an M.D. or lawyer. Now here I was, slick but not smart, in a cell. I was past forty with counterfeit glory in my past, and no marketable training, no future. I had been a bigger sucker than a square mark. All he loses is scratch. I had joined a club that suckered me behind bars five times.

A good pimp has to use great pressure. It's always in the cards that one day that pressure will backfire. Then he will be the victim. I was weary of clutching quicksilver whores and the joints.

I was at the end of the ninth month of the bit. I got a front office interview. I was contesting my discharge date. I was still down for an eleven month bit.

An agent of the joint had been in the arresting group. I spent thirty days in County Jail before the transfer to the joint to finish out the year. I knew little or nothing about law. I was told at the interview I had to do eleven months. I wasn't afraid I'd crack up serving the extra month. By this time I had perfect control of my skull.

Mama might die in California at any time. I had to get to her before she died. I had to convince her I loved her, that I appreciated her as a mother. That she and not whore-catching was more important to me. I had to get there as much for myself as for her.

I lay in that cell for two weeks. I wrote a paper based on what I believed were the legal grounds for my release at the expiration of ten months. It had subtle muscle in it too. I memorized the paper. I rehearsed it in the cell. Finally I felt I had the necessary dramatic inflection and fluid delivery. It was two days before the end of the tenth month. I was called in two weeks after I had requested the second interview.

I must have looked like a scarecrow as I stood before him. I was bearded, filthy, and ragged. He was immaculate seated behind his gleaming desk. He had a contemptuous look on his face.

I said, 'Sir, I realize that the urgent press of your duties has perhaps contributed to your neglect of my urgent request for an interview. I have come here today to discuss the vital issue of my legal discharge date.

'Wild rumors are circulating to the effect that you are not a fair man, that you are a bigot, who hates Negroes. I discounted them immediately that I heard them. I am almost dogmatic in my belief that a man of your civic stature and intellect could ill afford or embrace base prejudice.

'In the spirit of fair play, I'm going to be brutally frank. If I am not released the day after tomorrow, a certain agent of mine here in the city is going to set in motion a process that will not only free me, but will possibly in addition throw a revealing spotlight on certain not too legal, not too pleasant activities carried on daily behind these walls.

'I have been caged here like an animal for almost ten months.

Like an animal, my sensitivity of seeing and hearing has been enhanced. I only want what is legally mine. My contention is that if your Captain of guards, who is legally your agent, had arrested me and confined me on such an unlikely place as the moon for thirty days, technically and legally I would be in the custody of this institution. Sir, the point is unassailable. Frankly I don't doubt that my release will occur on legal schedule. Thank you, Sir, for the interview.'

The contempt had drained out of his face. I convinced him I wasn't running a bluff. His eyes told me he couldn't risk it. After all, surely he knew how easy it was to get contraband in and out of the rotten joint. Getting a kite to an agent would be child's play. I didn't sleep that night. The next day I got a discharge notice. I would be released on legal schedule!

22

Dawn

I had amazed cons and guards alike, I had survived it. I was getting out in twenty-four hours. I was almost forty-three sitting in a cell.

I thought, 'I have been in a deadly trap. Have I really escaped it? Does fate have grimmer traps set? Can I learn to be proud of my black skin? Can I adjust to the stark reality that black people in my lifetime had little chance to escape the barbed-wire stockade in the white man's world?'

Only time and the imponderables inside me would answer the questions.

I had no one except Mama. They dressed me out. My clothes flopped around on my skeletal frame. I still hadn't told them how I had escaped. Cons cheered me as I shuffled toward freedom. They knew how I had suffered and what the awful odds had been that I wouldn't have made it.

A friend of Mama's had sent me my fare. As the plane flew over the sea of neon, I looked down at the city where I had come so many years ago in search of an empty lonesome dream.

I thought of Henry and the sound of that pressing machine. Of Mama when she was young and pretty. How wonderful it had been back there in Rockford. She would come into my room at bedtime, a tender ghost, and tuck me in warmly and kiss me good-night. It seemed a long time before I finally got to her.

When I walked into her room, death was there in her tiny gray face. Her eyes brightened and flashed a mother's deathless love. Her embrace was firm and sure. My coming to her had been like a miracle. It was the magic that gave her strength.

She clutched life for an added six months. I never left the house for those six months. We would lie side by side on twin beds and talk far into the night. She made me promise that

I would use the rest of my life in a good way. She told me I should get married and have children.

I tried hard to make up for all those years I had neglected her. It's hard to square an emotional debt. That last sad day she looked up into my eyes from the hospital bed.

In a voice I could scarcely hear through her parched lips, she whispered, 'Forgive me, Son, forgive me. Mama didn't know. I'm sorry.'

I stood there watching her last tears rolling down her dead cheeks from the blank eyes. I crushed her to me.

I tried to get my final plea past death's grim shield, 'Oh Mama, nothing has been your fault, believe me, nothing. If you are foolish enough to think so, then I forgive you.'

I staggered blindly from the hospital. I went to the parking lot. I fell across the car hood and cried my heart out. I stopped crying. I thought Mama had really gotten in the last word this time.

These stinking whores would have gotten a huge charge if they could have seen old Iceberg out there wailing like a sucker because his old lady was dead.

Epilog

I am lying in the quiet dawn. I am writing this last chapter for the publisher.

I am thinking, 'How did a character like me, who for most of his life had devoted himself to the vilest career, ever square up? By all the odds, I should have ended a broken, diseased shell, or died in a lonely prison cell.'

I guess three of the very important reasons are lying asleep in the bedroom across the hall. I can see their peaceful, happy faces. They don't know how hard and often discouraging it is for me to earn a living for them in the square world.

This square world is a strange place for me. For the last five years I have tried hard, so hard, to solve its riddles, to fit in.

Catherine, my beautiful wife, is wonderful and courageous. She's a perfect mother to our adorable two-year-old girl, and our sturdy, handsome three-year-old boy.

In this new world that isn't really square at all, I have had many bitter experiences. I remember soon after my marriage how optimistic I was as I set out to apply for the sales jobs listed in the want ads.

I knew that I was a stellar salesman. After all, hadn't I proved my gift for thirty years? The principles of selling are the same in both worlds. The white interviewers were impressed by my bearing and apparent facility with words. They sensed my knowledge of human nature.

But they couldn't risk the possible effect that a Negro's presence would have on the firm's all white personnel. In disgust and anger, I would return home and sulk. Bitterly I would try to convince myself to go back into the rackets. Catherine always said the right things and gave me her love and understanding.

There was another indispensable source of help and courage during these hard times. She's a charming, brilliant woman.

She had been a friend to my mother. She functioned as a kind of psycho-therapist. She explained and pointed out to me the mental phases I was passing through. She gave me insight to fight the battle. To her I shall always be grateful.

The story of my life indicates that my close friends were few. Shortly before I started this book I met a man I respected. I thought he was a true friend. I was bitterly disillusioned to discover he wasn't. I'm glad in a way it turned out the way it did. I've always come back stronger after a good kick in the ass.

I have had many interesting and even humorous experiences in this new life. They will have to wait for now. I see my little family is awake. I'll have to light the heater. I can't let them get up in the early morning chill.

How about it, an Iceberg with a warm heart?

THE END

Glossary

[ICEBERG SLIM'S ORIGINAL]

BANG	injection of narcotics
BEEF	criminal complaint
BELL	notoriety connected to one's name
BILL	a hundred dollars
BIT	prison term
BITE	price
BLACK GUNION	powerful, thick, dark, gummy marijuana
BOO KOOS	plenty
BOOSTER	shop lifter
BOOT	Negro
BOSS	very good, excellent
BOTTOM WOMAN	pimp's main woman, his foundation
BOY	heroin
BREAKING LUCK	a whore's first trick of working day
BRIGHT	morning
BULL SCARE	blustering bluff
C	cocaine
CANNON	pickpocket
CAN	derriere
CAP	a small glycerin container for drugs
CAT	female sexual organ
CHILI PIMP	small-time one-whore pimp
CHIPPIED	light periodic use of heavy drugs
CHUMP CHANGE	just enough money for basic needs
CIRCUS LOVE	to run the gamut of the sexual perversions
COAST	somnolent nodding state of heroin addict
COCKTAILED	to put a marijuana butt into the end of a conventional cigarette for smoking

COME DOWN	return to normal state after drug use
COP AND BLOW	pimp theory, to get as many whores as leave him
COPPED	get or capture
CRACK WISE	usually applied to an underworld neophyte who spouts hip terminology to gain status
CROAK	kill
CROSSES	to trick or trap
CRUMB-CRUSHER	a baby
CUT LOOSE	to refuse to help, to disdain
DAMPER	a place holding savings, bank, safe deposit box, etc.; to stop or quell
DERBY	head, refers to oral copulation
DIRTY	in possession of incriminating evidence
DOG	older, hardened whore, or young sexual libertine
DOSSING	sleeping
DOUBLE SAW	20 dollars
DOWN	a pimp's pressure on a whore, or his adherence to the rules of the pimp game; when a whore starts to work
FIX	to bribe so an illegal operation can go with impunity; also an injection of narcotics
FLAT-BACKER	a whore who gets paid for straight sexual intercourse
FREAK	sexual libertine
FRENCH	oral copulation
G	one thousand dollars
GANGSTER	marijuana
GEORGIAED	to be taken advantage of sexually without receiving money
GIRL	cocaine
GORILLA	to use physical force
GORILLA PIMP	no brains, all muscle
H	heroin
HARD LEG	an older, street-hardened used-up whore

HEAT	police, or adverse street conditions for hustlers
HIDE	wallet
HOG	Cadillac
HOOKS	hands
HORNS	ears
HYPE	addict
JASPER	lesbian
JEFFING	low level con
JIB	mouth
KEISTER	derriere
KITE	note
KITTY	Cadillac
LARCENY	to turn against by vocal condemnation
LINES	money
LIP	lawyer
MACKING	pimping
MARK	victim; sucker
MITT MAN	a hustler who uses religion and prophecy to con his victims, usually the victims are women
MUCKTY-MUCKS	a contemptuous term applied to the rich and privileged by the poor and underprivileged
MURPHY	con game played on suckers looking for whores
NUT ROLL	a pretense at stupidity or unawareness
OKEE DOKE	a con game
OIL	pay-off money to the police
OUTFIT	hyperdermic kit used by addicts
PACIFIER BULB	the rubber top of a baby's pacifier used by addicts to draw up drugs through the eyedropper
PEEL OFF	removal of only a portion of money from a wallet or roll
PIECE	measurement of narcotics; usually an ounce
PIECE OF STUFF	one ounce of narcotics

PINNING	looking
POKE	wallet or bankroll
PRAT	to pretend rejection to increase desire
ROLLER	policeman, usually plain clothes
ROUST	stopped, harrassed by police
SAW	10 dollars
SCRATCH	money
SHAKE	extort
SHEET	police record
SHIELD	badge
SHIV	knife, usually made by convicts from various objects
SHORT	car
SIZZLE	narcotics carried on the person
SLAT	one usually refers to money or length of prison term
SLUM HUSTLER	a phony jewelry salesman
SNATCH	female sexual organ
SPADE	Negro
SPEEDBALLS	a combination of heroin and cocaine injected
SPIC	Mexican
SPIELING	talking, a term used by older hustlers and pimps
SQUARE UP	get out of the life
STABLE	a group of whores belonging to one pimp
STALL	an accomplice of a cannon
STAND UP	to endure or survive
STING	rob
STRIDES	trousers
STUFF ON	to play on or con
SWIPE	penis
THREADS	clothes
THREE WAY	orally, rectally, vaginally
TO PULL COAT	to inform and teach
TURNED OUT	introduced to the fast life, or drugs
UP TIGHT	in trouble, financial or otherwise

VIC	mark, victim
VINE	suit
WHALE	throw, usually applied to throwing dice
WIRE	information, message, etc.
YEASTING	to build up or exaggerate
YELLOW	a yellow capsule containing barbiturate powder

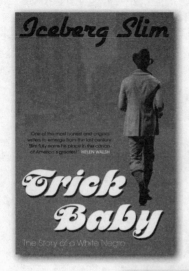

'Iceberg Slim's prose was, and is . . . ecstatic
and original' *New York Times*

CANON█GATE